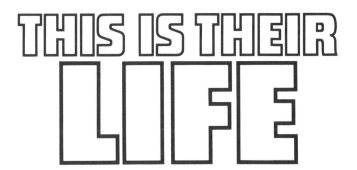

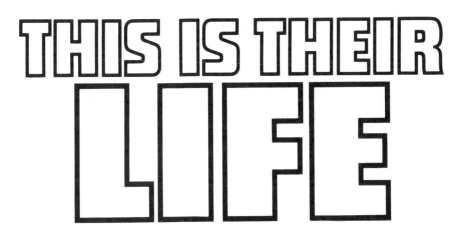

THIS IS THEIR LIFE

Foreword by Mike Yarwood

Written by Jonathan Meades

a Salamander book

Published by Salamander Books Limited
LONDON

A Salamander Book

Published by Salamander Books Ltd
Salamander House
27 Old Gloucester Street
London WC1N 3AF
United Kingdom

© Salamander Books Ltd

ISBN 0 86101 0422 2
   0 86101 045 0

Distributed in the United Kingdom by
New English Library Ltd

Credits

Editor: Martin Schultz
Designer: Rod Teasdale
Picture Researchers: Barbara Peevor and
Irene Reed

Filmset: Modern Text Typesetting Ltd, England

Printed in England: Fakenham Press Ltd

Foreword

Let me ask you a question.
What have Dr. Magnus Pyke,
David Bellamy, Russell Harty,
Eddie Waring, Magnus Magnusson
and Michael Parkinson in common
—besides earning me a very good
living?
Give up?
Well, for starters, none of them
are showbusiness people . . . yet
they are all big stars. They are
certainly not singers, nor dancers,
comedians, or actors. Yet they have
all become very big personalities
through their exposure on
television. All six are brilliant
people in their own fields . . . experts
at their trade, who would still have
been at the top of their professions
without television.
What television has done, is to
establish them all as household
names. TV today has become the
biggest entertainment medium in
the world. And the people who

watch it have created their own personalities . . . whom they regard very simply as 'friends' . . . whether they be actors, singers, newsreaders, footballers, commentators or what have you.

It is a very personal relationship and, as such, the fan thirsts for information—facts and figures—about his favourite star. He will go to great lengths to gain such information. That's why personality biographies have become a publishing company's dream—whether they are from the world of sport, showbusiness, politics, or journalism—because books about famous celebrities are always in the best-selling charts. And that's why 'This Is Your Life' has become one of Britain's most-avidly watched TV shows.

Television is entertainment. And fans are what entertainment is all about for, without them, we would all be unemployed. Fans are marvellous people and very loyal.

But then, television can only present the personalities before the public. It can't, it doesn't and, quite honestly, it shouldn't delve into their backgrounds, their family life and highlight the things that make them tick. Yet this is just the kind of information that the fans want to know about. And I should know . . . I'm a great fan at heart myself and I've hundreds of my own favourite personalities. But that's another story. . . .

This book starts where television switches off. Featured within its pages is a mass of information—background details, facts and figures, family statistics, birthdates,

and a wealth of biographical data on hundreds of our best-loved television personalities. It's a television addict's delight; a brilliant reference work for the avid fan.

For instance: Did you know that Dave 'Goodnight, and may your god go with you' Allen was christened David Tynan-O'Mahoney—the vicar had hiccups at the time—and he started his professional career as a journalist? Or, did you know that Eamonn Andrews once wrote a play and had it performed, called 'The Moon Is Black'? And were you aware—I sound more like Michael Caine every day—that John Cleese's family name almost turned out to be cheese!? I certainly wasn't.

These are just three examples of the fascinating information that this book reveals about people who have all become household names through the medium of television. And it doesn't really matter if they are singers, newscasters, or producers, does it?

So, please read on . . . and when you glance through the following pages, I'll bet you will see your own personal favourite 'star' in a completely different light next time he's on the 'box'.

That reminds me . . . I'd better have a word with the Editor about my own entry. . . .

The entries in this book are presented in alphabetical order. An index to entries for quick and easy reference will be found on pages 126 and 127.

JOSS ACKLAND

Born: 1919.

Ackland appears so frequently in all sorts of plays and series, that only the eagle-eyed can be sure to spot him. Indeed, it is his versatility and the extraordinary flexibility of his features which, perhaps, cause him to be less celebrated than he merits. His most acclaimed recent role was that of Peron in Tim Rice's and Andrew Lloyd Webber's musical *Evita*.

Mr Ackland's research for this role was extensive and took him to Argentina and, eventually, to Lobos, where Peron was born. Hardly surprisingly, no one there wanted to talk about the discredited dictator. It was, says Ackland, 'like going to Stratford and finding nobody wanting to talk about Shakespeare'. Not to be outdone, he resorted to professional guile. Disguising himself as an author (how? With a pocketful of pens), he approached one of Peron's closest friends, a brain surgeon, who failed to see through his cover and granted him an interview.

Though he has, incredibly, been constantly in work for 18 years, his early career, which began when he was 15, was not so easy. In fact, he became so despondent about achieving a living, let alone success, that he quit the profession for three years in 1954 and worked as a tea planter in Central Africa. His personal life, too, has not all been plain sailing. A few years ago, his uninsured house was burned down, his wife broke her back trying to escape the blaze, and five of his seven children were injured. Though his busy life allows him little time for recreation, he does enjoy collecting cartoons of himself and owns ten originals by Punch's Bill Hewison.

MARIA AITKEN

Born: September, 1945.
Educated: Sherborne and Oxford.

The daughter of one MP, Sir William Aitken, who sat for the Conservative interest in Bury St Edmunds, and sister of another, Jonathan, the Tory former journalist who represents Thanet, Maria Aitken seems forever to be billed as a 'bluestocking' or 'egghead'. Actually, this may not be too far from the truth. She actually reads things other than scripts and contracts, and was, albeit briefly, a teacher of logic at a Suffolk crammer's. Her earliest creative endeavours were not Thespian. As children, she and her brother produced a magazine of which she was 'Lady Contributor'. At the age of seven, she wrote a play called *Havoc among the Lovers*.

RAY ALAN

Ventriloquist.
Born: 1931, Lewisham.

Alan, who generally appears alongside the boorish and drunken Lord Charles, is reckoned by many of his colleagues to be the most technically adept ventriloquist in Britain. The son of a tally clerk in the docks and the grandson of a rat-catcher, his first job in show biz was working the spotlight at the old Lewisham Hippodrome. He then went on to become an impressionist and ukelele player. He abandoned these acts after finding himself on a bill at Chatham, where Jack Warner did impressions better than he could, and the Fabulous Dunstables played the uke with greater flair.

He has performed with dummies other than Lord Charles (motto: *Sempra* (sic) *inebriate*). They include a

10ins—almost deterred her from embarking on a professional career: 'I thought I was a female grotesque, doomed to play lesbian Spanish governesses'. When at last she took the plunge, she found herself in a company with a young actor called Richard Durden. She married him in Manchester before the matinée of a pantomime: 'The family couldn't bring themselves to attend, so they sent the spaniel on the train to represent them'.

The pressures of rep and of trying to build reputations conspired against the success of that marriage, and Miss Aitken is now married to Nigel Davenport, whom she met when filming *Mary Queen of Scots*. They have a six-year-old son called Jack and live in the Sussex countryside, where they raise guineafowl, geese and pigs (which have names such as Amin) for sale to restaurants.

Miss Aitken, who has recently been in *Company and Co* on BBC2, began her stage career at Oxford, where she was the first woman elected to the OUDS and where she appeared in the famous Burton-Taylor *Dr Faustus*. Her size—she is 5ft

ALAN ALDA

Born: 1935.

Alda is just completing his eighth series as Hawkeye Pierce in M*A*S*H. During all the years that it has been on the screen, he has commuted weekly to Los Angeles, some 3,000 miles away, from his home in Leonia, in rural New Jersey. He lives there with his wife Arlene (who was a clarinettist in the Houston Symphony Orchestra when they met) and their three daughters—Eve, 21, Beatrice, 19, and Elizabeth, 17. He could have chosen years ago to take his family with him to California, but 'it would have meant pulling the children out of school' and, anyway, he knows the legendary strains placed on family life in the film capital. He jealously guards his family's privacy and rarely allows any member of it to be photographed for publicity purposes.

Living with three women has turned him into a keen champion of women's rights. He writes and lectures on the subject, exploiting his own undoubted sex appeal to draw in listeners and readers who might otherwise give the matter a miss.

'Masculinists' might find this a bit much, but they should know that Mr Alda, even when preaching, uses humour as the main weapon in his armoury.

pageboy, Steve; Tich and Quackers, and Ali Cat, who is scared of mice and hates milk. It is with Lord Charles, who made his first stage appearance at a Wormwood Scrubs concert, that Alan shares the odd off-stage relationship to which ventriloquists are supposedly prone. On one occasion at an M3 filling station,

it was the dummy which ordered a pump attendant to fill the tank of Alan's Mercedes. The attendant, who apparently didn't recognise Lord Charles, said 'Yes, sir' and doffed his cap while the car drove off. Lord Charles lives with Alan in a flat in Wimbledon. He is divorced but would like to remarry if Miss Right appears.

JOHN ALDERTON

Born: 1940, Hull.
Educated: Kingston High
School, Hull.

Makes up half of the most popular show biz married couple since Micki and Griff— or, perhaps, Pearl Carr and Teddy Johnson. Alderton and Pauline Collins, who don't much like the husband-and-wife tag (though they have certainly courted it), would probably name Michael Dennison and Dulcie Gray as their 'legit' precursors. They met in the late 'sixties, when they both had parts with Donald Churchill in something called *One Night I Danced with Mr Dalton.* Some time later, their paths crossed again when, one Christmas, Alderton was recording the part of Octavius in a disastrous BBC production of *Julius Caesar.* They married just over a year later, in 1970.

This was Alderton's second marriage. His first had been to Jill Browne, with whom he co-starred in *Emergency Ward 10* back in the mists of time. Now he and Pauline Collins have three children (Nicholas, Kitty and Richard), a nice line in choosing the right show at the right time, a £200,000 house in Redington Road, Hampstead, and the prospect of many further years of conjoined success following *Upstairs, Downstairs; No Honestly; Wodehouse Playhouse,*

Thomas and Sarah, etc. They also have a valuable knack of knowing when to get out of a series—before the public gets bored with them.

Alderton's father was a Yorkshire grocer, and he, too, has something of the canniness and sharp-wittedness for which the sons of that county are well-known. Among his friends is the great Geoffrey Boycott. And like Boycott he is very much his own man or, put another way, he can be awkward when he feels like it. On two occasions he has become involved in disputes with the writers of series in which he performed. Both Keith Waterhouse (*The Upchat Line*) and Alfred Shaughnessey (*Thomas and Sarah*) took exception to alterations that he had made to their scripts and requested that their names be removed from the relevant episodes' credits. This was after he had spent his own money in pursuit of the ideal script for *Thomas and Sarah* and had thrown away the result.

He has a well-developed flair for publicity. Announcements that he and Miss Collins are to cease working together have virtually become part of the TV calendar, as regular as Frank Sinatra's farewell performance.

The couple know as well as anyone— indeed, better than anyone— that the public loves to find hints of their private selves in the way they perform together, and that this is an important part of their appeal. They pretend to wish not to reveal much about their private life. They enjoy buying each other presents, and Alderton likes playing, as well as watching, games. In addition to cricket (which he watches avidly and fanatically if Yorkshire is playing), he plays golf and football. And, yes, he actually uses orange lavatory paper.

DAVE ALLEN

Born: 1936, Templeogue,
near Dublin.

It was only because he regarded himself as something of a failure as a journalist that David Tynan-O'Mahoney became Dave Allen, comedian and raconteur extraordinary. He was thus able to become a television journalist and collector of oddballs on both sides of the Atlantic.

His background was literary and journalistic. His grandmother was editor of the Dublin newspaper, the *Freeman's Journal*; his aunt was the poet, Katharine Tynan, and a friend of Yeats; his father was managing director of the *Irish Times*, and his brothers are both journalists. He started on the *Irish Independent* when he was 16, moving on later to the *Drogheda Times*. He came to London when he was 20, convinced that Fleet Street was ready for him. It wasn't. He met some relatives of some people he knew in Dublin— they had worked at Butlin's on occasion and suggested that he do the same. Off he went to Skegness to be a redcoat. He did several seasons there, worked during the winter as a toy salesman in Sheffield, and began to get work on the club circuit. On a tour of Africa in 1963, Sophie Tucker

RONALD ALLISON

Born 26 January, 1932.
Educated: Weymouth Grammar
School; Taunton's School,
Southampton.

Allison returned to TV a year ago, with a weekly sports show for Thames. For the previous five years he had been the Queen's press secretary, spanning the time from the wedding of Princess Anne

suggested that he try his luck in Australia. He did so, and ended up with his own TV show. He also found a wife, the English actress, Judith Stott. They now live near the Thames at Wargrave, and have two children.

His willingness to use anyone and anything as the butt of his humour has sometimes resulted in his becoming the object of a certain amount of abuse. Objections from Catholic priests are the predictable echoes of his Pope jokes. He has little time for those who unquestioningly accept the tenets of any creed or system of thought. He is also wary of political organisations, and withdrew his support for the Anti-Nazi League when he formed the view that it was simply the respectable face of the totalitarian left.

Though Sir Charles Curran, the former Director-General of the BBC and himself a

Catholic, defended Allen's right to make cracks about the inanities of the Church, such tolerance has not been extended towards him in Eire. Telefis Eireann has never, in fact, transmitted any of his British material, though, of course, it denies that he is proscribed. He rarely visits his native country nowadays. Like most exiles, he retains a great fondness for it and for the mentality manifest in, for instance, a sign like one he spotted in a jeweller's window: 'Ears pierced while you wait'.

He is an obsessive taker of notes and writes down everything that he observes. He also scours newspapers for possible material. One source of material that he would never dream of using is his family — 'Lemme tell you 'bout my wife', and so on. His children have only rarely seen him work, and he can conceive of no possible reason why he should talk about his family: 'If I go to a barrister or a brain surgeon, I'm not interested in his married life, or if he's a homosexual, or if he washes the dishes'.

Government health note: the cigarettes he smokes are Gauloises. Manual health note: the tip of the fourth finger of his left hand is missing. This makes him a natural for the villain in the next remake of *The 39 Steps*. How did he lose it? Well, that's another story. . .

 A

PETER ALLISS

Born: 1931, Berlin.

Golf is the Alliss's family trade. Peter's father, Percy, was working as a professional in Berlin when his son was born. Percy was a Ryder Cup star and has the reputation of being the best British player never to have won the open championship. Peter's best year in the British Open was 1954, when he was only four strokes behind Peter Thomson's winning 283 at Birkdale. Two years later he gained the first of three consecutive victories in the Spanish Open.

Like his father's, his putting often left something to be desired, and he has a permanent reminder of this in the number plate of his maroon Rolls — PUT 3. Peter's son, Gary, who began his professional career at his father's old club, Parkstone, feared for a long time that he might have inherited his father's and grandfather's weakness in this department.

When Peter quit playing professionally, it was taken for granted that he would step into the two-tone, studded shoes of the BBC's famous golf specialist, Henry Longhurst, and so he has. He also writes about the game, runs a golf course design business and is president of the Women's Professional Golfers' Association.

and Mark Phillips to the Jubilee celebrations. He describes this time as 'the most rewarding period of my life'. He cannot mean materially, for his salary was a comparatively meagre £10,000 a year, a great deal less than he could have made in TV. The kudos to be gained by working in such a priviledged post is, of course, considerable and it was widely rumoured that when he left the Palace, he would be

appointed to an executive position with his erstwhile employers, the BBC.

It seems then extraordinary that a man who had travelled the world, both as a leading foreign correspondent and as a royal aide should now be applying his professional talents to a magazine programme — a far cry indeed from denying Prince Charles's connection with this or that foreign princess, confirming Prince Charles's interest in

Three Degrees or issuing bulletins on Captain Phillips's career prospects.

Ronald Allison lives with his wife and two daughters (one of whom ran away from home a few years ago, causing her father to return early from a royal tour of Canada) in Hampton, in the county of Middlesex.

Watching football is a recreation as well as a job. He is also a keen photographer and painter.

MOIRA ANDERSON

Born: 1940, Ayrshire.

Stars on Sunday is only a part of Moira Anderson's life. She is constantly touring Britain to give concerts and, on a couple of trips, has been the star entertainer on the QE2. On these working cruises her accompanist takes along 'about eight tons of music', to satisfy the tastes of all sorts of passengers.

The big things in her life are her husband and her country. She lives in Glasgow, where her husband, a consultant anaesthetist, is an elder of the Church of Scotland. He is also a teetotal non-smoker, whose talents include playing the trumpet and piloting light aircraft. They have been married for eleven years, and always try to see each other at least once a week when Moira is away on tour. They have no children. Moira says: 'If I had a child, I would have to devote my life to it, because I couldn't be a part-time mother.'

Proud of her Anderson tartan (and, presumably, of the MacDonald, to which clan her husband belongs), she loves visiting different parts of Scotland, and is especially fond of Perthshire and of Sutherland, where her father, a deep-sea diver, used to take the family on holiday.

ANTHONY ANDREWS

Born: January 12, 1946.
Educated: Royal Masonic School, Bushey.

Although he is now inevitably associated with roles of an 'aristocratic' sort—like those he played in *The Pallisers, The London Assurance* and the soon to be seen *Bridehead Revisited*—Anthony Andrews' background is far from gilded. His parents were both in show business. When he was born his father was a musical arranger and conductor who worked with, among others, Vera Lynn, and his mother was a dancer. His father, who died when Andrews was only five, was a freemason. Had he lived, Anthony Andrews would probably not have received a public school education and the rather steely accent he has traded on ever since! However, the Royal Masonic School offered scholarships to the sons of masons who had died, and he took up one of them.

He was encouraged to go into the army but declined, preferring to take odd jobs

before knocking on the door of the Chichester Festival Theatre and being taken on, to his complete amazement, as a stage hand.

His wife has a career of her own with which he admits that he competes. She is Georgina Simpson, daughter of the hormone specialist, Leonard Simpson, who owns the Piccadilly store, of which she heads a section. They live in Wimbledon with their children, Joshua and Jessica, where Andrews spends his time between roles hatching plans to set up a production company.

EAMONN ANDREWS

Born: 1923, Dublin.
Educated: Synge Street Secondary School, Dublin.

Of the 'personalities' of TV's early days in this country,

none has survived so well as this resilient former boxer who, for 30 years, has been an invariably bonhomous presence on the screen, manifesting a touchingly ingenuous curiosity about a wide range of subjects. In 26 of those years he's been accosting unwitting people with his shy smile and the traditional statement: 'Thess is *yer* layfe'. In his book, *The Surprise of Your Life*, he wrote about the problems faced by the team preparing a show whose leading character is in ignorance of his role till the programme starts.

Heaven alone knows the secret of his success. A patently good nature? Being 'the one true unsophisticate

FRANCESCA ANNIS

Born: 1945, Kensington.
Educated: Convent.

For some years Ms Annis, who owes her looks to a Brazilian mother, was associated with the actor Jon Finch, who is never slow to remind the world of his reputation as a tearaway, high-liver etc. Nowadays her life has slowed down somewhat. She lives in Fulham with the photographer, Patrick Wiseman,

and their eight-month-old baby, Charlotte Emily. She made news at the tender age of three weeks when, slung round her mother's neck, she accompanied her on a promotional tour for *Lillie* in the USA.

Francesca Annis's previous experiences of America were not entirely happy. After her success in Polanski's *Macbeth,* she received numerous offers from Hollywood, but found the place stifling. 'The studios want to

run you, choose your friends for you'. She's well-known for her independence and common-sense, and even maintained her down-to-earth attitude during her first film part—no mean feat, considering that it was in *Cleopatra,* when 'Burton Tayloring' was taking on a new meaning.

Her recreations nowadays are enforcedly domestic— cooking, reading, listening to music. A far cry from the days when she travelled around India on her own.

JOHN ARLOTT

Born: February 25, 1914, Basingstoke.
Educated: Queen Mary School, Basingstoke.

Year after year, after a winter spent devoting himself to his other love—wine—Arlott reappears in April, in order to commentate on the first rained-off cricket match of the season. His face is now as famous as his voice, and for many viewers and listeners he is synonymous with the game, which has honoured him by electing him president of the

Cricketers' Association.

Arlott didn't begin his working life describing a seagull strutting about a muddy wicket; far from it. Until the age of 31 he was a

detective in the Hampshire Constabulary. A rather unusual policeman, to be sure, one who published poetry and topographical works about his native county.

Hampshire still means as much to him as it has always done, and among the many local matters with which he currently concerns himself is the Winchester and Alton Railway. He is on the unpaid board of this enterprising company, which has revived the 'watercress line' between Alresford (where he lives) and Ropley with the aid of many volunteers and the army.

left in showbiz? His willingness to display himself as just an ordinary guy? His ability to persuade others to do so? On this last count he is remarkably successful. Only two people in the history of *This Is Your Life* have ever refused to co-operate: Richard Gordon and Danny Blanchflower. The extraordinary thing is that Andrews, who commands up to £1,000 an appearance, is just as successful a businessman as performer. His prowess then, belies his screen image.

His capacity for work is well-known. Even as a teenage fighter—he was All-Ireland juvenile middleweight champion at the age of 16—he doubled as a radio commentator, sometimes dashing from the ring to the

microphone to commentate on the next bout. It was because of his reputation as 'an astute business head' that he was hired to present *Time For Business* for Thames TV, after the company replaced him on the *Today* show. His business interests, most of them based in his native Dublin, are varied. They include TV and radio studios, dance halls, 'leisure complexes', country clubs, theatres, an hotel, artistes' agencies. His first partner in these ventures was his father-in-law, Lorcan Bourke. He was also a consultant to the Irish Government when Telefis Eireann was set up.

Andrews and his wife, Grainne, were married in 1951. They have three

adopted children: Emma, Fergal and Nieamh, and divide their time between Portmarnock (outside Dublin) and Chiswick. He plays golf—with a handicap of 18—to relax, and fantasises about acting in a crime or Western series. He once wrote a play called *The Moon is Black,* which his father, who was keen on amateur dramatics, produced.

Whether the dismal failure of the exhumed *Eamonn Andrews Show* earlier this year will mark the beginning of the end remains to be seen, but the man who would count Andrews out is rash indeed. The very fact that he is so variously nicknamed (Seamus Android, Mr Bland, The Irish Joke) surely testifies to his endurance and popularity.

JAMES ARNESS

Born: 1924.
Lake Harriet, Minnesota.

Arness holds a record of which many of his fellow actors would not necessarily be proud. His Matt Dillon walked tall (6ft6ins, actually, and his eyes are blue) for 20 years in *Gunlaw* and *Gunsmoke*, becoming the longest-running of all charac-

ters—although the older residents of Coronation Street are not far behind.

Off screen, Arness rather lives up to the rough, tough role he played in *How The West Was Won.* He left his Norwegian-descended parents' comfortable home near Minneapolis when he was 16, and worked as a lumberjack, seaman and soldier. He was wounded at Anzio and then further injured, when the stretcher-bearers carrying him to an ambulance dropped him, causing him to spend a year in hospital. He drifted into films after the war at about the same time as his brother, Peter Graves, star of *Mission Impossible.*

His family life has been not only stormy, but touched by great misfortune. His first marriage, to Virginia Chapman, broke up in 1963. Soon afterwards, she slashed her wrists in a Hawaiian motel room.

She survived, but later took an overdose and died at Malibu two years ago. Two years previously, their daughter, Jenny, had committed suicide —another overdose—after breaking up with the rock star, Gregg Allman.

Arness remarried a year ago and lives with his new bride, Janet Surtees, in the Los Angeles suburb of Brentwood. He sees a lot of the two sons of his first marriage. One of them, Rolf, is a former world surfing champion. He likes to get away to the 1,000-acre ranch at Santa Barbara which his father runs for him, and is shy of publicity. In one of his rare interviews recently, Arness looked back with nostalgia to the good old days of *Gunsmoke,* when 'we'd have half a dozen killings and a few bar-room brawls every week .... Now they cut down on the violence and replace it with sexual activity'.

MICHAEL ASPEL

Born: January, 1933, London.

Aspel is, of course, well-known for being well-known. His early ambitions were to be a journalist (both his brothers write on motor-cycling) or, perhaps, a cartoonist or an actor. It was as an actor that he got his start—in radio, in Cardiff—and acting is something he has had the opportunity to turn to again in recent years. He has appeared in *Cinderella* and *Sleeping Beauty* in Croydon, toured the country as the narrator in *Side by Side by Sondheim* and played in *Private Lives* at Eastbourne. It was in this production that he met a local girl, Liz Power (Ellen Terry in *Lillie*), who became his wife in July, 1977. She is in her early thirties—the age which he likes to think of himself as being. Hence the carefully shaggy haircut, rather young for the face

on which it perches; hence the sneakers and denims and frequent admissions that he is 'highly sexed'. He is also prone to make remarks like: 'Sex should be dirty and furtive . . . I don't believe in monogamy'. This is as well, since Liz Power is his third

wife, though not long before they wed, he announced: 'I don't think I am marriageable material' and vowed that he would never marry again.

In his autobiography, *Polly Wants a Zebra*, he reveals what all his friends have known for ages. That he can never get over having had no 'teenage years' in the modern sense, and has been trying to make up for it ever since. Actually, this Peter Pan has two grown-up children by his first marriage—they are both at university in Australia now—and twins by his second marriage. They live nearby and often visit him and Liz at home in Wimbledon. They even accompanied the Aspels on their honeymoon.

Meanwhile Aspel's future looks as though it may owe a lot to his past. He is planning a story based on his experiences during the war, when he was evacuated from Tooting to Chard, in the county of Somerset.

DAVID ATTENBOROUGH

Born: May 8, 1926, Leicester.
Educated: Wyggeston School,
Leicester, and Clare College,
Cambridge.

Attenborough's is among the most successful of all careers in post-war British broadcasting. Just as now, when he stands gazing at a totem pole or polecat and seems to grant it a sort of censor's thumbs up — there, that's OK for you at home — so, for a period of eight years, from 1965 to 1973, he exercised similar control in a rather more straightforward manner.

After years as the BBC's house naturalist, closer to a nineteenth-century gentleman explorer than to the boy scout as which he is often characterized, he became the first Controller of BBC 2 and subsequently Director of Programmes. He has since profited from one of his innovations of this period — the 13-part series of a more or less educational character. Both *The Tribal Eye* and *Life on Earth* filled such slots to great acclaim from all quarters. He is a notably modest man who, when not travelling — he spends at least three months each year out of the country — lives quietly in Richmond with his wife Jane, not far from his brother, Sir Richard. The David Attenboroughs have two children, and their son is currently lecturing in anthropology at Oxford. The family has always had an academic bent — David Attenborough's father was Principal of Leicester University, and he himself has much respect for academic scientists, describing himself by comparison as a 'nature jockey' with no speciality.

PAM AYRES

Born: 1947, Stanford in the
Vale, Oxon.
Educated: Farringdon
Secondary Modern School.

The best selling poet of 1977 (the late Marc Bolan was the best-selling poet of 1971) lives nowadays in an alarmingly modern house at Standlake, a few miles from the village on the Oxfordshire-Berkshire border where she was born and where her family still lives. She has four brothers (two electricians, one plumber, one bricklayer). Her father used to work for the regional electricity board. Life has changed a bit since she became a household name and a person worth inviting to open a supermarket. But it hasn't changed that much, although she has acquired an MGB, a labrador and a secretary to help out with the bundles of fan mail that clog the postal system of the east Cotswolds.

It all seems pretty modest, you might think, compared with the weighty luxuries of certain stars, but that's Pam's style. Not that she has ever lacked ambition; she has it written all over her, though she went an odd way about achieving her current celebrity.

She left school when she was 15, and after a series of dreary jobs, joined the WRAF to see the world. In Singapore she began to take an interest in amateur dramatics on a nearby base and had a few walk-on parts in such classics as *Boeing Boeing* and *Collapse of Stout Party.* Infected by the show biz bug, she returned to England and resolved that she would get to the top, starting at the time-honoured bottom rung of Butlin's. What she didn't know was that Redcoats have to empty chemical toilets. (Remember that, next time you shake hands with Des O'Connor.) Pam left that job in short order and became a secretary, spending much of her spare time reading her poems in folk clubs in the south Midlands. At one such club she met an American teacher called Lawrence Strauss, who encouraged her to try to sell her work.

Full of confidence after having received the normal rejections, she published a volume herself and managed to sell 7,000 copies. She had already made a bit of a name for herself on *Woman's Hour* and Radio Oxford, and so had some professional savvy by the time Hughie Green put her on *Opportunity Knocks.* The rest is history; that is to say, she has her own show, scores of guest appearances, tours all over the world. . . .

Away from the stage, Pam enjoys cycling, country life and litigation. (She won 'substantial' libel damages from the *Sunday Express.*) She is currently at work on a new volume of verse to be published shortly.

BARBARA BACH

Born: 1948.

The lowest paid of Charlie's Angels, on a mere £20,000 per episode, Barbara Bach was an ideal choice to take over from Kate Jackson, who complained so frequently to the producers about having to strip, that she was fired.

Though she is American, born of an Irish mother to an Austrian father, she began her screen career in Italy after a brief stint as a model in New York. In Italy, she married the wealthy industrialist, Augusto Gregorini, and had two children (Francesca and Gianandrea) before they separated. Her name has since been linked, as they say, with the producer, Dan Rissner, who is vice-president of Warner Brothers Europe.

Among her most notable attributes is that of growing younger as the century grows older. The year of birth given above is generous.

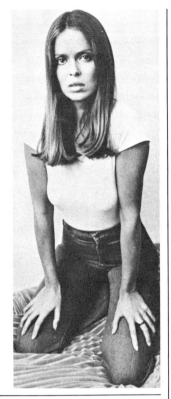

ROBIN BAILEY

Born: October 5, 1919. Hucknall, Nottinghamshire. Educated: Henry Mellish School, Nottingham.

Not only is Robin Bailey physically quite different from the shambling, ghastly, Uncle Mort he portrays, he is as far as can be from a philosophising, cunning misogynist. The word that everyone uses of him is elegant, and this he undoubtedly is. He prefers highly tailored suits, a clean shave and claret to a muffler, mutton chop whiskers and a pint. He was not born to this style, to which he has become accustomed. In fact, during his childhood, he got to know all sorts of families a bit like the Brandons in the village where his father had a small shop.

Bailey became a familiar face in 1957, when he was the actor chosen to present the British version of the $64,000 Question. Before this, he had worked in theatres all over the country, after a false start in the Civil Service. His next period of maximum exposure was in the successful soap opera, *The Newcomers,* in the mid-'sixties. The years hence, who knows? He lives in Wimbledon with his wife, Patricia, and enjoys playing tennis and travelling in Italy.

RICHARD BAKER

Born: 1926, Willesden. Educated: Kilburn Grammar School and Peterhouse, Cambridge.

Baker's interest in music was fostered from an early age by his parents, though he wasn't always a willing pupil and certainly cannot have imagined, when he was a 'cellist in his school orchestra, that he would one day become one of the best known presenters of music in the country.

He began as an actor. His Cambridge career – he was an exhibitioner in history, French and Italian – was interrupted by service in the Royal Navy towards the end of the war, and when he returned to university, he found his time increasingly taken up with theatrical activities. He abandoned his former ambition to become a teacher and went into rep. A few years, though, were enough, and he was taken on by the Third Programme as an announcer. In July, 1954, he became television's first news-reader and has been at it ever since. In 1977, myopia got the better of vanity, and he wore glasses on screen for the first time.

Music apart, Baker's overriding fondness is for the Navy, in which he rose to 'the dizzy height of Sub-Lieutenant'. He is now a Lieutenant-Commander in the RNVR and spends two weeks a year at sea. He made a short film about the Reserve's activities last year. He is also the author of biographies of the late First Sea Lord, Sir Michael Le Fanu, and Vice-Admiral Sir Gilbert Stephenson.

Baker lives in Radlett, near St Albans, with his wife, Margaret, and their two teenage sons, Andrew and James. He is publicly renowned for his hard work. Privately, he is renowned for his prodigious capacity for sleep.

TOM BAKER

Born: 1934, Liverpool.

The fourth Dr Who is a some-time Rasputin—on Laurence Olivier's recommendation, he played the role in the film *Nicholas and Alexandra*. He is also a sometime Don Quixote's horse—both ends. Baker has also written revues, served in the RAMC and been a hod carrier. He was actually work-ing on a building site when the BBC offered him the part of the doctor. He was glad to get it, not only because it afforded him a degree of fame and financial security, but because the show is one of which he approves: 'Dr Who doesn't shoot anybody or beat his wife, and has a heroic appeal to children. I think the biggest bores are James Bond, Kojak and footballers who do nothing but kick other people in the balls'. A typical comment.

Although not himself Irish he was a Catholic and was brought up among Irish Catho-lics in the tough Scotland Road area of Liverpool. He was for a time a novice with the Order of Ploermel in Jersey. At least one of his recreations, drinking Guinness, is typically Liver-pudlian. Another, 'beautiful women', is universal. He tends nowadays to spend less time in afternoon drinking clubs than he used, and devotes more time to making long train journeys, going to the cinema and collecting books. He is especially fond of diction-aries and reference books, and rues the fact that posses-sion of a large library rather inhibits his nomadic existence. He was, he says, not much encouraged to read as a child, and that is why he takes such pleasure in the YTV show, *The Book Tower*, which he intro-duced.

Baker used to be married to Anna Wheatcroft, niece of the late Harry Wheatcroft, the dundrearied rose grower. They have two sons who live with their mother in Nottingham. Tom Baker himself lives contentedly in Notting Hill.

JOAN BAKEWELL

Born: 1935, Stockport.
Educated: Stockport High
School and Cambridge.

Destined to be forever saddled with the epithet 'the thinking man's crumpet' after her eight years as an interviewer on *Late Night Line-Up* in the 'sixties, Miss Bakewell still manages to look just as young as she did then. Less earnest, though, and rather less inclined to promote her persona of daunting, all-purpose, popular thinker. She is, in fact, quite playful in her pronouncements nowadays, talking about all sorts of things like sex in aircraft, and writing a series of books on subjects as diverse as holidays and tombstones.

The change seems to coincide with her new career and new marriage. Her first marriage was to BBC pro-ducer Michael Bakewell, who is nowadays responsible for, among other things, the dub-bing into English of foreign-language films. They have two children, Harriott, 20, and Matthew, 16. They divorced after 15 years, soon after Miss Bakewell had lost her job on *Late Night Line-Up*.

In 1975, she married Jack Emery, and her general loosening up is attri-buted by friends to his influ-ence. Nowadays, she is a ubiquitous journalist and broadcaster, with a particular and profitable line in the Bronte trade, although, as a freelance, she has to put up with a certain amount of bloody-minded snubs. Her rival Esther Rantzen's omnipuissant husband, Des-mond Wilcox, recently referred to her publicly expressed disappointment at being dropped from a film in the kind of language we all under-stand: 'It's her bloody fault if she assumed that she had been chosen'. Still, that's just the sort of thing that someone who claims to have lost her Manchester accent sitting on the loo at a Cambridge party can ride with no trouble at all.

NICHOLAS BALL

Born: 1946, Hastings.
Educated: Harold's Eye
Secondary School.

The East End Wisenheimer in a twin tab collar, 'azell, is impersonated by an actor who is a Londoner only by adoption. After he left school at the age of 15, Ball went through a variety of jobs in his native Hastings, where his father was a bookie. He was a lorry driver, labourer and, during the sunny months, a deck-chair attendant. At the age of 20 he went off to the Bristol Old Vic School and on into a score of small TV parts, playing characters a lot younger than himself. None of them brought him much recognition and it wasn't till the ill-fated series *The Crezz* that producers began to notice him as a potential star.

Ball now enjoys a prosperous, unflashy life-style, whose only concession towards celebrity is an ex-directory 'phone—he was forever being pestered by admiring female fans—and a wallet as thick as a Bible.

RONNIE BARKER

Born: September 25, 1929.
Educated: Oxford City
High School.

Barker, the most notable of British comic actors, owes much to his having been an actor before he was a comic. It wasn't until the late 'sixties that, with exposure on shows like *The Frost Report*, he started to specialise in exclusively comic parts, and his characterisations still testify to his training and long experience as a straight actor. Indeed, his admission—not to be taken altogether seriously, perhaps—that: 'I haven't a personality of my own. I have to be someone else to be happy' is characteristic of an actor. It is not the sort of thing that a comedian, who has to rely so much on his own personality, would be likely to say.

This 'comic teddy bear' still recalls his earliest visit to the theatre at Aylesbury and High Wycombe—his parents' car couldn't safely get any further. Places like that do not smell of grease paint and success, but of 'tatty curtains and disinfectant'. It was the smell that attracted him to the stage. And

it was at Aylesbury that he got his first professional engagement, after working as a trainee architect and a bank clerk. His early fortunes in the theatre were typically mixed. On one occasion, a company with which he had been touring in Cornwall went bust, and he had to get back to London without a penny in his pocket.

Memories of such incidents seem to plague him. He still fears that it could all end tomorrow, and still cannot really believe his success, although tangible evidence of it is plentiful—a couple of houses (one in London and

PETER BARKWORTH

Born: January 14, 1929,
Margate.
Educated: Stockport
and R.A.D.A.

A regular on TV for close on twenty years, Barkworth has become a name only with the success of such comparatively recent enterprises as *Professional Foul* and *Telford's Change*. The latter was his own idea. He formed a company to make it, using several of the team who had been involved with his earlier successes, *The Country Party* and *The Saturday Party*. To start a company and become

involved in a project from its outset, might seem uncharacteristically forceful for a man who has said of himself that he is 'totally without ambition'. On the other hand, he is—as his work consistently demonstrates—something of a perfectionist, and perhaps the only way to ensure the right conditions is to establish them for yourself. Still, even in the flawed environment of run-of-the-mill TV production, he has had some notable successes, receiving a top-actor award for his *Edward VIII* five years before Edward Fox did so in the same role.

Barkworth is a bachelor, something of a loner, whose

the other at Littlehampton), a huge car and an even huger collection of Victorian objects and postcards. He has profited from his hobby, producing two books, one on period bathing beauties, the other on boudoir beauties. He describes himself as a 'delti-ologist' – collector of cards. Something else of which he has a more unusual collection is fan mail from prisoners and prison officers enthusing about *Porridge*. He has not always been overly keen on the character of Fletch, of whom he used strongly to disapprove, but Fletch has been good to Barker and he knows it. Others who have been good to him are Gerald Wiley, Jonathan Cobbold and Jack Goetz. These three gentlemen are scriptwriters for Barker and Ronnie Corbett, and it was some time before Corbett discovered that they are all pseudonymous incarnations of his partner.

While Fletch and his seedy family inhabit Muswell Hill, Barker and his respectable brood (one wife, three children) live not far away in Pinner, a fitting place for a conservative achiever – all prosperity and pretty laburnum and not a screw in sight.

rather contemplative style of acting is mirrored by his somewhat introverted pursuits – walking by himself and listening to music (he is a great opera buff) – and by the thoroughness of his life. He keeps a diary with meticulous care. It is soon to be published under the title *An Actor's Diary*. He also has a most receptive memory, in which he stores all that he might use professionally. His preoccupation with his art is total. He taught at R.A.D.A. for seven years (one of his pupils was Diana Rigg) and is currently writing a book on acting technique, rather modestly entitled *Tricks of the Trade*.

MICHAEL BARRATT

Born: January 3, 1928, Leeds.

Known, not entirely affectionately, as grumpy, this professional tyke is a less common sight on the screen now than he was a few years ago. That is to say, he is only on once a week, rather than hogging the box daily with his characteristic mixture of rude charm, rudeness and gruff, no-nonsense, direct mawkishness. Barratt's current slot is *Songs of Praise*, which might suggest that he has been put out to grass with God and the lads.

The rest of the time he devotes to his 'communications consultancy' (among his clients is Rentokil) and to his PR business. His partner in these enterprises, which he runs from near his Bryanston Street home, is the second Mrs Barratt, his sometime *Nationwide* co-presenter, Dilys Morgan. He married her on the Carribean island of Grenada two years ago, and she co-presented him with a son (his seventh child) sometime earlier this year.

Oddly enough, Barratt also met his first wife, Joan, at work. They were fellow reporters on a Loughborough newspaper in the early 'fifties. Their marriage ended suddenly after 24 years, when Barratt announced that he was in love with Miss Morgan. The first Mrs Barratt, who has worked as a barmaid since the divorce, said of her years with the grey-haired Lochinvar: 'I didn't exist as a person during our marriage. He took all the decisions, he was dominating'.

Barratt was just as able to get his way at work as he was at home. For some reason which has never been satisfactorily explained, the BBC gave him a send-off from *Nationwide* that it is never likely to repeat – it hired a train to conduct him on a quasi-royal progress round the country. The general public was somewhat put out by the extravagance of this gesture. Not a bad farewell present to a man who refers to himself as being 'amazingly ignorant on some subjects'.

RAYMOND BAXTER

Born: January 25, 1922, Ilford.
Educated: Ilford County
High School.

The year 1977 was something of an *annus terribilis* for the former Spitfire pilot who was part of the BBC's backbone of ex-officers who had joined the corporation by way of forces broadcasting. In 1977, he was subjected to much unwelcome publicity, when the gardener he sacked from his small estate at Denham, Buckinghamshire, brought an action against him at an industrial tribunal. The gardener's case was dismissed, but not before Baxter had displayed considerable emotion. The £35-a-week gardener and his wife refused to move from their tied cottage, and Baxter had to seek an eviction order against them.

Just a few weeks later, a row blew up between Baxter and the editor of *Tomorrow's World*, Michael Blakstad, who described Baxter as 'the last of the dinosaurs'. The two men had different views about a number of questions relating to the presentation of the programme and Baxter declined to continue because of this antipathy to the form that it was to take.

His appearances are now restricted to outside broadcast commentaries and the infrequent documentaries made by one or other of the BBC old-timers. His legacy is apparent in the odd, robot-like speech of his successors on *Tomorrow's World*, who evidently consider 'Baxter-speak' the correct mode for the presentation of things technological.

NORMAN BEATON

Born: October 31, 1934,
Georgetown, Guyana

The star of *Empire Road* is among the first black actors in this country to establish himself as something other than a local colour man. He is neither a grovelling Uncle Tom nor a finger-clicking hipster. He calls himself 'a black with a fragile public image', and it is enhanced by frequent

TOM BELL

Born: 1933, Liverpool.

Some idea of the conservatism of the British film industry (RIP) can be gained from the case of Bell. Sixteen years ago, he heckled the Duke of Edinburgh during a speech at the British Film Academy Award dinner. He had recently been much lauded for his part in *The L-Shaped Room*, and he is not alone in thinking that his gaffe probably cost him certain prize parts which would otherwise have come his way. Not, mind you, that he has done badly. Shortly after that incident, he made a good small-budget film called

STANLEY BAXTER

Born: May 26, 1926, Glasgow.
Educated: Hillhead High
School, Glasgow.

Baxter never stops acting. His wife, Moira, is used to his arriving home in the middle of the night after rehearsals, confronting her with yet another impersonation and asking her who the victim is. Mrs Baxter is a long-suffering person, who has given up a lot for her husband's singular career. They met in Scotland in 1952, when they were both extras in a comedy called *Bunty Pulls the Strings*, and after they married, Moira continued with her career for a while. Baxter had other ideas, however. He couldn't see her getting to the very top, and so encouraged her to quit the business, which she did. He now rather regrets that she took his advice.

One thing, though, that neither of them regrets is their lack of a family. They have both seen the burden placed on other stage marriages by children and, anyway, Baxter is not that sure whether he likes them: 'We hire relatives from time to time. When you get fed up with them, you return them to the fold'.

His own childhood was happy enough and pretty normal. He hated school, spent a lot of time at the cinema (where his favourites were Rogers and Astaire, and where he ate his mother's banana and marmalade sandwiches) and was encouraged in his theatrical aspirations by an understanding teacher. He began broadcasting at the age of 14, on children's programmes—where Mrs Mary

reports of his slightly un-
predictable and somewhat
eccentric life.

He worked in Guyana for
Radio Demerara and on a
local paper, and was a calypso
champion during the heyday
of the craze for such songs in
1957. Three years later, he
came to Britain to train as a
teacher in Liverpool at a time
when it was the centre of
Britain's nascent pop-culture.
During his time in that city, he
got to known Scaffold and

Adrian Henry, and began to
perform with them. He then
went on to writing musicals
and took to the stage in the
production of one of them, *Sit
Down Banner*, in 1968.

Beaton has subsequently
appeared in such things as
LWT's *The Fosters*, in Ron
Hutchinson's excellent TV
play *The Last Window Cleaner*
and in the film *Black Joy*. For
his role in this film,
that of a sort of Mr Fixit,
he won the Variety Club's

film actor award. Another
independent production with
which he was involved, in a
different capacity, is *The
Outsiders*, a documentary about
West Indian life in Britain
which he produced and into
which he put £7000 of his
own money. He is also the co-
founder of a black theatre
group based in Brixton.

Beaton is divorced, has
four children and lives in
the Birmingham suburb
of Moseley.

He Who Rides a Tiger, and
has been producing work of
consistently high quality ever
since.

However, it wasn't until *Out*,
which he has so far refused all
offers to repeat, that he really
showed the TV public just how

good he is. He realised the
potential of the part as soon as
he saw Trevor Preston's
script: 'I knew I was Frank
Ross. I'm not an actor anyway,
I just play myself'. Like Ross,
he comes from a hard background—Liverpool during the
depression.

He got a taste of something
different from a life of privation—
he was one of seven children
of a seaman—when he was
evacuated to Morecambe. He
learnt a kind of toughness in
those days which has stayed
with him ever since. His father
wanted him to acquire a trade,
but the young Bell had been
bitten by the acting bug, and
went off to a drama school in
Bradford.

Bell's toughness manifested
itself in his reputation for being
a difficult actor. Some producers don't thank him for the
sort of publicity he gives the
works he has appeared in. He
was openly critical of *Holocaust*
and has made clear his antipathy to appearing in it on
stage, although his last major
role, in *Bent*, received excellent notices. Evidently com-
fortably off, his life is quite
modest. He shares a house in
Camden Town with his girl
friend, Frances Tempest, and
their baby Polly, spends some
time half-heartedly gardening,
and follows with pleasure the
progress of his 17-year-old
son, Arran. He enjoys smoking
an occasional cheroot.

Whitehouse would be glad not
to see him again.

He has lived in Highgate for
20 years, and still finds time to
make frequent visits to his
native city, whose language
and edgy life still excite him.
He is less happy about the
way much of the place's
monumental Victorian centre
and Edwardian suburbs have
been swept away to accom-
modate a row of ring roads.
However, this is not simply out
of some sort of local partiality.
He is a great devotee of the
flashy architecture of the turn
of the century and was among
the leaders of a campaign, a
couple of years ago, to prevent
the destruction of Manchester
Opera House.

DAVID BELLAMY

*Born: 1932, Marylebone.
Educated: Chelsea Polytechnic,
Bedford College, London.*

The Arthur Mullard of natural
science was inspired to take
up the career he has pursued
so profitably by one George
Fluck, a cousin of Diana Fluck
(alias Diana Dors). This was
fairly soon after he had left
school and was working as a
junior laboratory technician at
Ewell Technical College, in
Surrey. After a tardy but
successful career as an
undergraduate and, later,
graduate student, he was
offered a job at Durham
University and moved north in

the early 'sixties. His specialities
have included peat, on which
he has written a text book, and
marine biology. An improbable
background for a TV star.

He and his wife, their son
Rufus and three adopted
daughters, still live near
Durham, although he gave up
teaching three years ago to
concentrate on TV.

There is some irony in the
fact that 'Dayweed Behwormy'
got his TV break as a result of
an ecological disaster—the
wreck of the tanker, Torrey
Canyon. He was frequently
pulled in to give an expert
opinion on the effects of the
oil spillage, a slick with a silver
lining which he could not
then have envisaged.

RITCHIE BENAUD

Born: October 6, 1930, Sydney.
Educated: Parramatta High
School, Sydney.

Renaud was one of the greatest cricketers of his generation (which included Cowdray, May, Truman, Harvey, O'Neill, and so on) and the first man to take 200 wickets and make 2,000 runs in Test cricket. This is a distinction now shared by the only all-rounder with whom he can be compared, Sir Gary Sobers. First capped for Australia against the West Indies in 1951, Benaud represented his country 63 times during the next 12 years, and succeeded Ian Craig as captain during the series against England in 1958-59. This was notable for England's persistent failures and for the performance of the Australian left-arm fast bowler, Ian 'Chucker' Meckiff. The business surrounding Meckiff, whom he strenuously defended, was not the first controversy in which Benaud had been involved. Indeed, as long ago as 1956, when fielding at gully at Lords (he held a catch from Cowdray which has passed into cricket lore as 'the catch of the century') he had begun to feel the antipathy of

the Australian cricketing authorities and was rather surprised to be appointed captain. He made a great success of the post and, of the 28 Tests in which he led his country, lost only four.

A reason for the authorities' mistrust of him was his profession. He was a journalist who never made any secret of his championship of players against the Establishment. It was his conviction that players were still getting a rough deal that prompted him to throw in his lot with Kerry Packer, predictably becoming the butt of the righteous indignation of many of his journalistic colleagues (who have, of course, not been cricketers). During his playing career, which ended in 1964, and ever since, he has tended to side with those who have a reputation for being 'difficult' – Ray Illingworth, Ian Chappell and Brian Close, for instance.

Despite being as high-powered off the field as he was on it – he still holds the record for the number of wickets taken in Test cricket by an Australian bowler – he leads a modest life and says that what he and his wife enjoy doing more than anything is 'sitting down with a few friends and drinking wine'.

LENNIE BENNETT

Born: 1939, Blackpool.

Bennett must be the only part-time show biz journalist who has crossed the footlights and achieved success on the other side. As Mike Berry – his real name – he worked for years as a journalist on a local paper in Blackpool, often reviewing the shows of those artists alongside whom he now performs. This has had its embarrassing moments, as Des O'Connor recalls: 'He

TONY BLACKBURN

Born: Parkstone, Dorset, 1943.
Educated: Millfield
School, Street.

Contrary to what one might believe, the ceaselessly smiling, pudding-coiffed, U-certificate disc jockey does think about his job. He admits that his strength lies in 'inane chatter', but in a world which demands such a thing and is choosy about the level of inanity and the chattiness of the chatter, it takes a real pro to deliver the goods. Blackburn is a child of Radio One, which he joined after a spell on Radio Caroline. He is not, however, uncritical of the

HYWEL BENNETT

Born: April 8, 1944, Garnant,
South Wales.
Educated: Henry Thornton
Grammar School, Clapham,
and R.A.D.A.

Bennett's career is now enjoying a great renaissance. In the 'sixties he was the star of countless forgettable films which earned him a fortune, a Rolls, a Queen Anne house in Richmond, and so on. He enjoyed the sort of popularity and acclaim that is more often the lot of a pop star. He married Cathy McGowan amid a blaze of publicity and

once reviewed me and said I was promising, but needed new material. Six years later, I saw him on stage using my routine. He told me afterwards: "I know it's dreadful, but it gets laughs'".

He was still a journalist when he began doing the rounds of the clubs with his act. Eventually, the two careers began to interfere with one another, and after consulting his wife, Margaret, to whom he has been married since 1958, he decided to chuck scribbling and become

a full-time entertainer. When he was getting started, he continued to provide material for, among others, Lonnie Donnegan and — would you believe— Des O'Connor. The world he entered was a far cry from that of the junior on the *West Lancashire Evening Gazette*, who once fell asleep at Lancaster Assizes and was roundly admonished by the judge.

A two-year contract with the BBC, a claim for Bennett and Stevens as the successors to Morecambe and Wise, a

£100,000 house in the exclusive Blackpool suburb of Cleveleys— these are the results of a partnership which came about by accident. Lennie and Jerry had known each other for two years, but had never thought of working together until a couple of years ago. BBC producer Ernest Maxim put the idea to them. It came at just the right time because, as Lennie rightly says, you don't really make it as a first-class TV comic until you are well into your thirties.

station that has made him famous. It isn't commercial enough, he considers. That's right. He'd like to see it limited to playing only 40 records a day— the same ones over and over again. In this way, he thinks, audiences would get larger and larger. They might also get brainwashed, but he

says he doesn't mind.

Since his separation from Tessa Wyatt— they have since divorced— Blackburn has been seen with a number of attractive young women, most of them ten or so years his junior— though you wouldn't believe it to look at him. All 32 of his teeth are his own, and he takes notably good care of his complexion.

His break up with Tessa Wyatt was, of course, too public for anyone to bear. He pleaded with her over the air waves, insisted for a long time that they were undertaking a 'trial separation', and was instructed by the BBC to 'rest'. He has lately become rather more acrimonious about the

whole business. If Miss Wyatt were to remarry, he says, he might be forced to apply for care and control of their son, Simon, six. He does not even now make a point of keeping up with her other TV appearances preferring *Crossroads,* which he never misses. He lives alone now, in the former family home at Cookham, and is very deeply concerned about what he considers to be the deterioration in the quality of life— to which Radio One has evidently not contributed— and the breakdown of law and order. He claims that a disc jockey's work is actually more risky than that of a miner and votes Tory.

they had a daughter called Emma, who is now eight years old. After a particularly dreadful film called *Percy*, in which he played a man who suffered a penis transplant, the decent parts began to dry up: 'I wish I'd never made it. It took two years for people to take me seriously again'. By that time, no one was making films in this country, and although Hollywood beckoned, Bennett demurred: 'I couldn't see myself ageing as a juvenile and turning up as a young punk in Kojak'. There followed a not uncommon series of misfortunes— his marriage broke up, he was

constantly asked to do carbon copies of old performances (notably the psychopath of *Twisted Nerve* and the innocent of *The Family Way*), and the tax man clamoured for payment.

Bennett's new career as a character player coincides with the adoption of an almost vagrant way of life. The house has been sold and so has the Rolls, in favour of an old Renault. He has also fulfilled his desire to be a director. He has been responsible for a number of productions at various rep theatres, including Birmingham.

His divorce from Cathy

McGowan was amicable enough, but he is wary of committing himself again: 'The rules I operate with mean non-involvement. I don't want or need any problems'. Bennett, whose father was a policeman and whose brother is the actor Alun Lewis, is now not only more choosy about what sort of work he does, but also less liable to dismiss offers at a glance. In 1971 he was offered the part in *Cabaret* which eventually went to Michael York, and he is still kicking himself for turning it down without really bothering to read the script thoroughly.

CHRISTOPHER BLAKE

Born: 1949, London.
Educated: Central School of
Speech   Drama.

Blake's introduction to the theatre was a familiar one. A girl friend of his in Brighton, where he was living with his parents and working as a tin-plater ('the acid burnt the clothes off my back'), told him that the theatre group he was in needed a scene painter. All that prevented him from going on the stage was a dense Cockney accent overlaid with Strine he had acquired during ten years of emigration.

He met his Liverpool-born wife, Wendy— they now have three children and live in Twickenham— when he was at drama school. Early on in his career, their financial position was a bit akin to that of the couple in *Mixed Blessings*. He wasn't actually out of work, but she was earning twice as much as he was. Before he got his starring role opposite Mel Martin in *Love for Lydia*— he had read the book and wrote to the producer suggesting himself for the part— he had been seen in a couple of other TV series, *Death or Glory Boy* and *Anne of Avonlea*.

A keen Arsenal supporter, he named his first daughter Charlotte after Charlie George, whose transfer must have been a source of some worry to him.

JAMES BOLAM

Born: June 16, 1938,
Sunderland.
Educated: Bede Grammar
School, Sunderland

Bolam is a markedly reticent man who is loath to say anything about himself or his work. For years, reports appeared to the effect that he was a ringer for Terry Collier, the Likely Lad who made him

REGINALD BOSANQUET

Born: September 9, 1932,
Surrey.
Educated: Winchester and
New College, Oxford.

The measure of this unlikely pin-up's popularity can be gauged by the fact that, last year, a Liverpool nurse claimed that he was the father of her new-born son. (The claim was unfounded, the

FRANK BOUGH

Born: January 15, 1933,
Fenton, Staffordshire.
Educated: Stoke-on-Trent,
Merton College, Oxford.

Grandstand could have been created for Bough, who's been at it for 11 years now. He played hockey for Shropshire, cricket for anyone who would have him, and football for Oxford— which makes him the only BBC commentator other than Bob Wilson to have played at Wembley. Sad to say, the team he was in at

famous. It's a fame he could have done without. He detests the idea of being 'identified' with the character. He also considers it nonsensical that he should be expected to show some sort of gratitude to Tyneside for his success. When he turned up late for a reception in Newcastle to celebrate the shooting of a Likely Lads film, he outraged local worthies by announcing: 'There is no special sentiment

paternity suit was dropped and Bosanquet was awarded libel damages against the *Daily Star*, which had seized upon the story with characteristic relish.)

Further evidence of his popularity is the fact that he is 'Reggie' to the world, a cuddly, red-faced reprobate who is undeniably a sort of minor national institution. His dalliances, his hairpiece and his pranks are all incessantly chronicled by columnists. They characterise him as a hard-drinking *bon viveur* who, for all his foibles, is a great bloke and a handy person to have around a bar.

Under the transparent alias of 'Ronnie Beaujolais', he is the hero of *Private Eye's* 'After the Break', which purports to recount the tale of Anna Ford's infatuation with him. During the past year, he

centre half lost 3 — 2 to Cambridge, but at least he felt the turf and all that. The sort of stamina required to get through 90 minutes on an infamously fatiguing pitch is what keeps him going, day in day out, year after year. During the 1976 Olympics, he stayed round the corner from the BBC, at the Shepherd's Bush Roundabout Hilton, and hardly saw his wife, Nesta, and their three sons. While he was rehearsing lines like 'The British girls . . . didn't quite qualify', his seventeenth wedding anniversary occurred. So

about coming to the North-East. A job is a job'. Local councillors duly made predictable noises about Bolam's being ungracious, ill-mannered, and so on.

Bolam, who has a three-year-old daughter, Lucy, by his co-star in *When the Boat Comes In*, Susan Jameson, is clearly unrepentant about this and similar incidents in his career. He points out, incidentally, that he left the North-East

when he was in his teens, and that, anyway, the idea of regional loyalty is one which offends him. Also, to the amazement of all who are unable to distinguish between an actor and the character he portrays, he sees no reason why he should pretend that Rodney Bewes is anything other than a colleague he met at work. Bolam used to live in Fulham. Now, he and Miss Jameson live in Surrey.

---

made news when, tired after a hard day's work, he left a Royal charity show before Prince Charles had arrived; when, on another evening out, he found himself being photographed with a topless model; and when he attended Victor Lownes's extravagant party to mark the 25th anniversary of Hugh Hefner's empire.

The son of an eccentric Edwardian test cricketer credited with the invention of the googly (an off-break bowled with a leg-break action) still known in Australia as a 'Bosie'), he was orphaned at the age of seven and evacuated to Canada. He was an academic success at school and took up a scholarship in English at Oxford after doing his national service as an officer in the Green Jackets. While still an undergraduate, he married for the first time.

The daughter of that union, Abigail, is now 22. His other daughter, from his second marriage, is 11. He inherited from his father a fondness and aptitude for sports. He enjoys cricket, claims to play tennis daily near his home in World's End, Chelsea, and is also very much at home beside a snooker table. He is president of the All England Bar Billiards Association.

One of his most endearing qualities is a lack of pretension (he wears a hairpiece for medical reasons, he says). While other news-readers tend to claim that they really want to be campaigning journalists or committed film-makers, Bosanquet seems quite happy with his lot. This may be because he has already done what so many of his colleagues aspire to.

---

preoccupied was he with commentating matters, that he forgot, for the first time ever, to give Nesta a present. The effort was all worth it though, for the following year Bough received the Richard Dimbleby Award for his unflappable linking of the events.

Sometimes confused with ex-ITN man Andrew Gardner, Bough learnt the ropes in broadcasting when he was in the forces. During his national service, he was commissioned in the Second Tank Regiment, where one of his fellow officers was the mountaineer, Chris

Bonnington. After he left the army he worked for ICI at Billingham in organisation and methods, played football in the competitive Northern League, and acted in local dramatic society productions. After besieging BBC Newcastle with letters, he was eventually granted an audition and was taken on to start the magazine programme, *Look North*. He's been around ever since, commuting to the BBC for the last few years from his house at Dorney, near Maidenhead where, on his one day off a week, he digs the garden.

MAX BOYCE

Born: 1945, Glyn Neath, South Wales.

Boyce trades on his Welshness in the same way as, say, Billy Connolly trades on his Scottishness. His particular brand of folkloric cosiness is rooted in the rugby-mad mining communities round Merthyr. He still lives there, in the village of Glyn Neath, close by the rugby club and not far from the terraced house that he owned when he was a miner. The fact that his father was killed in a mining accident a month before he was born did not deter him from that dark way of life, although he was always anxious to escape. He did so by studying to be an electrical engineer, but when he qualified he couldn't get a job, so he sang for his supper in clubs, using as material songs he had composed to entertain his friends. These same songs have now sold millions of copies and made him a rich man. This must please him no end and probably pleases his fans, but it does not by any means please all of his compatriots.

It is not just his gung-ho nationalism and his ceaseless digs at the English, appealing as they do to the lowest of all common denominators— chauvinism— but the way he turns the Welsh into a nation of quaint scoundrels and scroungers, that causes him to be less than totally popular. Still, those who complain are in the minority, and the extent of his appeal can be judged by the prices that tickets for his concerts fetch at venues as far apart as Penzance and Newcastle.

He is convinced that his success outside Wales shows that nationalism and rugby may be the apparent subjects of his songs, but that these are really anthems to companionship and good cheer.

KATIE BOYLE

Born: 1928, Italy.

Undeterred by an anonymous correspondent who threatened to murder her 25 years ago, if she did not quit appearing on TV, the Marchesa Caterina Imperiali de Francabilla has made a marvellous career out of being plain Katie Boyle. She was first seen on the box in 1953.

Her tonsils, beauty hints, and personal misfortunes have rarely been out of the news. From 1946, when she arrived in this country from her native Italy and was 'discovered by the egregious Beverley Nichols', to the present—when she claims to be in constant touch with her late husband—she has captivated the world with a sort of up-market triviality and determined charm.

The messages that she receives from her husband—Greville Baylis, an underwriter and racehorse-owner who died three years ago—are not the first sign that she is prone to para-normal experiences. Some 15 years ago, she was suffering from paralysis of the neck and left arm, and had given up hope, when she was recommended to a faith healer called Edward Fricker. Mr Fricker put on a record, made her stand on a stool and laid on his hands. The treatment worked, and Miss Boyle was able to dispense with her surgical collar.

She is soon to publish her autobiography, to which she has been putting the finishing touches at her Kensington home. Among the revelations it will contain will be the story of her tyrannical Italian father, who once committed her to a loony bin for nine months; the story of her tumultuous first marriage to the present Earl of Shannon; how she witnessed the rape of a woman by three soldiers in a dusty Italian street, while traditional Neapolitan folk songs played and mongrel dogs salivated on the curb, and the secrets of her perennial youthfulness.

RICHARD BRIERS

Born: January 14, 1934, Raynes Park.
Educated: Wimbledon and R.A.D.A.

When he was 16, Briers was sacked from an amateur theatrical company and, he says, deserved to be. But his determination was such that he didn't allow this setback to deter him, and eventually got into R.A.D.A. There he was a contemporary of Peter O'Toole and Albert Finney, beside whom he felt, well, a bit awkward. But again he didn't let comparison with his contemporaries get him down, progressing slowly but surely up the theatrical ladder. This wasn't viewed with much enthusiasm by his father, who himself had had numerous jobs and was anxious that his son should do something less chancy—banking rather than mountebanking.

Richard Briers realises that what makes him so special is also what makes him such an

MELVYN BRAGG

Born: October 6, 1939, Wigton.
Educated: Nelson Thomlinson School, Wigton, and Wadham College, Oxford.

The Cumbrian sage began his career at the BBC, in radio. He recalls being awed by some of the great names of wireless who were still around when he started, and by the ghosts of others who had stumbled along the corridors of Broadcasting House and round the corner to the Stag's Head—Louis MacNeice, Dylan Thomas, Julian MacClaren Ross. It was in this rather special atmosphere that he wrote the first of his nine novels. They are mostly set in Cumbria, where he now has time to go to write during some of his time off. It was in Cumbria, too, that he began

to develop his ideas about populist arts coverage in the broadcasting media. He later moved to TV and was eventually the subject of a 'transfer deal', when London Weekend lured him away with the promise of untold swimming pools and as much Jennings

Ale as he could drink. He is now openly critical of his former BBC colleagues. They are not, so far as one can gather from his pronouncements, sufficiently down to earth for his taste: 'An arty-farty bunch', he calls them.

Famous for his tie-knots, which are as large as anything a professional footballer could contrive, and for his eccentric elocution, Bragg is chairman of the Arts Council literature panel, and one of his more remarked-upon actions has been to withdraw the subsidies from the *New Review*. His chief recreation is walking. He lives with his second wife, their daughter, and about 10,000 books in a late-Victorian terraced house in Hampstead. His self-confessed weaknesses are an elephantine egocentricity and a well-known inability to stop working.

unusual person in the theatre: 'I'm really just the bloke next door . . . everybody's neighbour'. His life bears this out. His pursuits are quintessentially suburban — gardening, sitting in the garden, drinking in the garden with his wife Anne (whom he met when they were in rep in Liverpool), and walking their dog, Paddy, in local parks. They entertain only rarely. Alan Ayckbourne and Ronnie Barker are among their friends.

He describes his background as one of 'genteel poverty' and, although he is now among the most highly rewarded British actors — not least on account of all the commercials for which he does the voice over — his life is still unmistakably genteel, even though his particular patch, Bedford Park, where he lives in a house designed by Norman Shaw, still has about it something of the air of the 'artistic' suburb that it was intended to be, and is so represented in Chesterton's *The Man Who Was Thursday*.

TONY BRITTON

Born: June 9, 1924, Birmingham.

Though he has been around on the box for years, Britton's preference is the stage, and he spent half of this year touring in a Leicester production of *My Fair Lady* backed by the Arts Council. It was not the first time that he had played Professor Higgins — he had a two-and-a-half year stint in the part during the 'sixties.

Tony Britton's career began as an amateur in Weston-super-Mare and was interrupted by the war, during which he served in the Royal Artillery. Peace found him back in uniform in a variety of film roles, which he alternated with spells at the Old Vic. He made a lot of money, earned a reputation as something of a hell-raiser and spent a great deal of time with colleagues like Peter Finch and Trevor Howard. He put some of his money into a wine business in Fulham Road, where he is sometimes to be found serving astonished customers. The rest went on 'Fast cars, women, night clubs. I had a great time.'

Britton has two grown-up daughters by his first marriage, and a son by his second wife, the sculptress, Eve Castle, with whom he lives in Chelsea. He is not, he claims, anything like his *Robin's Nest* character: 'old fashioned, pompous, very, very conservative'. He is himself merely Tory, quite a long way to the right of the feckless MP he played in *The Nearly Man*. His recreations are gardening and travel.

ELEANOR BRON

Born: March 14, 1940, Stanmore.
Educated: North London Collegiate School and Newnham College, Cambridge.

When Miss Bron published her delightful *Life and Other Punctures*, which purports to be simply an account of two cycling trips (one round Normandy, the other through Holland), but is really a sort of informal autobiography, some fool reviewing it referred to her as 'a thinking man's Marianne Faithful'. Presumably, a heavy-handed reference to *Girl on a Motorcycle* was the intention, but, in fact, no reference could have been less apt. Miss Bron's life has certainly not been avidly and censoriously recorded in the *News of the World*, and her private life, so

far as she is concerned, is just that. She is unmarried, doesn't smoke or drink alcohol, cooks well, cycles a lot and visits the Zoo, of which she is an Associate Member.

Her professional activities are startlingly varied. She rose to fame in the 'satire' boom of the early 'sixties, of course. She had made her stage debut as a witch in *Hansel and Gretel* at primary school, acted in Chekhov and Shakespeare during her teens, and

written a review called *Minus Minus* before she arrived in Cambridge to read languages. There, she was in *Footlights* When she came down, she appeared with Peter Cook (who had struggled to have her the first woman elected to Footlights), John Bird, etc., at The Establishment. She also toured America for a year, before making her first appearance on the box in *Not So Much a Programme*.

She is well-known now as a straight actress, scriptwriter (she even does Crown Court) and composer of light verses — she has made a record reciting them to music by Saint-Saens. It is released by Bronze, owned by her brother Gerry, who used to manage the Bonzo Dog Band. She also performs concerts of a kind, as well as lecturing on anything and everything.

TIM BROOKE-TAYLOR

*Born: July 17, 1940, Buxton,
Derbyshire.
Educated: Winchester and
Cambridge.*

Another member of the 'sixties
'satire' Mafia, Brooke-Taylor
last year returned to the West
End for the first time since
1963, when he played there in
an undergraduate review called
Cambridge Circus. He hadn't
thought at the time of becoming a professional entertainer.
He had taken a degree in
economics and law, and
seemed set to follow in the
footsteps of his older brother,
Martin, who is a solicitor. But
he was already hooked on the
smell of the crowd (which is
rank) and was soon making a
name for himself in radio. In
1967, he starred in one of the
best of all TV comedy shows,
At Last the 1948 Show. Incidentally, he still considers
video the best medium for
comedy—'It can be extremely
rude'. He is worried about not

being able to be extremely
rude. He complains of the
Goodies: 'We can't get in
some filthy bits, because we
have such a large audience of
kids. It's a terrible strain being
good all the time'. Brooke-

Taylor wasn't always so good.
At the age of five he was expel-
led from school, and regrets
that he was consequently
unable to become a Brownie
and then a Girl Guide. Who
knows where he would have
been today?

Later on, he claims, he was
responsible for ruining a
Trevor Nunn production of
Much Ado at Cambridge.
Taking umbrage at being cast
as Third Night Watchman, he
determined to make the most
of the part and reveal Shakespeare's hitherto unnoticed
intention of having the Watchman as a major role.

Although his wife, Christine,
comes from near the Derbyshire spa town where he grew
up, they met in Switzerland,
where he spotted her on a ski
slope and determined to get
her, even if it meant crashing
into her. They have a son
called Benedict, and it is still
Tim Brooke-Taylor's intention
to play the other important
part in *Much Ado.* Definitely
not to be missed.

FAITH BROWN

*Born: May 28, 1947,
Liverpool.*

Faith Brown is not to be confused with Janet Brown. Both
are impersonatrices, both do
Margaret Thatcher, and Faith

sometimes does Janet doing
Maggie. Faith is the one with
the 41-inch bust. She first
realised that she had an aptitude for mimicry, when she
was a demonstrator of oven-
cleaners in a Liverpool store:
'Every time I did a demon-
stration, I used a different
accent. By the end of the day,
the audience was blocking the
aisles'.

She began as a singer in a
group managed by her hus-
band, Len Wadey. Eventually
she went solo and was billed
rather unflatteringly as the
female Tom Jones. We can
reveal that she has no hair on
her chest. One night, her
dress split on stage. In a
panic, she called out in a
funny voice for Len to bring
on safety pins. The previously
bored audience was reduced
to stitches, and Faith had
found a new career as a
comedienne. Until recently,

she and Len lived in Lydiate,
near Liverpool, but they have
been forced to move south
through pressure of work. The
apple of their eye is their baby
daughter, Danielle. For twelve
years they tried to have a
child, and Faith, although
assured by gynaecologists
that everything was all right,
often despaired of ever being
a mother. When she learnt
that she was pregnant, she
could hardly believe it.
Danielle now goes everywhere
with her mother and father.
Len is still managing Faith,
and often has to combine his
business with child-minding
when Faith is on-stage. Len
also has to cope with a lot of
gents who ask him if he could
fix up a date with Faith. In
these circumstances, he
simply points out that he is her
husband, rather than demon-
strate his talents as her
bodyguard.

JANET BROWN

Born: 1927, Rutherglen, Glasgow.

Janet Brown had her most famous subject thrust upon her by Eamonn Andrews. When Margaret Thatcher was elected to the leadership of the Tory Party four years ago, Thames TV's *Today Show* couldn't very well call on Mike Yarwood for an impression. Janet was contacted and arrived in the studios five minutes before she was due on the air. It was then that she revealed to Andrews that she had never done Thatcher before. All went well though, to the relief of Andrews and to the continuing profit of Miss Brown. She not only impersonates the Prime Minister in front of the cameras and on stage, but is often asked to stand in for her at functions. If we can't get Thatcher, goes the thinking, we can always try Janet Brown. Margaret Thatcher herself appears to enjoy the knowledge that she has a double—so much so, that she invited Janet to the Commons for tea. This engagement turned into a sort of lesson, with Thatcher advising Brown on the finer points of speech, gesture and hairdo.

That Janet admires her model is evident from her reaction to *Viva Magazine's* use of her Thatcher impersonation in a radio advertisement. She had completed the project ('First ladies everywhere are discovering *Viva* magazine'), when she discovered that *Viva* was to carry a piece by its editor, Bel Mooney, which was sharply critical of Thatcher. Janet Brown hastily wrote to Thatcher dissociating herself.

Though Thatcher's election victory was, of course, a great boon to Janet, this year began sadly for her, with the death of her husband, Peter Butterworth. After much heart-searching, Janet and her children—Tyler, 20, and Emma, 17—agreed that two shows he had recorded just before his death ought to be shown. Meanwhile, she has kept working, believing that it's the only way to keep her mind off her loss.

ALFRED BURKE

Born: February 28, 1918.

Burke's war was most unlike that of Richter, the character he plays in *Enemy at the Door*. He was a conscientious objector who worked as an agricultural labourer. He doesn't much like the perpetual British preoccupation with the war, but on the other hand reckons that the sort of role he plays—that of a civilised German who is neither National Socialist nor butcher—may help to redress the balance of previous series and films: 'It's terrible how we condemned a whole nation out of hand'. Burke's main objection to the role initially was that he would be obliged to shave his beard. However, he did a spot of self-interested research and found a photo of a German army officer with a full set, and so was allowed to keep his.

Burke, who is married, lives in Barnes and has two sets of twin sons. He achieved a huge following in the sixties as Marker, the ineffably seedy private detective in *Public Eye* —still, perhaps, the most subtle of all British telly sleuths.

Among other parts he has played in the last few years is that of Long John Silver in BBC TV's eccentric adaptation. With a Leeds University lecturer, Brian Wilks, he is co-author of a one-man show about the life of the Rev Patrick Bronte, father of the three sisters.

JAMES BURKE

*Born: December 22, 1936,
Londonderry.
Educated: Maidstone
Grammar School and Jesus
College, Oxford.*

'A nervous butterfly on a windy day', TV's sexiest-looking scientist' or — and this is surely the most likely — 'The man the BBC sent off to 20 countries and 150 locations, in the hope that he would never come back' — that's Burke. Only rarely has a man got such a pasting from all quarters as did Burke for his preposterous confection, *Connections* — what links a woman from New Zealand with hard boiled eggs, a plumber with a garrulous brother and the Berkeley Hunt?

Well, James Burke's wife, Madeline, comes from New Zealand. She enjoys getting away from her husband, and spends as much time as she possibly can visiting friends in different parts of the world. She is, he says, 'very independent'. Burke, for all his professed scientific and technological *nous*, can't cook. Like the Spanish, he can't even time an egg, so he lives on hard-boiled eggs. Being a man of many parts, he has a modicum of medical savvy, and knows what such a diet can do to a man. One of Burke's brothers is a plumber. The other two do what he calls 'ordinary jobs'. They came to England in the late 'thirties, when their parents (one is a Catholic and the other a Protestant) found the sectarian bigotry in Ulster too much to bear. Oh, and the Berkeley Hunt. Well, this is rhyming slang and gives us the epithet berk'. But this is a red herring. He used to be a teacher and has, in a way, never stopped. He was teaching English when he got a job as a TV reporter in Rome. Why science? Well, for the good reason that his subject was Eng Lit. OK?

ALASTAIR BURNETT

*Born: July 12, 1928, Sheffield.
Educated: The Leys School
and Worcester
College, Oxford.*

Burnett's father was cricket mad — more precisely, Yorkshire cricket mad. Now, we all know that Michael Colin Cowdrey was named by a similarly obsessed father, so that his initials would be appropriate to the career into which he would be pushed. Burnett's father went further in a way. A man can only play for Yorkshire if he has been born in the county, so Burnett père despatched his pregnant wife to Sheffield, in order that their off-spring should qualify. Heaven alone knows what would have happened had she given birth to a daughter. His reactions to his son's failure to make the grade as a cricketer have not been recorded.

If Burnett never shared his father's fondness for cricket, he certainly inherited his capacity for obsession. Burnett's is, of course, politics. He is a walking encyclopaedia of political information, and is at once both playful and very serious about the subject.

His ITN election guide was witty and impressively comprehensive. It was, perhaps, his inability to trivialise politics which made his period as editor of the *Daily Express* something less than a total success. He was notably unsympathetic towards the 'human-interest' approach the paper's readers were presumed to want. He has few recreations — racing (he gambles moderately) and reading thrillers — and hardly allows himself time for them. He leads an excessively private life with his wife, Maureen, in Kensington.

His background is Tory and vaguely religious — his uncle was a well-known Edinburgh divine. Though he manages to keep his views fairly well under cover when broadcasting, there are often hints — during the 1970 election he drank a lot of champagne in the studio when it became evident that a Conservative Government was going to be returned. His celebrations this year may have been tempered by the fact that he was an enthusiast of Heath, whose brand of Conservatism he much preferred to that of Mrs Thatcher. Like many exiles, he is very proud of his Scottishness and still maintains a house in Glasgow, the city where he began his journalistic career after failing to get the first class degree expected of him. This is sometimes attributed to his youthful lack of interest in subjects not exclusively Scottish.

A few years ago, when editor of the *Express*, he was critical of the way in which the police were handling the spate of IRA bombings in Britain, suggesting that suspects were being allowed free after insufficient questioning. For his troubles, he received a letter bomb, which he was lucky enough to spot. Experts defused it, which is as well, since he has a way of wanting to tackle such thing himself.

HUMPHREY BURTON

Born: March 25, 1931, Trowbridge.
Educated: Judd School, Tonbridge, and Fitzwilliam College, Cambridge.

Burton is surely Britain's most ardent amateur of opera. Whenever there is a singer exercising his larynx on the BBC, you can be sure that he will not be far behind – or, rather, you can be sure that he will be in front introducing whoever it is with his customary enthusiasm. Burton is also one of Britain's most, perhaps *the* most, prolific letter writers. He is forever popping up in the nation's newspapers and magazines, putting matters straight. If he is not defending himself against the jibes of critics or suggesting

very sensibly, that Muzak should be banned in public places, he is denying that he was responsible for coining the term that has gone down in history, 'simulcast', and so on.

As well as presenting operas and writing letters, Burton is boss of BBC TV's Music and Arts Department, a job which Russell Harty describes as 'the second best in television' – the best, presumably, being Russel Harty's. Harty also describes Burton as a 'Henry Kissinger of the arts', capable of anything – producing films, persuading the normally reticent to appear on the box, etc. It need hardly be said that he's a very energetic man, with a useful – some would call it paranoid – memory for everything that is said about him. He's very possibly the nearest

thing to a mogul that the BBC has got.

Burton plays squash, chess and cards, and enjoys competition. Music evidently plays a big part in his home life. He coaches his cello-playing daughter, Helena, every morning before he leaves for work. The family home is a Regency house on Richmond Hill. Burton's wife, Christina, was the first woman newsreader on Swedish TV in 1966. Since moving to London (they married in 1970), she has built a new career for herself as a photographer. Her husband's contacts have proved invaluable, and she does portraits of musicians for record covers. As well as Helena, they have a son, Lukas. Burton also has two children from an earlier marriage.

MAX BYGRAVES

Born: October 16, 1922, Rotherhithe.

'If television is a holy church', wrote an Antipodean critic, 'Max Bygraves should be at the door selling plastic effigies'. Max, of course, could not care less about what the critics think of him. 'I mean, I don't take any notice of their taste. After all, have you seen their wives?' The public appears to adore the man, and so do his fellow entertainers. Ernie Wise calls him 'businesslike, very rich, thoroughly relaxed, confident, fearless'.

Last year, he celebrated 30 years in the business, which has made him a sterling millionaire and allegedly the biggest single tax-payer in the country. At the Variety Club lunch in his honour, all the usual faces paid the usual compliments, while Arthur Askey revealed that Max's real name is Walter. He took the name Max – 'Wally Bygraves sounds like a flash book-

maker' – from Max Miller, whom he used to impersonate in wartime RAF shows. Wally served as an aircraftsman second class. Among his friends was Cliff Michelmore, who was after the same girl, a WRAF sergeant called Blossom. Wally got her, and they have been married now for 37 years. During this time, they have had three children and 'lots of laughs'. They live at Bournemouth in a house which is like a Hollywood version of Versailles. It was there that Max wrote his autobiography called, of course, *I Wanna Tell You a Story*. It made the top of the Scottish

best-seller list, but upset a lot of the people he grew up with in Swan Road, Rotherhithe. He was one of nine children of a poor family, and trained as a carpenter. He has also written a novel called *The Milkman's on his Way*, which makes use of some material that he considered too near the knuckle for a family entertainer's autobiography. He often says that he'd still be a chippy, had he not taken part in those wartime shows. After he was demobbed, he actually went back to his old trade, and then played the halls till he got his radio break on *Educating Archie*. Incidentally, he hated the dummy – as did Tony Hancock – and said of it recently: 'I hope he's got Dutch elm disease now'. Soon afterwards, a new career as a recording artist opened up for him, due he says, to 'having turned east and prayed to Decca'. During his career he has had a few dust-ups – and regrets one or two opportunities he would like to have taken, especially the chance to act in Hitchcock's film, *Frenzy*.

C

MARTI CAINE

Born: January 26, 1945, Sheffield.

Although Lynda Crapper, the estate agent's wife and mother of twins—for whom butcher Malcolm ('I'm fed up with being Mr Marti Caine') Stringer left Marti—has now left him, there is no chance of the couple coming together again. Malcolm now lives with the sons of his marriage to Marti, Lee, 17, and Max, 16, in a flat above his shop in Sheffield, having sold the Peak District house where he and Marti used to live. Marti, meanwhile, tends to live out of a suitcase in hotels, or at the home of her manager, Johnie Peller, and his wife.

Her personal misfortunes have forced her to alter her act. For all the years that she was a comedienne in shabby northern clubs, and even after she won the *New Faces* grand final four years ago, she built her material around gags about her husband and child-

ren. The price of fame is that such stuff would now no longer have any credibility. It has simply encouraged her to move farther from comedy.

She admits to loneliness now, though she is more often than not occupied by as much work as she can manage. She is a superstitious person, and extremely nervous. When she stopped smoking 80 cigarettes a day, she not only put on considerable weight, but found that her hair was falling out. 'I'd rather me lungs dropped out than me hair, so I went back on the fags'. Her favourite pastime, believe it or not, is housework.

KEN CAMPBELL

Born: 1941, Ilford.
Educated: R.A.D.A.

Actor is a meagre handle for someone who is also an impresario of the bizarre, a director and playwright, and a sometime guardian of a large ferret colony. He is the man who brought you, in association with the Liverpool School of Language, Dream and Pun, *Illuminatus*, which lasted for 10 hours—or maybe it was 20. He is the man who used to put a ferret down his trousers—'Once they bite, they don't let go'. His record was 50 seconds with one ferret, nothing to the man on the Bernard Braden show who placed two ferrets in his trousers for two minutes. The only trouble is that this licensed jester is restricted on the

box to acting in other people's stuff—*Laura Norder, The Last Window Cleaner,* and an advertisement for Dunn's menswear shops are among his recent appearances.

Campbell was encouraged to become an actor by his father, with whom he became very close after the death of his mother when he was 12. He worked with a well-known amateur group called James Cooper's Ilford Renagades, went into rep after R.A.D.A., and began his odyssey of hijinks with a production of *Treasure Island* done in the public swimming baths at Bournemouth. In this, he directed 14 aqua-lovelies and played Long John Silver. Campbell's wife is the actress, Prunella Gee; his daughter is the baby, Daisy; his dog the mongrel, Werner, and his home is in Hampstead.

PATRICK CAMPBELL

Born: June 3, 1913.
Educated: Rossall and Pembroke College, Oxford.

One of the few men in history to have turned a stammer to good account—it's not what he says, it's how he manages not to say it—Campbell is the third Baron Glenavy and the brother of Michael Campbell the novelist, author of *Lord Dismiss Us,* etc. He is a journalist who has worked for the *Irish Times* and *Sunday Despatch,* was assistant editor of the short-lived and much mourned magazine, *Lilliput,* during the late 'forties, and became known for his massive speech impediment on *Not So Much a Programme,* where he sparred with such specimens

HARRY CARPENTER

Born: 1925, South Norwood.

'Not as dumb as he looks' is Mohammed Ali's opinion of the boxing commentator, whom he first met during the 1960 Olympics in Rome. Carpenter had, of course, been around for a while before that tournament. His father, who was vice-president of a boxing club, taught him to appreciate

JASPER CAROTT

Born: March 14, 1945, Acocks Green, Birmingham.
Educated: Moseley Grammar School.

Seen in a fog or through the smoke in the clubs where he used to perform, Carott looks a bit like Trevor Francis, who provided him with so much material. Sport, especially football, and especially Birmingham City ('lose some, draw some, that's us . . .') is his second priority in life. His wife and family come first, he says, and show business—which he just drifted into—comes third,

of elocutive perfection as Norman St John-Stevas, the late Harvey Orkin and, of course, David Frost. He was for 18 years a columnist on the *Sunday Times.* He is not the author of a book called *You Want to Write for Television?* That is another Patrick Campbell, the Patrick Campbell whom the 'real PC', Lord G, might refer to as the 'unreal PC'. Got it?

The journalist Campbell inherited his title from his father in 1963. His family is distinguished in politics and the law. His father was Secretary to the Irish Department of Industry and Commerce from 1922 to 1932, while his grandfather was Lord Chancellor of Ireland and first Chairman of the Senate of the Irish Free State.

Campbell was doubtless too lazy to follow in such august footsteps. At the age of 15, he announced to his father his intention to retire, and has done his best to achieve that ambition throughout his life. He prefers TV to writing, because it is less strenuous, although he admits to a gulf between his previous conception of himself ('Debonair, sporting') and what he sees on the screen. He and his wife, Vivienne, abandoned their Belgravia basement a few years ago, and are now shacked up on the Riviera, where they spend their days avoiding the other expatriates who inhabit the scent town of Grasse. He has actually been an expatriate all his adult life, living in Germany before World War II.

---

the sport. When he left the Royal Navy at the end of the war, he worked on small newspapers that specialised in greyhound racing and speedway, before moving on to the *Daily Express,* whose boxing correspondent he was until 1962, when he went full time into TV.

As a young reporter, Carpenter saw Freddie Mills, Bruce Woodcock and Randolph Turpin gain their world titles, but he is not starry-eyed about that period, recalling in his pictorial history of boxing that the boxers were tested to the limit, and sometimes beyond, by their promoters. For all his knowledge and enthusiasm, he has never himself boxed. All he plays is golf, and that with a handicap of 22. It is an understandable choice for a man who dislikes team games and prefers one-to-one confrontations, which

accounts for his enthusiasm for tennis.

Carpenter has a son of 24 and lives with his wife in Crystal Palace, not far from where he was born. He was once introduced on the air thus: 'Harry Commentator is your carpenter', and he himself is not innocent of such slips. He once rather unfortunately described an Irish boxer as 'the blonde bomber from Dublin'.

---

even though it has brought him fame, a Panther Lima (which is a car) and a big house at Knowle. His wife, Hazel, was a journalist on a Solihull paper, and they have

four children who are not called Carott—his real name is Robert Davies.

He was an agent—of sorts—before he was a performer. Before that, he was all sorts of things: market trader, driver, sales rep, lampshade maker. Then there was this agency—he was determined to set up in some kind of business. Among the acts he booked were Stephane Grapelli and Billy Connolly. When the agency began to fail, Carott went on stage himself to support it, and at a number of clubs, including one which he ran himself, called The Boggery, he built up a reper-

toire and a reputation.

His original interest in folk music was promoted by his friend, Bev Bevan of the Electric Light Orchestra, but it wasn't till 1975 that Carott had any sort of success—with his record, *Funkie Moped.* All this time, his mother was complaining that he didn't have a proper job, and she still keeps up that tune, even though her son now commands £6,000 a performance. That's her worry. His is that he's going to run out of material: 'In six hours of television I've used up seven years of material, which represents 20-odd years of experience'.

VIOLET CARSON

Born: September 1, 1899.

'She's taken over. She rules my life. I begged them to bury the old girl and let me go, but they won't'. That is Violet Carson on Ena Sharples, the character who, she claims, has 'destroyed her'. She has never been terribly keen on the character of Ena. It is Ena, she maintains, who is famous, not Violet Carson. She almost turned down the part when she auditioned, because of the bitchiness it involved – and when she learnt that Coronation Street was to run for 13 weeks, she was aghast. The odd thing is that Ena almost didn't exist at all. When the show was being prepared for its first run in 1960, it was touch and go whether the scriptwriters would actually include her.

She is now, of course, a sort of national institution, perhaps not as famous as during the 'sixties but still, it is claimed, more recognised than the Queen in certain obscure corners of the damp north-west and in Australia, where 150,000 people turned out to welcome her when she was on a tour there in 1968. All sorts of changes have taken place in the street and away from it – not least the demolition of Archie Street, Salford, which was the model for the place. Violet Carson is quick to point out others. She thought the show was better when it was in black and white, but welcomes the technical innovations which allow it to be pre-recorded scene by scene. She is impatient with some of the new, younger directors.

Miss Carson's constant companion is her sister, Nelly Kelly, with whom she shares a house in Blackpool, where she grows roses. Just as she has remained loyal to the north, so has the north honoured her. Manchester University conferred an honorary degree on her, and her effigy replaced Marlene Dietrich's at Blackpool waxworks. A world away from the days when she thumped a piano as accompaniment to silent films, before moving on to do the same for Wilfred Pickles and Mable at the Table.

JUDITH CHALMERS

Born: 1936, Didsbury, Manchester.
Educated: Withington High School, Manchester.

Judith Chalmers made her broadcasting debut at the age of 13 as an announcer on *Children's Hour*. A dozen or so years later, she became one of the BBC's 'glamour hostesses', and her engagement, marriage, and confinements were followed with the sort of interest granted today to, say, Anna Ford. Her husband is former

GRAHAM CHAPMAN

Born: January 8, 1941, Leicester.
Educated: Cambridge and St. Bartholomew's Hospital.

The gangly actor was first seen in *At Last the 1948 Show* with Cleese, Feldman and Brooke-Taylor, only three years after he had qualified as a doctor. He subsequently completely abandoned medicine on the advice of, believe it or not, the Queen Mother. She encountered Chapman over a cup of tea at Bart's, when he was president of the Students' Union. He recalls that she had 'lovely skin' and that she thought it would be a good idea if he went to New Zealand with a revue, which thus became a sort of Royal Command Performance.

ROY CASTLE

Born: August 28, 1932, Scholes, Yorkshire.
Educated: Holme Valley Grammar School.

Castle can do practically anything in variety and often does. He is in the *Guinness Book of Records* for his interesting feat of playing *Whistle While You Work* on 43 different instruments in four

minutes, and for doing 24 tap-dance beats in one second. He has been tap dancing since he was a child, and calls his former self 'a Yorkshire Jimmy Osmond'. He was delighted when, at the première of *That's Entertainment*, he actually touched Fred Astaire, Gene Kelly and Donald O'Connor, the idols of his childhood and youth in Huddersfield. He learnt tap dancing from the age of eight,

BBC sports producer Neil Durden-Smith, and her children, Emma and Mark, are now aged 12 and 10. As hostess of the holiday programme *Wish You Were Here*, she gets free trips all over the world, and is eagerly hoping to overtake the number of places visited by her husband during his years in the Navy. One place that won't count in that quest is Blackpool, which she was delighted to show off to her daughter as the place where she spent her holidays as a child, when it was still the natural resort for Mancunians.

Chapman was one of the first actors to talk publicly and entirely straightforwardly about being a homosexual. He is, as you'd expect, quite funny about the aftermath of such a declaration. 'A brewery wanted to put me in an advert as a barman, but decided they couldn't. And a lady from Newcastle wrote to me and told me I should be put to death. Eric Idle wrote back to her and said that this had already been done'.

GEANETTE CHARLES

Born: 1929.

One of Mrs Charles' most persistent and rather comical fantasies is that she is likely to be attacked by some assailant who mistakes her for the Queen, when she is out shopping or in a public loo. In fact, her anxiety about being the target of a bomb attack is such that she will never go into a public loo by herself — hoping that any potential pseudo-regicide will be a humane person who does not want to kill innocent bystanders and so will not throw his diabolical device. Mrs Charles, who lives at Danbury, near Chelmsford, has heard from somewhere that the Palace is quite amused by her activities, which include 'knighting' people. This is popular with German and Japanese tourists. Appearing at functions in full regalia, she is paid about £100 an appearance and insists: 'We are not greedy'. She has also appeared in a film called *Secrets of a Super Stud* — but this, according to the producer, Morton W. Lewis, has nothing to do with her resemblance to Her Majesty. 'I wouldn't dream of doing anything to embarrass the Royal Family. I'm a loyalist (sic). It's just a coincidence', he said.

Mrs Charles' career was for some time hampered by the failure of Equity, the actors'

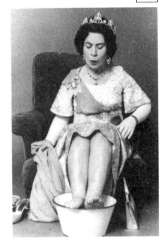

union, to acknowledge that looking like the Queen involves acting skills, although in her twenties she had worked in rep. Since being accepted for membership, she has appeared in *Queen Kong*, in which she is chased by an ape.

Throughout her life, Mrs Charles has been mistaken for her double. Woman have curtseyed to her in the street, and she has been given unsolicited police escorts. She has never met the Queen, though she came near to it when her husband, an oil executive, was to be introduced at the opening of a pipe-line. However, for the peace of mind of all concerned, her husband did not attend the ceremony and so both ladies must still content themselves with mirrors.

and when his fellow pupils heard about this extra-curricular activity, he was teased so consistently that he had to pick fights to prove that he was as much a man as any of them. Though his parents were not professional entertainers — his father was in insurance, and his mother was a hairdresser — his mother's family formed an amateur show band, and no one objected when he went straight from school at the age

of 15 into a Blackpool summer show. Much of his instrumental prowess he owes to an uncle, who was a stalwart of several brass bands.

'This is Fiona, she's in love with you'. Thus Eric Morecambe introduced Roy Castle to Fiona Dickson during a TV show in 1963, then promptly walking off and leaving the embarrassed couple facing each other. A year later the two of them were married and

Castle now puts family before business, since constant separation from Fiona and their three children, threatened at one time to break up their marriage. They are both committed Christians and regularly attend the Baptist church near their home in Gerrards Cross. Not content with the exercise he gets on stage — he reckons to lose 1,000 calories a night — he also jogs with his dog and plays squash.

C
JOHN CLEESE

Born: October 27, 1939,
Weston-Super-Mare.
Educated: Clifton College,
Bristol, and Cambridge.

Cleese describes himself as 'happily unmarried'. He owes this condition, he says, to the group psychotherapy which he and his former wife, Connie Booth, practised during the time that they were splitting up. Though it didn't prevent their divorce, it did at least mean that the couple remained on friendly enough terms to make a second series of *Fawlty Towers,* which was transmitted earlier this year. You're quite right, everyone else thought it was about the fifth series, too. It must be the ultimate in compliments to a situation comedy to suffer because of such a delusion as the result of what has simply been a series of repeats.

With daps on his feet he stands 6ft 6ins — big John. Another inch, and he would be medically classified as a 'giant'. Norwegian TV is evidently not too fussy about such things. This year, the comedy prize at the Montreux TV Festival went to a show called *To Norway, Home of Giants,* starring Cleese, who found himself competing against himself in *Fawlty Towers.* Not that he thought the BBC's show would have had even a remote chance of

winning anyway.

Had John Cleese's grandfather, a sensitive, easily embarrassed man, not changed the family name, John Cleese would be called John Cheese. It has even been suggested that what fired his ambition to be a comic was missing out on instant laughs when he introduced himself. Like many another comic, he began by accident, first realising his potential when cast as Lucifer in a school production of Goethe's *Faust.* As soon as he made his 'tremendous entry', the entire audience fell about laughing. He then trod the familiar path through Cambridge, where he read law and devoted his time to revues. (For years his parents expressed their disappointment that he had not become a solicitor.)

At Cambridge, he met Bill Oddie, Brooke-Taylor, Graham Chapman and, of course, David Frost, who put him on *The Frost Report.* He went on to *At Last the 1948 Show, Monty Python* and celebrity.

Cleese lives near his ex-wife and daughter, Cynthia, off Kensington High Street, a quarter of London which probably has more over-priced, pretentious, third-grade restaurants than any other. He says that, now he lives alone, he wastes all his money in such places and loves watching the waiters, most of them rather less agreeable than Manuel. He reckons that there is little so inspiring as the smooth discourtesy and evasiveness of waiters. One of the classic lines in *Monty Python* was addressed to two customers in a restaurant: 'The head waiter will be here to abuse you in a minute'. However, even that hardly matches the reply Cleese got when he asked in a hamburger joint if they had any mineral water. 'Not as such', said the crafty waiter.

The rewards of his reputation are offers to work with such people as Mel Brooks and Jacques Tati, the money to establish a highly successful firm making comic training programmes for industry, and a Rolls. The price is that he can no longer travel anonymously on the Tube and fake a fit or an uncontrollable twitch.

MAURICE COLBORNE

Born: September 24, 1939,
Sheffield

Colborne's theatrical career began with a meeting with Tom Courtenay. At that time he was hanging about London, living on the bread line in Bow, and working as what he calls 'a pavement artist', i.e., laying paving stones. He never

managed to get the knack of it, somehow. When he was accepted at the Central Drama School, he moved to Hampstead, and is living there again nowadays. After a period in rep, he became involved in the burgeoning fringe theatre of the late 'sixties. he worked with David Hare's portable theatre, and then helped to establish the Half Moon in Aldgate, where he lived till his house was condemned. Though gang-

ster and supporting roles have given him a measure of fame, his heart is still in the theatre, where he enjoys having to exercise a multitude of talents — singing, clowning, dancing, etc. He claims that he is fed up with being cast as a villain, because 'it's second division', even though such roles have revealed him as about the only British actor who can rival Delon and Eastwood for the cool machismo that is the hallmark of their personas.

GEORGE COLE

Born: April 22, 1925, Tooting.
Educated: Morden
Council School.

Cole is often to be found wearing a pair of blue suede shoes—a rather sober, rather scuffed pair to be sure, but with an undeniable suggestion of a raffish past, of having trodden some dodgy paths in their time, of having made some quick flits at midnight. These are the shoes that he has had for getting on for 30 years, the shoes he wore as Flash Harry of St. Trinians, or so he says. When he made the first of those films, he had already been an actor for 15 years.

He started in 1939 at the age of 14. He was a newspaper boy about to leave school and with no job to go to. Glancing through the defunct *Star* before he dispatched it into the letterbox of a house in deepest South London, he read of a vacancy for a 14 year-old-boy to lead two goats across the stage in a West End production of *White Horse Inn*. He applied for the job and got it.

It was the great teacher turned actor, Alastair Sim, who took Cole under his wing and taught him to talk and to act. Until his death a couple of years ago, Sim lived near Cole's house at Nettlebed, in Oxfordshire, and the two of them were frequently cast alongside each other, not only in the St. Trinians films, but also in plays like *The Bargain*. His most famous partner, though, was Percy Edwards, who played Psyche the dog in the radio series, *Life of Bliss*, during the 'fifties. Psyche got more fan mail than Bliss, he recalls. He says that he is frequently accosted by 'terrible old women in supermarkets', who tell him that they used to listen to him when they were at school. Cole still lives in Nettlebed, with his second wife, Penny, and their two children.

DAVID COLEMAN

Born: 1927, Cheshire.

Although he is now more famous for his amazing slips of the tongue ('Wales are bidding for their cripple crown'), statements of the obvious ('There's no score, it's Hibs nil, Rangers nil') and penchant for hyperbole ('That's it, number 3, goals pay the rent'), Coleman is still the BBC's top commentator.

He has always had the reputation of being 'a man in a hurry'. He was Cheshire's champion miler when he was 23, the age at which he attained his first editorship—of the *Wilmslow Alderley Express*. During his time in the editor's chair he was once assaulted by an irate councillor, stories of whose professional malpractice he had run in the paper. As well as being a fine runner, he was also something of a footballer. In his early days, he was once recruited by Stockport County Reserves to make up their team for a match he was attending in order to report it.

He raced through the BBC ranks very quickly and, four years after joining the Corporation as an assistant news editor in Birmingham, he became the first presenter of *Grandstand*. All went well until he felt that he was being passed over for important commentaries (just as Kenneth Wolstenholme, his predecessor, had been passed over, so he knew the signs). He sued the Corporation, and was off the air for a year before the dispute was settled by 'amicable discussion'.

During this period, he was tipped as a candidate for the chairmanship of the Sports Council—he has served on Sports Aid Foundation committees and was a member of the Royal Commission on Gambling. He was also, inevitably, rumoured to be on the move to ITV. His return to the BBC caused some worry to those younger commentators who, during his absence, had become used to covering major events themselves. The members of Coleman's family—he and his wife, Barbara, have six children—are not sporting slouches. The most successful to date is his daughter, Anne, who was the youngest ever British Ladies Show Jumping champion at the age of 16 and is a consistent prize-money winner at top events.

C

PAULINE COLLINS
(see also John Alderton)

Born: September 3, 1940, Exmouth.
Educated: Sacred Heart Convent, Hammersmith.

Pauline Collins' Liverpool Irish parents were both teachers, and so is one of her sisters. One of her grandmothers was Elaine Reid, the opera singer. She compromised and trained as a drama teacher, but only because, if she had admitted she was training for the stage, she would not have been able to obtain a grant. She did, in fact, teach for a time, as well as working as a waitress at the Cromwell Road air terminal and as an assistant at Harrods. Her first

appearance was at Windsor rep. Soon afterwards, she had a small part in *Emergency Ward Ten*, where she first met John Alderton, though at that time she was going out with a cameraman, and he was married to Jill Browne.

So much of her professional life—and nearly all of it on TV—has been in collaboration with her husband, that her achievements by herself have been overshadowed. She has played in numerous West End National Theatre productions— *Engaged*, *The Erpingham Camp*, *Confusions*, etc. She also harbours the ambition to write, and finds herself getting up to scribble in the middle of the night—'But I'm not sure that I've got the proportion of inspiration and perspiration quite right'.

PETER COOK

Born: October 17, 1937, Torquay.
Educated: Radley and Pembroke College, Cambridge.

Whatever happened to the all-round entertainer of yore. A great bloke for a joke between the final curtain and Ovaltine time', recalls one of his friends from the clean

old days. On the ATV pop-show, *Revolver,* he was cast as an intemperate and intermittently foulmouthed dance-hall manager, and his Derek and Clive records (made in conjunction with Dudley Moore) are not notable for the moderation of their language. Cook has also permed his hair, got a divorce from his wife, Judy Huxtable ('sexburga') and announced his fondness for Margaret

TOMMY COOPER

Born: 1922, Caerphilly.

Though the comic's father was a Welshman and a former miner, he was born in Wales

only because his parents happened to be on holiday there at the time. He was brought up in Hamble, near Southampton, where his father had a poultry farm. His accent still owes something to this. He began to learn conjuring tricks at the age of 10, and gave his first canteen show to fellow apprentice shipwrights at the age of 17. Everything went wrong. Things continued to go wrong when he did similar shows as Trooper Cooper of the Horse Guards. But his audiences loved him, never knowing whether the mistakes were planned or the product of a fumbling oaf.

BILLY CONNOLLY

Born: November 24, 1942, Anderston, Glasgow.
Educated: St Gerrard's Secondary School, Gotham.

The tartan class warrior has found that £300,000 per annum brings all sorts of problems. Former fans find it difficult to 'identify' with the tenement cowboy, now that he has moved into a huge house north-west of Glasgow and near Loch Lomond, with its own fishing. And his resolve not to drive a Rolls ('a two finger symbol on wheels') doesn't cut much ice, since he drives a custom-built Mercedes station wagon. Connolly himself admits: 'I am not one of them any more'. Nonetheless, he still has an

He'd attribute them to the latter, but off-stage he is one of the most accomplished magicians in Britain, a member of the inner circle of the Magic Circle.

Cooper's wife, Gwen, whom he calls Dove ('I've never seen anything less like a dove', she says) was an ENSA pianist, and they met somewhere near Port Said. There was, she remembers, 'this lad with eyes the colour of the sea. Well, you have to say something nice about the bugger'. When they came back to England, he started to play in pantos and was voted the funniest man in Britain as long ago as

uncanny understanding of Glasgow, and his repertoire of stories about vomiting, excretion, lavatories, etc., is unlikely to change. A fortune has never prevented anyone from telling lavatory jokes. Indeed, Britain's Number One family is well-known to be fond of this type of humour.

Thatcher — he reckons that comics are naturally conservative.

Cook supports Tottenham Hotspur, which shows both a big heart for lost causes and an understandable devotion to the increasingly far past, when both Blanchflower's Spurs and *Beyond the Fringe* were going great guns. He also supports *Private Eye*, about which the hard-hearted might say the same.

1952. Soon afterwards, he bought a house in Barrowgate Road, Chiswick — just round the corner from Jimmy Young, actually — and the place is now a repository of theatrical props, with little room for its inhabitants. Both their children live there from time to time.

Cooper has had his share of accidents, and his health has been poor recently. He is, however, getting so used to being asked if he knows any heart-attack jokes, that he has at least one up his sleeve, if he can get it out: 'There were six ambulance men racing me to hospital. I came third'.

Some of his fans still show an extraordinary loyalty. One went so far as to have Billy autograph his arm and then have the autograph tatooed.

Sassenachs may be interested to know that 'big yin' means nothing more colourful than tall man ('big one'). Everything else about him is colourful and a bit larger than life, too. This is appropriate, as anyone who knows Glasgow will appreciate. He does not confine his comments on the city to his stage shows. A film he made about the slums of Partick and the new slums of Castlemilk caused local councillors to complain to the BBC. A more persistent complainant is Pastor Jack Glass, who follows Connolly about Britain holding banners with legends such as 'Godless Connolly'

and 'Connolly the blasphemer'. Connolly replies with an improvisation to the tune of *Jumping Jack Flash*: 'Pastor Jack Glass is an ass, ass, ass'.

Connolly was raised as a Catholic by a devout father. His mother had left home for Dunoon when he was four, but his childhood was, he says, a happy one. He met his wife, Iris, when he was a shipyard welder by day and a folk singer by night. During his time he has also been, rather improbably, in the Territorial Army as a paratrooper. He enjoyed the jumps, but was less keen on the bull. Like everything that has happened to him, it has been plundered for his stage act, which is, of course, a distillation of his life, as potent as a Banffshire local brew.

RONNIE CORBETT

Born: December 4, 1930, Edinburgh.

Exactly 5ft 1in, for those who want to know. And it's not for want of trying. When he was about 12, he realised that he was much shorter than most of his friends, and complained to his mother about it — after all it might be considered her fault. She was duly concerned and took him to a specialist. If there's one city in the world where there is someone who might have ruined the young Corbett's chances of a career as a very small man, it was Edinburgh. The trip was a failure. So was the ruse of an aunt, who paid two guineas for a course of exercises to make her beloved nephew grow. His size may have brought him frequent insults ('If you weren't so small you'd be good looking'), but evidently taught him cunning. In his *Small Man's Guide* he suggests that better than a course of self-defence is a box of appointment cards for a Kung Fu course. Just leave

them about wherever you go, and you'll get a reputation as a student of the martial arts. Bullies will be frightened off, and will not kick sand in your face.

Corbett's wife, Anne Hart — they live in Croydon with their two daughters, Emma and Sophie — is six inches taller than he is, but never for a moment thinks that he wants mothering. Among her wifely duties is that of buying her husband's shoes from Harrod's boys' department and ladies' gloves from Marks and Spencer. They met when they were on the same bill at a London night club. He had become an actor after meeting Sir Cedric Hardwicke's son during his time in the RAF, and one of his first jobs had been in a concert party run by Clive Dunn. When he returned to Edinburgh to polish up his Morningside accent, he sometimes passes the office where he used to work as an assistant at the Department of Agriculture, and thinks: 'I can't believe all the lucky things that have happened to me'.

JULIE COVINGTON

Born: 1947, London.
Educated: Homerton College,
Cambridgeshire.

Julie Covington was given to the world by Clive James. He's not quite old enough to have engendered her, but he did persuade her to act in a *Footlights* revue at the Edinburgh Festival in 1968. Singing came more easily to her than acting. Her taste in music is fascinating: Beethoven, Randy Newman, Nick Drake.

Her acting career has been quite notable for the publicity she has generated by shunning publicity. No one can have done more for *Evita.* The saga of 'will she, won't she' play the part ensured that the whole world knew of the show long before it opened. She has also quit other successful produc-tions early in their run simply because she felt that she had no more to contribute to them—*Godspell, The Rocky Horror Show, Rock Follies.* She also refused to make any promotional appearances for *Don't Cry For Me, Argentina.*

She looks like a cross between Julie Driscoll and Shirley Williams. The chutzpah of the one and the high seriousness of the other form a combination which infuriates certain people in show biz. Too smug, too arty, not professional enough, are some of the criticisms aimed at her. She feels, though, that she was exploited early in her career, when she made a record over which she now feels that she had no control. She does not want to repeat that sort of experience. Hence the choosiness and the apparently wilful way in which she directs her career.

WENDY CRAIG

Born: June 20, 1934,
Sacriston, Co. Durham.
Educated: Yarm Grammar
School and Central School of
Speech and Drama.

It is only during the last ten or so years that Ms Craig has become more or less exclusively associated with television sitcoms.

Earlier in her career, she played in *Room at The Top, The Servant* and the Bette Davis thriller, *The Nanny,* as well as in all sorts of plays.

She grew up on her father's farm, and was spotted acting in a school play by the aunt of the film director Anthony Asquith, who recommended that she should train for the stage at the Central School which was then housed in part of the Albert Hall. When she left, she went into provincial rep for a short while, but was soon back in London and made her West End debut in *Mr Kettle and Mrs Moon* (a truly Stoppardian title).

Her role in the sitcom *Not In Front of the Children,* for which she won an Actress of the Year award in 1970, was developed from a one-off show in which she teamed with Paul Daneman for the first time. She went on to the rather similar ITV series *And Mother Makes Five,* and has most recently been seen in *Butterflies.*

JOHN CRAVEN

Born: 1941, Leeds.

The title of Newsround comes from its presenter's days as a newspaperboy in Leeds, when he used to charge customers on his round a penny to read his handwritten broadsheet of local news. He and his wife have two daughters of their own and, after six years of Newsround, he has a pretty

MICHAEL CRAWFORD

Born: January 19, 1942,
Salisbury.
Educated: Oakfield School,
Dulwich.

Having left the BBC for Thames TV and *Chalk and Cheese,* Crawford was offered an extraordinary contract by an American TV station to do 120 episodes of *Some Mothers Do 'Ave 'Em*—a contract that would have enabled him to retire after five years and live the rest of his life in indolence. It can hardly have been a temptation for the boundlessly energetic actor who, when not putting himself through hoops as the world's most accident-prone man, was teaching himself to fly, for fun rather than for a stunt.

The temptation can hardly have been heightened by the offer of the fame it would bring him. He was a film star at the age of 22 in *The Knack* and

LESLIE CROWTHER

Born: February 6, 1933,
West Bridgeford,
Nottinghamshire.
Educated: Nottingham High
School, Thames Valley
Grammar School

When Crowther and his wife, Jean, were clearing out the house at Twickenham where they had lived since their marriage—and where Crowther

good idea of what sort of news children want to hear: that is, more or less everything apart from murder. Actually, he knows very well that children are as fascinated as anyone else by murder cases, but he sees no reason why he should have to carry them on his show.

He began his career in journalism at the age of 18 on the *Harrogate Advertiser;* previously he had worked for a couple of years as an industrial apprentice in a factory. He moved through the world of flower shows, funerals and inquests to Newcastle where he got a job first on local radio and then TV. He had no intention then of specialising in children's programmes, but that is what turned up, and it really couldn't have happened to a more apt man, father and journalist.

even before that, had a huge following as Byron, the wise-cracking motor-scooter rider who delivered a weekly soliloquy on *Not So Much a Programme*.....

Crawford used to frequent Chelsea and the clunk-click of chunky jewellery was not unknown to him. David Webb was one of his great mates and his ex-wife, Gabrielle, now lives with the sometime idol of Stamford Bridge (well, part of it), Tommy Baldwin. Crawford himself leads a reclusive sort of life at a 'fairytale' cottage in Bedfordshire.

had previously lived with his parents—they came upon some ancient albums with photographs of him as a child. The conviction that the rest of the nation would like to see them gave him the idea for his most recent shows. He has also brought before the cameras his collection of Victorian pot lids, on which he has spent a great deal down the years. The clear-out of the house was due to a move to Bath, and their two youngest children Charlotte, 16, and Nicholas, 13, have gone with them. One of their elder daughters, Caroline, has gone her own way.

Their eldest daughter, one of twins, has followed the family trade and gone into the theatre. Crowther's father was an actor and his mother a stage manager in Nottingham. He still enjoys returning to his native city.

Born: January 4, 1930, Glasgow. Educated: Aberdeen University.

Cuthbertson played the bluff Procurator Fiscal in *Sutherland's Law*, and this year revived the character of Endell, the villainous Glaswegian who was Adam Faith's antagonist in *Budgie*, in *Glasgow Belongs to Me*. He based this character on a hood who used to frequent a pub he used when he was at the Glasgow Citizens' Theatre and who once threatened him. Cuthbertson is not a man one threatens lightly. He stands 6ft 4in and weighs 16 stone, though maybe he was slimmer in those days.

He has managed to spend most of his life in Scotland. He is a devotee of Scottish architecture and monuments, and lives with his wife, the actress, Anna Kristen.

He began as an actor almost by accident. While at university, he did a few broadcasts in order to supplement his meagre finances and, when he returned from National Service in the Black Watch, and worked as a radio journalist and occasional actor in that medium. He was invited to join the Citizens' company and during his period there, taught Scottish dialect at the Royal Scottish Academy of Music and Dramatic Art. He moved on to Pitlochry and Edinburgh and, when he returned to Glasgow, it was as director of the Citizens'. He was subsequently an associate director of the Royal Court and of Nottingham Playhouse. For the last ten years or so, he has again concentrated on acting and has appeared regularly on TV, where one of his most memorable performances was as the British Fascist leader in David Edgar's haunting work, *Destiny*.

PAUL DANIELS

Born: 1938, Middlesbrough.

Daniels prefers the title 'un-usualist' to that of illusionist and, of course, he didn't get where he is today simply by performing tricks. His mix of comedy, variety and magic has enabled him to fill the gap left by the death of David Nixon. However, his prowess as a prestidigitator is such that he was once asked to act as a witness on behalf of the Magic Circle at an industrial tribunal.

His success has been achieved at some cost to his family life. A former clerk with Redcar Council and sometime owner of a grocery shop, he separated from his wife Jacky, who still lives with their three sons in Middlesbrough, when he turned professional. He began to take an interest in conjuring when, on a rainy holiday with his parents at the age of ten

and confined to a boarding house, he read a book on the subject lent to him by the land-lady. A year later, he began to do amateur shows and continued until he started in northern clubs nine years ago.

He owes much to his father. His parents share his rambling house in the Buckinghamshire countryside and there, in a garage, Paul's father builds many of his props. His mother decorates them. She is also, he says, 'the best cook in the country'. One thing that he won't allow his parents to do is open his mail: 'I get the most amazing sexy letters which make Mayfair and Penthouse read like Enid Blyton'. For the sake of his peace of mind, and that of his girl friend and assistant, Nikki Heard, he deters his more eager correspondents, although, like any other man of 5ft 6ins, he is, of course, quite flattered by their attentions.

BARRY DAVIES

Born: 1939, London.
Educated: Cranbrook School and London University.

Cranbrook School, in Kent, is evidently something of a breeding ground for commentators and sportsmen. Peter West, Brian Moore and the

Middlesex and England bowler, Phil Edmonds, all received their education there. The kind of mouth work that Davies anticipated doing when he left was not speaking into a microphone. At London University he qualified as a dentist. It was during National Service— he was among the last men to have done it— that he began broadcasting on Forces Radio. He later worked on BBC's Sports Report and for Granada TV, before joining *Match of the Day* ten years ago. His career there has not been entirely happy. He lost his job as presenter when Jimmy Hill was lured from ITV and has been the subject of some subsequent transfer deal rumours when he has been passed over for important commentaries in favour of various other commentators. His own sporting activities are rather less popular than those on which he commentates— he plays a lot of squash and tennis.

DICKIE DAVIES

Born: 1933, Wallasey.

It was Jimmy Hill who suggested that Richard Davies become Dickie Davies and indulge on screen the characteristics that made him notable off it— extravagant clothes, baroque hair-do, huge smile, etc. He does deep breathing exercises before he goes on screen, so that 'the smile should come naturally'. His preoccupation with clothes dates from his days at sea.

After National Service, he worked as a clerk in an amusement arcade at New Brighton, but was sacked. He joined Cunard and went to sea as an assistant purser on the Queen Mary. By the end of his ten years at sea, he was entertainments officer on the Queen Elizabeth. When in New York, he used to seek out flashy suits from the Suicide Shop on Third Avenue—a rather sinister joint which sold clothes acquired from the New York morgue.

Some of the suits he owned — he has fond memories of a one-buttoned drape which made him the beau of South-ampton— came off the backs of gangsters fished out of the East River.

It was in Southampton that he got his start in TV. He was beginning to tire of his 'wine,

LES DAWSON

Born: February 2, 1933, Collyhurst, Manchester

Inside every fat man there's a wraith anxious to show himself, and inside every comedian there's a serious geezer anxious to express himself. Dawson still admits to an ambition to become a serious writer. Soon after he'd left the army, he went off to Paris for a year in order to, well, write. He didn't. He came back to England, took a

LYNETTE DAVIES

Born: 1950, Tonypandy.

women and song existence' and recalled that his mother had once suggested that he 'should settle down and get a nice job like Eamonn Andrews'.

Little did he suspect that he would replace Andrews on *World of Sport*. Through the offices of Julian Pettifer he landed a job at Southern TV as an announcer. His future wife, Liz, was a production assistant at the station, though their first meeting hardly suggested what was to come: 'She looked on me as a ram home from sea; I regarded her as toffee-nosed'. They still live on the Hampshire-Wiltshire border in the village of Over Wallop, with their twin sons, Peter and Danny. Their home

is a 350-year-old cottage, to whose garden they devote a great deal of time.

Liz, since giving up work with Southern, has run a pub (often with her husband's help — his gregariousness makes him a natural landlord), a restaurant and a fashion shop. Dickie still loves the sea and has a 24ft cabin cruiser, which he keeps at Poole. He is also a keen, if sometimes unlucky, cricketer and a golfer. His business interests include a directorship of Fabergé and occasional stints as a model. A persistent, if enjoyable, business failure has been his racing greyhound, Front Man, which always 'seems to come in at the back'.

Lynette Davies' life could hardly be further from that of the high-powered bitch, Davinia Prince, whom she played in *The Foundation*. The daughter of a Welsh Customs and Excise official, she most certainly does not thrive on being pushy and competitive. In fact, she says that she loathed R.A.D.A. where she was a contemporary of Stephen Sheppard and Leigh Lawson among others, because it was so competitive. Before landing the plum role of Davinia Prince, she had worked almost exclusively in theatre.

variety of jobs (including Hoover salesman) and played the clubs. This experience formed the basis of his first novel, *A Card for the Clubs,* which gives as vivid a picture as you would want of the nether regions of show business.

During this period he met his wife, Meg. She it was who encouraged him to go on *Opportunity Knocks.* She is the source of much of his most effective material, like her mother, Ada Plant, who actually loved his gags about

her. So did her husband, who used to tape record them and play them back to her.

His wife is also resigned to being the butt of his act, but she knows that abuse pays bills and doesn't complain. Anyway, he says: 'I'm a man with two wives—my real one and the one I run down on TV'. They live with their three children at Lytham St Anne's, where he enjoys dreaming of winning the Open Golf Championship with a 44ft putt and drinking with a room full of his close friends.

ROBIN DAY

Born: October 24, 1923.
Educated: Bembridge School,
St Edmund's Hall, Oxford.

Though Day's only non-journalistic participation in politics was as a Liberal—he stood at Hereford in the 1959 General Election, he is a Conservative nowadays. Not that his views are intrusive, but there are some strong hints. He has left the National Union of Journalists which, he considers, pursues political policies, which many of its members consider irrelevant. He has been a target of unwarranted abuse from the Campaign against Racism in the Media, for whom he is an Establishment bogey man.

Privately less tetchy and more modest than his screen presence suggests, he regrets that he didn't get into Parlia-ment, though he says that he would never have been anything more than 'a useful back-bencher'. He is less regretful about the law career he abandoned. After Oxford (he was president of the Union), he was called to the Bar in 1952. Many of his contemporaries are now judges and QCs, but they do not have his singular power. No other interviewer would dare to address politicians, not even Mr. Norman St. John Stevas, with the attitude of lofty scorn that Day usually adopts. His refusal to kowtow to shifty, self-interested politicians ensures that he is rarely out of the news. He lives with his wife, Catherine, also a barrister, and their two small sons in St. James's Square, Holland Park. His eldest son, Alexander, has recovered well after a near-fatal fall at London Zoo last year.

JONATHAN DIMBLEBY

Born: July 31, 1944,
Aylesbury.

The biographer of his father, Dimbleby is shortly to embark on another biography. The subject is Harold Wilson, who —perhaps surprisingly—has agreed to be interviewed for the book, although it is not an 'official' biography.

DAVID DIMBLEBY

Born: October 28, 1938.
Educated: Charterhouse and
Christ Church, Oxford.

The elder of the Dimbleboys, as Bernard Levin called them, is not only an interviewer and commentator, but also Managing Director of the Dimbleby newspaper group, which owns the *Richmond and Twickenham Times,* the *Brentford* and *Chiswick Times,* and the *Thames Valley Times.* He took over the position from his father and is the fourth Dimbleby to occupy it.

Even before he became a professional journalist, he had to learn to live with accusations of privilege. At Oxford, where he took a third in PPE, his appointment as editor of *Isis* was opposed by the outgoing Editor, Kenith Trodd, who is now a noted drama producer, and his staff. Dimbleby countered with a swingeing attack on 'the left-wing clique'. A couple of years later, some journalists took it upon themselves to advise him publicly not to attempt to follow in his father's footsteps at the BBC. On the face of it it might appear that he has done just that, but, of course, his route and his approach have been very different from Richard Dimbleby's. Whereas

Dimbleby has the unusual distinction of being something of a national hero in Ethiopia. He owes this to his films, newspaper articles and appeal, which were designed to draw attention to the famine there in 1973.

His initial intention when he left school was not to enter the family trade. He wanted to be a farmer, and his father succeeded in getting him a job on the Royal farm at Windsor, where he trained to be a showjumper. His first job in journalism was with the *Evening Standard*, and then he moved on to the BBC in Bristol.

His wife is the author and editor, Bel Mooney. Their home is in Clapham and they have one son. Dimbleby also has a share with his two brothers — the younger, Nicholas, is a sculptor — in a large house outside Tiverton.

the father was ever reverential, the son — despite his looks and his smooth cap of hair — is rather an abrasive fellow. His arch-opponent was Sir Harold Wilson, a man who was famously sensitive about media coverage of himself and his chums. Dimbleby once described him, during a state visit by Richard Nixon, as 'hogging the limelight'. Not long afterwards, he incurred the sometime Premier's wrath by asking him about the money he had made from his memoirs.

He owes his ever-expanding frame to his wife Josceline's cooking. Her step-father was an ambassador and she picked up dishes all over the world, which she collected in a volume called *A Taste of Dreams*. They live in Putney, where he sometimes interests himself in environmental matters, with their three children. He enjoys travel, sailing, walking, reading, playing the piano, and looking at paintings.

KEN DODD

Born: November 8, 1927, Knotty Ash.
Educated: Holt High School, Liverpool.

Calling himself Kenneth Arthur Dodd, one-man business, the man with the tickling stick this year campaigned vigorously on behalf of the Conservatives in the North-West: 'Harold Wilson — I used to put him down on my tax forms as a dependant'. Dodd himself is loudly independent. He worked briefly for his father, who was a coal merchant. However, wishing to show that he could go it alone, he bought a barrow and hawked pots and pans in Liverpool back-streets.

He started entertaining at the age of 14, when he did a ventriloquist show at the Knotty Ash orphanage and was paid half-a-crown for his trouble. Thereafter he worked in small concert halls as an amateur and didn't make his full-time professional debut

until 1954. The venue for that show was the Nottingham Empire, which is one of several theatres which he has actively campaigned to save from destruction. Others include the Manchester Palace, Blackpool Grand, and the Morecambe Winter Garden. He grew to love such places during his childhood, spent watching such artistes as Sandie Powell and Tessie O'Shea in the Liverpool halls.

One of the many comics to whom the gag 'the trouble with Freud is that he never played second house at the Glasgow Empire on a Friday night' is attributed, Dodd spends a lot of time reading and thinking about the psychology of humour. This interest, he says, has broadened his range. Hence his excursions into Shakespearean comedy. Dodd is perhaps the last survivor of a genuine music hall tradition in Britain, and his act gives millions a taste of what their grandparents and great-grandparents enjoyed.

VAL DOONICAN

Born: 1927, Waterford.

Michael Valentine Doonican became Val at an early age— 'Every time my mam called in Mike for dinner, she found herself with a dozen little Irish boys to feed'. He was a devoted son and says that it is to his father that he owes his imperturbability—'He trained me never to lose my temper . . .

he had a way of making you feel ten feet high'.

Waterford is the home of beautiful glass, and the young Doonican was expected to work as a blower or cutter in one of the town's factories. However, his father died when he was in his mid-teens and, instead of serving an apprenticeship, he got a job in a steel construction factory and moved from there to making orange-boxes. The family had

been a musical one and, at the age of 20, Doonican decided to profit from the talents that he had acquired and played a summer season at the small seaside resort of Courtown Harbour. That was in 1946. A couple of years later, he was 'discovered' for the first time on Irish radio. It was not for a long while that he was to become famous as the toothy fellow with the world's thickest cardigan. During those years he worked at clubs all over Britain and Ireland, living a fairly penurious life based in south-east London.

His homely style has now earned him a huge house in Buckinghamshire at Seer Green. It used to belong to Jon Anderson, of the pop group Yes. He has a wife, Lynn, and two daughters— Sara, 13, and Fiona, 12. He has from time to time said that he would like to change his style, and has been able to afford during the last few years to take time off to work on a new sort of act—but he generally returns with the same thing. During these breaks, he plays a lot of golf with a handicap of five. Pressed to describe himself, he says that he is 'somewhere between *Stars on Sunday* and *The Old Grey Whistle Test* . . . I'd like to be a sort of Marks and Spencer of music'.

MICHAEL DOUGLAS

Born: September 25, 1944, Brunswick, New Jersey. Educated: Black Fox Military Academy and University of California.

Though he hasn't actually made an episode of *Streets of San Francisco* for getting on for two years now, Douglas is still about. His major activity nowadays is film production. At the age of 30, he was responsible for *One Flew Over the Cuckoo's Nest*, and since

then he has done *China Syndrome.*

'*Cuckoo's Nest*' was originally to have been produced by his father, Kirk, but that deal fell through and Michael took it over, launching himself on a new career. He never set out to be either actor or producer. At the University of California at Santa Barbara he studied English, though his great love was Indian art. Towards the end of his time there, he dropped out and went to live in a commune which adhered to the

principles of the Maharishi Mahesh Yogi. After he left the commune, he went to Norway, where his father was filming *Heroes of Telemark*, and was given a small role. He returned to California to study acting and got his first job from a director who didn't know whose son he was. He regards having a famous father as a disadvantage— we have all heard this before.

He has been married, for two years, to Diandra Zucker, whom he met at Jimmy Carter's inauguration party.

ROBERT DOUGALL

Born: November 28, 1913, Croydon.
Educated: Whitgift School.

The wholesomeness of Robert Dougall went professionally unexploited during his years as a news-reader. It wasn't until recently that an advertising agency paid for his patent trustworthiness and got him on screen to sell margarine. Thus was the general public's instinctive assessment of Dougall endorsed. During his heyday, he was left money in the will of an elderly female fan and used to receive up to twenty proposals of marriage each week. Both he and his wife Nan—they have an adopted daughter of 34 and a son, Alistair, who is 27—were thankful that the security at Alexandra Palace and Television Centre was tight.

Dougall's first job with the BBC was in the Accounts Department, having already gained some experience of accountancy with the eminent city firm of Deloitte, Plender, Griffiths. At the age of 20, he was transferred to radio news and became the youngest news-reader ever on the old Empire Service. In those days, news-readers wore evening dress. During the war, he was an interpreter with Russian convoys in Murmansk. His interest in Russia was fired by the time he spent there, though he didn't like much of what he saw. In fact, he describes his radio announcement of the death of Joseph Stalin in 1953 as the happiest news that he ever had to broadcast.

In and Out of the Box, his autobiography, was published in 1973, the year he quit his news-reading job. It gives a detailed description of 40 years of broadcasting, which brought all sorts of unsought rewards, from an MBE to three trophies from the Royal Institute for the Deaf. As well as the reputation for being 'the nation's clearest speaker', he was also the easiest to lip read. A less welcome side of celebrity was that he was constantly being pestered and pointed at in the street. He frequently used to wear plain glass spectacles and once grew a beard in his efforts to preserve anonymity.

Dougall divides his partial retirement between Swiss Cottage and a house in Suffolk which he bought because of its proximity to Minsmere bird sanctuary. Ornithology has for years been his greatest love, and he is a sometime President of the Royal Society for the Protection of Birds. His book, *A Celebration of Birds*, was well received when it was published last year. His well-publicised hobby has accounted for a staggering rise in the number of Britain's amateur ornithologists.

LESLEY ANNE DOWN

Born: March 17, 1954, London.
Educated: Mayfield Comprehensive School, Putney.

Lesley Anne Down lives with the actor and musician, Bruce Robinson, in Kentish Town. They met when she was 15 at a party given by Ava Gardner and have been together ever since. Every so often they announce their intention of marrying, and the last time that Robinson proposed was in the orange groves near Chopin's house in Majorca. They share the same pursuits —going to the cinema and collecting books and prints. He seeks first editions of Dickens and George Cruickshank; she, cartoons by Heath Robinson.

The daughter of the caretaker of a Territorial Army centre, she began her career at the age of 10 as a model and made her first film when she was 13. It was called *A Smashing Girl I Used to Know*. She went on to make a string of others during her teens. When she was 19, she got the part of Lady Georgina Worsley in *Upstairs Downstairs* and hasn't looked back since. She says that she would prefer to be known on account of her acting prowess —in her role as Phyllis Dixey she aged from 16 to 54— rather than for her looks. She still suspects that she owes her success to them alone.

NOEL EDMONDS

Born: 1948, Ilford.
Educated Brentwood
School, Essex.

The ubiquitous disc jockey is considered by a colleague to be 'a chillingly ambitious man'. Given the number of radio and TV shows he has been connected with that sounds like an understatement. When he left school, he angered his father, a headmaster, by turning down a place at Surrey University and going to work for Radio Luxembourg. His subsequent career with the BBC, by which he was first engaged ten years ago, is reputed to have made him a millionaire. It also came close to breaking up his marriage. His wife, Gill, and he underwent a widely publicised 'trial separation' a couple of years ago. During that time there was speculation in the usual quarters about his involvements. 'I went to the opening of Elton John's restaurant with a male friend. I later learnt that he and I were supposed to be living together'.

The first thing that Noel and Gill did when they got together again was to look for a new house. They eventually settled on a Queen Anne pile in the Buckinghamshire village of Weston Turville. Burglars please note—he is scared of being robbed and so their 10 acres are scanned by hidden infra-red video cameras, the pictures from which he watches on a screen in his study. Inside the house, he merely has ultra-sonic bugs in each room. The house is not far from Silverstone, and Edmonds sometimes hires the circuit at £400 for a day of speeding. He has an impressive fleet of motors: a Mark I Ford GT 40 with a 4.7 litre V8 engine that will do up to 180 mph, more modestly, two Jaguar saloons and an 'E' type. A year ago, he escaped injury when a tyre burst on his XJS at 70 mph. As well as cars, he keeps a few farm animals, a couple of cats, a tractor, a large dog and a supply of suits with very wide lapels.

DENHOLM ELLIOTT

Born: May 31, 1922.
Educated: Malvern College
and R.A.D.A.

Television's favourite remittance man actor trained for the stage in the '30s, but was kicked out of R.A.D.A. went into the RAF and was shot down over Denmark. It was in a POW camp that his career really began: 'The Germans were very culture-conscious, marvellous about putting on plays'. In costumes borrowed from the local opera house, the only half-trained actor in

the camp played Macbeth and Eliza Doolittle.

After the war, he started work at Amersham rep, rather to the chagrin of his family, who thought that he might have decided to follow some other profession; like, say, the Bar—his grandfather had been a well-known KC. As it was, he was signed up by the producer, Alexander Korda, on the then sizeable salary of £5,000 per annum. He didn't get many parts of note, but he did at least make a good living. During this period he married Virginia McKenna.

His popular following began with his role as the ineffably seedy, velvet-collared Charles Prince in *Nothing But the Best*. He is now married to Susan Robinson, by whom he has two children.

DICK EMERY

Born: 1918, Bloomsbury.

Emery's parents were a musical double act, Callan and Emery. His father also had a solo career as Laurie— 'The Aristocratic Navvy'— Howe. Emery was not born in a trunk, but he started touring at the age of three weeks and has rarely given up since. Not long ago, he complained that he had spent only a week of the previous year at home in Weybridge with his fifth wife, Jo Blake. The rest of the time he had been in Australia, New Zealand and Leeds.

He considers himself an actor rather than a comedian, and his parade of grotesques has been called 'a one-man repertory company'. Some of the better-known characters in that company no longer give him any pleasure. He has not done Mandy ('Oooh you are awful') for some years now, and regrets that he did not kill her off earlier. Before he followed his parents into show business, he was a farmer, a chauffeur in Hampstead, a journalist, an engineer and a driving instructor. One reason that he fought clear of the stage was that, at the age of eight, he was a witness to his parents' break-up.

It was during the war, in an RAF Gang Show performed on the back of a lorry, that he first realised his talent. He appeared then in drag, but his first TV appearance was in the opera *Aida*. He has a good tenor voice, and was heard for years singing: 'Esso sign means happy motoring'. During his early days, he appeared at the Windmill with Tony Hancock. They used to ride round Hyde Park together on a motor bike he bought on HP. He now owns a BMW 1000cc machine, as well as a Rolls—cars have always been a passion, though it wasn't until he got a job on *Educating Archie* that he could afford to chauffeur himself in the style to which he thought he should be accustomed.

KENNY EVERETT

Born: December 25, 1944, Seaforth.

Mrs Cole called her Christmas present to her husband, a scouse tugboat skipper, Maurice. Eighteen years later, young Maurice Cole called himself Kenny Everett, when he was trying to persuade someone, anyone, to make him one of the most popular disc jockeys in the nation.

In between times, he had grown to almost full size and had been sacked from a Catholic seminary, a bakery and an advertising agency, Kenny Everett in turn called his alter ego Captain Elvis Brandenberg Kremmen. Kremmen changed his name to. . . This serial pseudonymity suggests someone trying to escape from himself and, sure enough, KE wants to do just that: 'I've always wanted to be muscular and heavy and butch'. This of course is why KE's former neighbour Roger Walker, who draws the Kremmen cartoon strips and anima- tions, turned the space hero into a man who is stronger on biceps than on brain. Talking of brain, during the 'sixties, KE's preferred recreation was tattooing his chromosomes with liberal doses of LSD. Life became boring—an endless parade of discos and nightmares, which are approxi- mately the same thing. He announced one day that he was going to commit suicide. Billy Fury's girl friend, in whose house he was at the time, requested: 'Do you mind doing it outside, because I don't want you to spoil the carpet'. This admonition worked better than the usually caring, concerned approach, and KE decided against ending it all. He also married Billy Fury's girl friend, Lee, and they have lived happily ever after. Their current gaff is in Notting Hill, whither they repaired after a period in the Cotswolds. Her time is spent cooking and keeping her hus- band's books. His is spent doing housework, making TV commercials, playing with tape recorders, enjoying rounds of golf with some of his many fabulous show biz friends, and receiving an apparently endless series of awards for his *Video Show*.

PETER FALK

Born: 1927.
Educated: Syracuse University.

'Peter says he is leaving. It happens every year. We offer him half of California. He comes back'. So says an NBC studio executive about the world's shabbiest millionaire, who now receives up to £300,000 per episode of *Colombo*. His ex-wife's settlement of £1,200,000 is thus less staggering than it might seem at first. He divorced Alyce Mayo a couple of years ago, after 15 years of marriage. They have two adopted daughters—Jackie, 13, and Kathy, 9. They met when they were at university together in up-state New York. In those days, Falk had no intention of becoming an actor. He was studying public administration and wanted to be a businessman. He has succeeded. He has interests in 12 companies which he and Alyce set up.

He took to the stage in his late twenties in New York and went into films a few years later. For most of their years together, Falk and Alyce lived in a joke-oak pile in the older part of Beverley Hills. Both of them have now remarried, Alyce to a property man called Harry Derleth, and Falk to starlet and former beauty queen Shera Denes. He gave her a £1,000,000 house for their first wedding anniversary.

FRANK FINLAY

Born: August 6, 1926.
Farnworth, Lancashire.

Finlay, who's played Jesus, Napoleon, Hitler, Henry VIII, Casanova and Voltaire, and who will almost certainly get the role of God when Lord

CYRIL FLETCHER

Born: 1913, Watford.

Fletcher married Betty Astell at 1 pm on May 18, 1941, in St Martin in the Fields. Every year since then they have returned to the London church to repeat their marriage pledge. They met in 1940, in the gents' of a Bristol concert hall.

They live in a neo-Georgian house in Sussex, not far from where they used to live in a pukka-Georgian house which had no view. They bought a Victorian house with a view, cleverly pulled it down, and built a replica of their former home on the site. Gardening is one of the Fletchers' occupations—they grow all their own vegetables—but they are away from home so much, that it often has to be done by remote control from a hotel room, instructing one of several gardeners about what needs doing. Fletcher has an ambition to have a flower, a deep red rose by choice, named after him. When he is not working, he always spends his time at home. He claims that he has never been abroad, save for a day trip to

Ostend, which is, of course, enough to put anyone off 'abroad' for life. Among the many frequent visitors to the Fletchers' house are Esther Rantzen, her husband, Desmond Wilcox, and their baby, Emily. They love the house; Esther says it makes her feel so peaceful: 'Betty is so friendly, so—well—ordinary. A great person'.

The Fletchers own a company called Associated Speakers, which is the largest agency for after-dinner speakers in Britain. One of the most popular speakers on its books is, as you might guess, Fletcher himself. He is also a pantomime dame and longs to play the Palladium. A Conservative Party propagandist, his sophisticated,

urbane brand of preaching—he eccentrically refers to Clement Freud as a lefty—has made him a great favourite among the converted across the country.

Fletcher's is far from being a show business background. His father was a solicitor and Town Clerk of Watford, while his uncle was treasurer of another North London borough. He himself began life as an insurance clerk and dreamed of becoming a straight actor in the style of Gielgud. He was spotted at the age of 23 by Greatrex Newman, who ran a concert party called 'The Folderols', reciting one of his early 'Odd Odes'. Fletcher soon became established at top venues like the old Holborn Empire and on the radio. He also played in the first television pantomime, *Dick Whittington*. It was when the couple's daughter, Jill—now an actress—was born soon after the war, that they discovered that they had good business heads. In order to be together, the Fletchers set up a company to do summer shows. Their 'two-person cottage industry' has been thriving ever since.

Grade gets round to doing His Story, went virtually unrecognised until a few years ago. He doesn't much enjoy the loss of anonymity that *Bouquet of Barbed Wire* and its sequel cost him. Since then, sightseers have tended to park outside his Walton-on-Thames house and gape at him, and an American woman wrote asking if he would marry her and enclosed two dollars, presumably as some sort of inducement. Another American woman became so besotted with Finlay, that she flew to London for her holiday and watched 16 successive performances of the musical, *Kings and Clowns.* In this he did his impersonation of Henry VIII, a role in which he sang for the first time in his professional career—he had done some Gilbert and Sullivan during his amateur days.

The syphillitic Tudor monarch and Casanova might not be thought of as parts which could easily be played to near-perfection by a happily married man, but Finlay is an actor who seems to lose himself in his characterisations. He met his wife, Doreen, in Bolton at an amateur dramatic society. In those days he was, like his father and grand-fathers before him, a butcher. He still has his City and Guilds butcher's diploma. As well as acting he used to pick up the odd fiver as a stand-up comic and master of ceremonies.

When he was 25, he crossed the Pennines to Halifax, and ended up getting a job in rep. Two years later, he went to R.A.D.A. on a scholarship and found himself an elderly contemporary of Finney, O'Toole, Bates, etc.

His initial progress was a bit slow, and he spent many an afternoon with Edward Woodward signing on at the Chiswick labour exchange. They both used to tell their children that they were going to the library. Just as Woodward's son has gone into the theatre, so, too, has Finlay's, who is called Stephen. Finlay has two other children—Daniel, who is 13, and Kathy, 22, who is training as a Cordon Bleu cook.

ANNA FORD

Born: 1943, Tewkesbury, Gloucestershire.
Educated: Manchester University.

When Anna Ford courageously turned down Paul Raymond's extraordinarily generous offer of £75,000 to bare herself in Club International, she pointed out that she was the daughter of a vicar who had once been an actor. And, she added, her contract with ITN (£14,000 pa) stipulated that she should do nothing which might conflict with her role as a 'serious journalist'. It is doubtful whether the vicar's daughter argument cut much ice with Mr Raymond. His Trilby, Fiona Richmond, is also the daughter of a vicar (and former foot-baller) and, come to think of it, a serious journalist as well. Anna Ford's and ITN's idea of a serious journalist is presumably different—respectable, earnest, concerned, etc. She has often said that she wants to make documentaries and do more reporting, etc. One documentary in which she was involved was scuppered by ITN executives. It was

deemed to be too 'political'. It's subject was the *Sun* newspaper and in it Anna Ford would have interviewed a variety of that paper's gifted models. She has herself done some up-market modelling, for a Vogue publication called *Real Life Fashion.*

Mr Raymond's was not the first generous offer that she has rejected. To their disbelief, she declined the invitation of Messrs Morecambe and Wise to appear on their show and do a Rippon. She has, in fact, become understandably 'bloody sick' of being compared with la Rippon.

Miss Ford, a runner up to Joe Loss in the National Society of Non-Smokers poll last year, was married in 1970 to Alan Bittles, a research

chemist. He is an Ulsterman, and they lived in Belfast until 1974. During that time, she was a teacher at Rupert Stanley College and then joined the Open University as a tutor. She had actually been approached by the BBC when she left university, where she had been an active student politician, in 1967. After she and Dr Bittles separated, she worked for Granada TV before joining the BBC, whence she migrated to her present position.

All her family have now moved away from Cumbria, where she was brought up in Eskdale and Wigtown. She has four brothers—Inigo, a sculptor; Piers, an architect; Dominic, a teacher, and Adam a school chaplain. Her uncle is the Liberal peer, Lord Winstanley, who describes her as 'a perpetual student'. Since she has become well-known, gossip columnists have eagerly chronicled her suitors. These have included a guitarist and a couple of telly fellows—one of whom was so ungallant as to deny all rumours of a relation-ship. However, we now hear that she has become officially engaged to Jon Snow.

F

BRUCE FORSYTH

Born: February 22, 1928,
Edmonton, North London.
Educated: Latimer Grammar
School, Edmonton.

After 37 years in variety, a little flop like the *Big Night* will not deter Forsyth, who is due back in the New Year with another LWT show devised by Lance Percival. In the meantime, he has done his own one-man show in America, reckoning that it was time to find out whether he could make it as an 'international entertainer'. He was the first 'unknown' (on the other side of the Atlantic) to top the bill at New York's Winter Garden Theatre. He also hopes to offer the *Generation Game* to American TV audiences. In addition, it has been rumoured that he had his eye on Johnny Carson's chat show job at a cool £3,000,000 a year. He denied any ambitions in this direction, though after the less than total success of the *Big Night* and the *Travelling Music Show,* such diversification would surprise no one.

As everyone knows, Brucie is married to Anthea, who smokes in non-smoking theatres when watching him perform. They have two daughters, one of them adopted, and live in the golf links and rhododendron belt near Virginia Water. Their house has lots of flock wallpaper, like an Indian restaurant. He was formerly married to Penny Calvert, whom he met when they were performing together at the Windmill in 1949. They had three daughters, one of whom, Julie, is the singer in a group called Guys and Dolls. Another, Debbie, is married to the song-writer and recording mogul, David Martin, who was once involved in a legal tangle with Guys and Dolls. Complicated.

Forsyth has had more catch phrases than some stars have had face lifts. 'I'm in charge', 'Nice to see you, to see you nice', 'Didn't he do well'. They seem to have supported him soundly through a career that began when he was only 14. Billed at Bilton, Staffordshire, as Boy Bruce the Mighty Atom, he travelled north from Edmonton with his tap mat, ukelele and suits on to which his mother had sewn the sequins. He played seasons all over the country before he got his Palladium job in 1958. (He had previously had a double act with his first wife, with whom he lived in a caravan while touring India.)

He resuscitated his career with the *Generation Game* and has subsequently become one of the highest-paid entertainers in Britain. According to Eric Morecambe, he is pretty much the same off stage as he is on it. Odd. He says that he owes much of his energy to the fact that he is often the only sober person in the theatre. He is also a non-smoker. Anthea likes menthol cigarettes. Forsyth is about as superstitious as Don Revie—he is terrified of the colour green in dressing rooms, and never goes anywhere without a little sailor doll given to him by three grateful girls at the Windmill.

Forsyth only rarely reads a book, though he did dip into his former wife's baring of their marriage in *Darling, Your Dinner's in the Dustbin.* The portrait painted of him was not entirely flattering. As is well-known, he enjoys golf, and often pops out of the back garden of his house and straight on to the course. His golf friends include such show biz celebrities as Jimmy Tarbuck, Kenny Lynch, and Val Doonican. He is still ambitious, as his activities in America indicate. 'He will not rest', says a friend, 'until Sammy Davis is described as America's answer to Bruce Forsyth'. And if he never sees that in print? 'I always think that, even if nothing else happens, I have got lots of things to look back on and be thrilled about'.

EDWARD FOX

Born: April 13, 1937, London.
Educated: Harrow.

Described by his mother – herself an actress and the widow of the theatrical agent, Robin Fox – as 'the world's worst actor', Edward Fox was for years overshadowed by his younger brother, James, who was arguably the world's best actor, at least in certain roles. James Fox quit acting after the disturbing experience of making *Performance* with Mick Jagger and became a counsellor for the Navigators, a Billy Graham-inspired evangelical group in Leeds. Within a few years, Edward has become a film star, almost as if he has stepped in to fill the huge gap left by his brother.

Like him, Edward has various reservations about his job, notably about 'the questionable taste' of transmitting *Edward and Mrs Simpson* while the Duchess of Windsor was still alive. He was not, however, slow to refute Esther Rantzen's sanctimonious pronouncements about the show – pronouncements made before she had actually seen the show, though, of course, she was in a unique position to understand the Duchess of Windsor's feelings because of the way her own privacy has been invaded.

Edward Fox seems not to mind who knows about his private life. He is proud of his long-standing relationship with Joanna David, by whom he has a daughter, Emelia, and whom he has not the slightest intention of marrying: 'I married Joanna with my head and my heart, and that's good enough. I don't need to solemnise the marriage vows to a mere clerk'. He was previously married to Tracy Reed. His daughter of that marriage, Lucy, is now 19 and very pretty.

BARRY FOSTER

Born: 1930, Beeston, Nottinghamshire.
Educated: Hayes, Middlesex, and Central School of Speech and Drama.

Some measure of the reputation gained by Foster as the dour detective, Van der Valk, is indicated by the fact that, when fan letters arrive in London addressed to 'Van der Valk, London' or 'Herr Foster, England', the Post Office actually knows what to do with them. Foster has finished with VdV for good now. He learnt that the series was to finish from a BBC doorman (it was actually made by Thames TV) but doesn't reckon that there was much mileage left in it anyway. One thing, though, that he does miss about the show is location work in Amsterdam – 'one of the least hung-up communities in the world'. Not that Wimbledon, where Foster lives with his wife, the former singer Judith Shergold, and their three children – the eldest, Joanna has already done her first TV role – is a particularly hung-up place. It is certainly safe to go for a jog without getting mugged, providing one doesn't venture too far onto the common, although Foster is so fit that he could probably fight off all but the most determined assailants.

Barry Foster's intention when he left school was to become a chemist, and he began training as one. When literary ambition raised its head, he thought, well, actors have a lot of time off, so why not try it. Actually, he has been in work for nearly the whole of his career. His only long period of 'resting' he spent as a waiter at the National Liberal Club. One of the times in his life that he enjoyed most was immediately after leaving drama school. He toured Ireland with Anew McMaster's famous Shakespearian troupe, which also included the young Harold Pinter, alias David Baron.

Since then of course Foster has played numerous big roles on the box (Orde Wingate and Richard Hannay among them) and starred in Hitchcock's *Frenzy* as a psychopathic strangler. When he's at home, he plays the piano and sometimes accompanies his wife. His heroes are – and this provides a clue to his generation – Bill Evans, Stan Tracey and Oscar Peterson. He also plays golf. His pronouncement on his trade is not notably down to earth: 'An actor's duty is to be in the front line of human existence, bringing back messages from the front about what it's like'.

WILLIAM FRANKLYN

Born: 1926, London.
Educated: Haileyburgy College, Melbourne.

The man who said "Schhh" in 50 commercials over nine years and afterwards introduced *Master Spy* was born into the theatre. His father was the actor, Leo Franklyn, who toured Australia in a Pullman car while his son was at school. Among his forebears was Arthur Rigby, who worked with George Robey. Franklyn's only rule has been to accept anything that's going: 'I think actors really ought to be buccaneering characters. I act for money. Not for an ego trip'. This policy has brought him a wide variety of jobs, both in and out of his profession.

At one time, he was doing so badly that he became a totter, a smooth Steptoe, calling at houses in Chelsea to remove whatever junk he could get and selling it in a tatty shop that he owned. On another occasion, he was offered the chance to direct the first Italian production of *There's a Girl in My Soup.* He accepted, signed the contract, and then shot off to Berlitz to learn the language, of which he knew not a word.

He was actually scared stiff of the theatre as a child. He

associated it with being dragged, blushing, through dressing rooms full of half-naked women: 'It sounds very good news, but actually, it made me terrified'. As a young man he himself tried to bring terror into the lives of others as a fast bowler and was once granted a trial by Essex. He still plays cricket for a local club in Putney. He also has his own team, called 'The

Seargeant Men', which plays charity matches. His other recreations include stamps—he has a formidable collection—and playing squash. He still maintains a near-professional interest in antiques.

Married to the actress, Susanna Carroll, by whom he has two daughters, he also has a daughter by his first marriage.

RONALD FRASER

Born: April 11, 1930, Ashton-under-Lyne.

This splendid character actor, the star of *Spooner's Patch, The Misfit,* etc., is fortunate enough to be able to draw on a picturesque off-stage life for his creations. During the 'sixties, he was a popular figure about town and frequented many of the capital's better-known niteries. In his earlier days, he attended a party at

Errol Flynn's house, where that infinitely thoughtful host had provided a bevy of young models for the benefit of the male guests.

Fraser divides his time between the South of France and Hampstead, where he is a well-known figure in many hostelries. He likes to live at a decent standard and likes big cars and good-looking women, and *vice versa.* He has been divorced from his wife, Elizabeth, for 15 years and has two daughters, the elder of whom is 20.

DAVID FROST

Born: April 7, 1939.
Tenterden, Kent.
Educated: Wellingborough
Grammar School, Gonville
and Caius College, Cambridge

Frost's ambition, according to one of his erstwhile colleagues who knew him from Cambridge, was 'to become world-famous for being David Frost'. The extraordinary thing is that Frost achieved it. He seems to have been around for years, yet he's only forty, the biggest star that the British box has produced. Frost is, lest we forget, the man who once said that luxury was being able to throw away a shirt after wearing it only once. He is also the man who gave the world the breakfast party. The first was at the Connaught in January, 1966, and the guests included Harold Wilson (who came because he thought the Beatles would be there), the Bishop of Woolwich, Len Deighton (the then fashionable spyman), a couple of Fleet Street editors, etc.) Frost is the man who invented 'trial by television', with his relentless cross-examination of the insurance swindler, Savundra; the man who, at the age of 27, set up London Weekend Television with no more than some useful phone numbers and his usual boundless self-confidence; the man who ran more or less simultaneous chat shows on both sides of the Atlantic and became such a prisoner of the airlines that he gave jet lag a new meaning.

Frost's heyday was the 'sixties. Appearing from nowhere and amazing everyone, he fronted *TW3*, *Not So Much a Programme*, *BBC3* and a variety of other shows named after him. He was a national figure at the age of 23. The 'seventies have hardly treated him unkindly, but have prompted the

question that used to be asked of a more exquisite sort of gilded youth—what happens when they grow old? Do whiz kids become whiz persons, or just grow chins and become forgotten? Frost's recent projects have not lacked ambition and efforts like the Nixon interviews ('the most fulfilling thing I've done'; fantastic, fantastic') and *Global Village* are mirrors of their begetter—media phenomena which are interesting mainly because they *are* media phenomena. His activities outside TV have been ill-starred. He is reported to have lost a lot of money with the collapse of Jim Slater's empire, and various 'leisure industry' projects came to nothing.

But he is still a very rich man and he retains some of the qualities considered to have been behind his extraordinary ascent. One is his capacity for being star-struck. He is proud to show off the wrist watch that Sammy Davis Junior gave him, and somehow can't believe that he is the man who has shaken hands with and addressed by their first names the rest of the world's famous men. 'Seriously, though', he says, 'I wouldn't like to be anyone else. I love being David Frost'. It's hard not to believe him.

Frost is less widely recognised than he used to

be. Oddly enough, he looks more like he used to than he has done for ages. Understand? He strongly denies having had cosmetic surgery. This year's activities have been marginally less grandiose than those of a few years ago—co-producing a Bee Gees spectacular, putting together a show for the United Nations Children's Fund. One of the problems, of course, is that there is no one world-famous left to interview— a series of interviews with himself would surely die an ignominious death.

He has had a number of woman friends. Some who have left him (Karen Graham, Caroline Cushing, Diahann Carroll, Jeanette Scott) claim that his inability to slow down has been the cause of this. Others hint that he is inhibited from committing himself by his mother Mona who was the guest of honour at his fortieth birthday party in Los Angeles. He has recently resumed a relationship with one of his companions of the 'sixties, Carol Lynley.

God—likely to be a guest on a future show when we will learn His Christian name—alone knows what Frost will get up to in his forties. Anything is possible, since, as he says, 'Life is a *theme of opportunities*'. There may be some hint in his admission that: 'I am interested in making a contribution to the welfare of the human race', although this may, of course, simply mean more TV shows. Or, perhaps, he means to produce another book. His record of the negotiations surrounding the Nixon interviews was a commercial success, even if it was regarded with less than enthusiasm by some very unkind reviewers: 'Told with the self-satisfied air of someone who has bought a secondhand car from Nixon and lived to tell the tale'.

G

JAMES GALWAY

Born: December 8, 1939, Belfast.
Educated: Mount Collyer Secondary School, Belfast; Royal College of Music, London

'A twentieth-century gypsy with a caravan run by Swissair' is how the gnome-like flautist describes himself. He needs the caravan to transport himself to engagements all over the world; not surprisingly, he has too many offers to be able to accept them all: 'I could play 365 days a year'. It probably makes his lost childhood worthwhile after all.

Galway was brought up in the back streets of Belfast. Both his father and grandfather played the flute. He was encouraged to do so as well from infancy, and began with the 39th Old Boys' Flute Band. At the age of 10, he won three cups in the Irish flute championships, and thereafter abandoned such pursuits as football, in his

effort to attain mastery of his instrument. He still retains a fondness for the music he played in his Orange band and for the music of bars and parties. Hence his association with such folk bands as the Chieftains. Hence, too, his huge repertoire of non-classical music, some of which he used to play as a busker.

He began his professional career in the orchestra at the Royal Shakespeare Theatre, Stratford-on-Avon, and worked with several other orchestras before becoming principal flautist of the Royal Philharmonic. He then made his name with the Berlin Philharmonic under Herbert von Karajan, who could hardly believe his ears when Galway announced his intention of pursuing a solo career independent of an orchestra: 'Nobody leaves the Berlin Philharmonic'.

Seriously injured and subsequently forced to rest for a year after being knocked down by a car near his home three years ago, Galway has,

he thinks, also been hampered in his career by the lack of first-class music for the flute. Tiring of adapting scores intended for other instruments, he commissioned the Spaniard, Joaquin Rodrigo, to compose a flute concerto for him. This was a remarkable collaboration between a man who is blind and has to compose in Braille, and a virtuoso who speaks no Spanish. Galway actually considered *Concierto Pastoral* 'the most difficult piece' he had 'ever had to play'.

It was to his Swiss wife, Annie, that he dedicated his hugely successful recording of *Annie's Song*. He met her in Berlin. They now live just outside Lucerne with their three children, the younger two of whom are twins. Galway also has a son by his first marriage. His recreations include chess, about which he reads as much as he plays, and Lizst, whom he describes as 'the Mick Jagger of his day'. He also finds time to conduct master classes.

ANDREW GARDNER

Born: 1932, Beaconsfield.

Reginald Bosanquet saw his relationship with Gardner as resembling that of Spencer Tracy and Katherine Hepburn. Which was which he did not make clear, but it's a rather touching sort of picture, even if the roles are hopelessly confused. Comparing himself with his somewhat extravagant former colleague, Gardner describes himself as 'ordinary'.

After 16 years with ITN, Gardner left to join Thames TV as a smoothish replacement for Eamonn Andrews. He was attracted by the offer of a salary even bigger than the one ITN was paying him, and by the challenge of a new sort of role. He was also believed to be worried about the future of *News at Ten* as we all know

and love it. Furthermore, he had a poor opinion of ITN's chauffeurs — he was involved in two crashes in 10 days, and was not entirely light-hearted when he talked of demanding

a helicoper to get him home safely. One disadvantage of spending one's public life seated is that the audience doesn't get the full picture — in this case, 6ft 5ins.

JAMES GARNER

Born: April 7, 1929, Norman,
Oklahoma.
Educated: Berghof School,
New York

Rockford is easy-going, James Garner is not. 'I have a flashy temper. It's kill or be killed. People seem to want to pick fights. It usually happens when I'm sitting down. When I stand up they generally back off'. Garner is 6ft 3ins tall and 14 stone in weight. 'I have no qualms at all about decking someone with a baseball bat. I'm very physical. I'll pick somebody up and throw him right through the door'. It is surprising that anyone wants to get close to him, but Doris Day did, and he cracked her ribs. But, you guessed it: 'I'm a shy fella'.

Before getting into films, he was a salesman, carpet, layer, bathing suit model and oilfield worker. He has put much of the considerable fortune he has earned from acting into real estate. He is also president of the Silver Lake National Bank. One of his regrets is that he never enjoyed the super-star status of his successor in *Maverick,* Roger Moore, or of another telly cowboy, Clint Eastwood. His film career included such things as *Grand Prix.* He was also Marilyn Monroe's choice for the male lead in her last, ill-fated film, *Something's Got to Give.* Garner lives with his wife, Lois, in Los Angeles. They have two daughters, Kim and Greta. 'People seem to think that there ought to be a Hamlet lurking inside me. But there isn't'. Perhaps not, but he, nevertheless, remains popular.

BAMBER GASCOIGNE

Born: January 24, 1935,
London.
Educated: Eton; Magdalene
College, Cambridge.

'When you come to Christianity, there are very few Lord Clarks around'. So said the producer of *The Christians.* That is, no doubt, why Gascoigne—who is neither Lord Clark nor Christian—got the job of writing it, presenting it and, presumably, making himself a few pence along the way. It was, perhaps, the first indication for many members of the general public that Gascoigne was not simply a sometimes stern, but more generally genial, face saying: 'No, Keele. I was looking for Piers Gaveston, you were thinking of Tom Driberg. Good try. Your starter for ten'.

Gascoigne is, or has been, variously a playwright, theatre critic, novelist and historian. While in his early twenties and still at Cambridge, he wrote a revue called *Share My Lettuce,* which ran for the best part of a year at the old Lyric, in Hammersmith. A subsequent play, *Leda Had a Little Swan,* had the interesting distinction of being banned in this country by the Lord Chamberlain, who claimed that the theme was 'offensive', and of closing before its opening night on Broadway. After another couple of unstageable plays, he began writing novels, *Murgatreud's Empire, The Heyday,* etc.

He owes his name to an ancestor who was one of the last MPs to oppose the abolition of slavery. This gentleman represented a Liverpool constituency, and Liverpool was doing well out of that trade. He comes from a well-to-do Knightsbridge family and now lives in Richmond. His father was a stockbroker, his uncle—Lord O'Neill—was once Prime Minister of Northern Ireland. He met his wife, Christina, who is a photographer, at Cambridge, where he took a first in English, having gone up after a spell in the Guards. Among his contemporaries were Michael Frayn, Andrew Sinclair (another Guards officer) and the delightful cartoonist, Timothy Birdsall, who died in 1963, soon after having made his name on *TW3.* Gascoigne contributed the introduction to his posthumously collected work, which can still be found and which pungently evokes the era of Harold MacMillan and embryonically swinging London.

JUDY GEESON

Born: September 10, 1948.

Described in her early career as 'the new Julie Christie', Judy Geeson (elder sister of Sally, who was in *Bless This House*) never quite became that. She was widely known by the time she was 18, thanks to the soap opera, *The Newcomers,* in which she played on and off for two years. From there she went on to *To Sir With Love* and a string of films in the late 'sixties and early 'seventies. With the collapse of the British film industry, she went to Hollywood – but not for long. Like many other British actors and actresses, she was soon back in this country.

During the last three years of his life, she was the constant companion of the great stage designer, Sean Kenny, and was with him when he died of a stroke at the hopelessly young age of 40, six years ago. Since then she has been a close friend of the actor, Pip Miller (son of Garry, the 'fifties crooner), although she now lives alone in Fulham with her menagerie

– an eight-inch-high terrier called Tarra, a cockatoo and six canaries. She is delighted by the tailored clothes she wore in *Danger UXB* and wears them off-screen too – a sartorial world away from the mini-dresses in which she was forever jumping in and out of mini-cars in the 'sixties.

JOHN GIELGUD

Born: April 14, 1904.
Educated: Westminster and R.A.D.A.

'Acting is my only interest. I have nothing else to do, except directing. I have no hobbies or sport. I am not political and no good with my hands'. Gielgud, the theatrical knight, is evidently a modest man. In this, his 76th year, he has filmed LWT's Agatha Christie thriller, *Why Didn't They Ask Evans,* seen his autobiography published and filmed Thames TV's series on the history of the garden. Not bad for a man who once said – modesty again – 'I thought I would end up

playing ambassadors in Hollywood'. Gardens are one of his pleasures, and those of the houses he has inhabited have been notable. His present home near Aylesbury is no exception.

He admits to few professional regrets. He would like to direct films, and once had plans to do a film of Graham Greene's play, *The Living Room.* He also hoped to do a film of *The Tempest.* His latest film was made in Poland under the direction of Andrej Wojda. Gielgud is actually of Polish extraction. His great-grand-parents fled the country in 1831. His younger brother, Val, who used to be head of BBC drama, was a frequent visitor to the country.

PAUL MICHAEL GLASER

Born: March 25, 1943, Cambridge, Massachusetts. Educated: Tulane and Boston Universities.

David Soul, the blonde part-time singer who plays Hutch, describes his relationship with Glaser as being akin to a marriage: 'We don't always agree with each other, but we have enormous respect for each other and can have dis-agreements openly'. Soul, who has been married and divorced twice, presumably knows what he's talking about. Glaser himself has never been married, and says that there have been but two women in his life – an earlier girl friend and a former school teacher, Elizabeth Meyer, with whom he has lived for four years. He met her in a most unorthodox way. Her car drew up alongside his at a traffic light, and when she moved off again, he pursued her, stopped her and asked for her driver's licence as if he were a speed cop. This was before the days of Starsky and Hutch, so he has evidently always felt

HANNAH GORDON

Born: April 9, 1941, Edinburgh.

Hannah Gordon's voice is as distinctive as her looks. *Can You Hear Me at The Back,* the play she went into with Peter Barkworth at the Piccadilly Theatre, after their successful partnership in *Telford's Change,* is the sort of question she, of all actresses, need never ask. Her voice is extra-ordinarily resonant and so deep, that she has been mistaken for a man on the telephone. One can imagine no other circumstance in which such confusion might occur. Radio plays and readings and commercial

at home as the hip hand of authority.

Glaser had a lonely childhood—he says that his father was so preoccupied with his architectural practice that he had no time to devote to home life. A veteran of many psychiatrists. couches, he attributes to his childhood his introspection and his frequent despair. Stardom hasn't helped, he says—anything but: 'My trouble is, I never know whether people see me as a commodity, as a property.... I don't like playing at being a film star, I can't be doing with all that crap'. His antipathy towards playing at being a film star leads him to do such characteristically film-star things as breaking news photographers' cameras. He works hard at keeping his private life as private as can be and shuns the trappings of even the new laid-back Hollywood. His car is a six-year-old Mazda, and the house where he lives with Elizabeth is the one he has had since he arrived in Hollywood as a fairly unknown New York theatre actor in the early 'seventies.

BRIAN GLOVER

Born: April 2, 1934, Sheffield. Educated: Barnsley Grammar School; Sheffield University

Glover is England's leading wrestler turned teacher turned actor turned writer. His parents didn't marry till he was 22: 'My father came into the gym looking sheepish and said: "I've done right by your mother"'. They kept a corner shop in a village near Barnsley, where the young Glover went to school with that town's most famous son, Michael Parkinson. Glover père made a bit of extra money as a wrestler. This was the first trade that Glover aspired to. Using the Red Devil (his father wore a mask in the ring) as a reference, he got on to an agent's books and was eventually offered a bout in Wilmslow, in place of a wrestler who hadn't turned up. Getting into the ring, he was surprised to hear himself announced as the missing grappler, Leon Arras. He has stuck with the name throughout his career.

He then outraged his family by neglecting his wrestling in favour of gaining an education. He was making £3,000 a year in the days when £3,000 was £3,000. The education authority paying him a £200 a year grant was not impressed, so he left his geography course in Sheffield after a year. However, he enrolled on a teacher training course and went on wrestling, taking a plane from Leeds to Paris each week-end, fighting there on Saturdays and in Zurich or Basle on Sundays. He continued with this double life—which he had by now learnt to keep a secret from his Barnsley employers—until one of his fellow school teachers, Barry Hines, the author of *Kes,* suggested that he should play the bullying games master in the film.

Glover has been an actor ever since. He hasn't given up wrestling, though, and has a further string to his bow in his regular TV scripts—many of them drawing on his extraordinarily varied experiences, which include being beaten up by John Wayne in the film *Branagan* ('Good publicity photographs for a wrestler') and doing the voices in the Tetley tea commercials.

voice overs have provided her with a good living that is not dependant on her looks. She is still, after several years in the public gaze, rather surprised that she is considered a sort of sex symbol. Of course, the parts she has had have contri-buted to this: 'I was always playing mistresses, so being an ex-wife is a step up'.

Considering the amount of work she has done, it might be hard to believe that she puts her family first, but she is adamant that this is so. TV work enables her to get home to Weybridge without much difficulty. However, she took some persuading to accept the role in *Can You Hear Me,* because it means that she doesn't get home until after midnight. She says that, because she married 'late'—she was actually 28—she appreciates marriage and motherhood that much more. Her husband is the cameraman, Norman Warwick, whom she met when they were both working on the film *Spring and Port Wine*: 'He asked me to dinner —it was as simple as that'. They have a son called Ben, who is six years old and thought *Telford's Change* 'terribly boring'. Although she took a year off after he was born, it seems not to have had any adverse effect on her career. Indeed, her best-known TV roles have come since.

Personally and professionally, she says, she has never been happier than she is now. She adds that she did not much enjoy her twenties, when she supported her acting career by running a stationery shop, which she acquired along with a flat.

NOELE GORDON

Born: December 25, 1921 (?)
East Ham.
Educated: R.A.D.A

Marlon Brando with a mouth full of cotton wool is not, perhaps, the first person one is prompted to think of by Noele Gordon, but there it is—the star of *Crossroads,* the Queen of the Midlands, is known in certain quarters as 'The Godmother'. Is this, then, the true secret of Sandie's legs—crushed by the Sharples mob from Salford with frozen cow heels during the infamous war of the ratings? One thing that Miss Gordon really hates is jokes about *Crossroads.* She thinks that the show's critics forget the conditions under which the cast is required to work. She, for instance, gets up at 7.30 in the morning, in preparation for an 11-hour day at ATV's Birmingham studios. She lives not too far away and drives to work in her cherished-number Roller—NG 10. The

car is her only luxury. She lives in a ground floor flat in an unflashy Birmingham suburb. Her mother, Jockey, who is her closest companion, lives in the flat above—and is, she claims, still very strict with her.

Noele Gordon owes her Christian name to having been born on Christmas Day. Her mother had wanted to be an actress but had never had the chance, so she pushed her daughter onto the stage at an early age. Her early career was mostly spent in musicals, and she made her West End debut in 1941 in *Let's Face It.* She was also in many pantomimes, including

Humpty Dumpty at the Palladium in 1953. Her agent was Lew Grade, and he it was who gave her her first job ATV in 1955. With a sure eye for her future, she had gone to New York to study television technique at university, and when she returned she became responsible for a wide variety of programmes—sport, chat shows, outside broadcasts, etc. She moved in front of the cameras with a magazine programme called *Lunchbox,* and started in *Crossroads* in 1964.

She says that her personal life has often been lonely. At the age of 18 she was engaged to an army officer who was going to read for the Bar. His family objected to his marrying an actress, so the match was called off. She will not name this fiancé, simply stating that he is now a High Court judge. Nor will she name her subsequent loves, one an actor, the other an impresario, both dead. Her abhorrence of critics (easily

ALEC GUINNESS

Born: April 2, 1914, Maida Vale.
Educated: Roborough,
Eastbourne.

Sir Alec's TV appearances have been rare. Considering that he is so superb a miniaturist, this is, perhaps, surprising. Indeed, the scale of his performances in films like *Kind Hearts and Coronets* and *The Lavender Hill Mob* is admirably suited to TV, as is

evident when they are transmitted in that medium. Those films and the others of the late 'forties and early 'fifties which established him as Britain's leading character actor were, of course, made at Ealing, and it was in the same studios (now owned by the BBC) that parts of *Tinker, Tailor, Soldier, Spy* were shot. He admitted to no nostalgia upon returning there for the first time in a quarter of a century: 'Working at Ealing was not particularly happy. It was a good studio for technicians, not for actors. They rather thought actors got in the way. They would have preferred puppets'. This, unkind to say, is very likely why the films were so good.

He is an admirer of John Le Carré and says that he is convinced 'for various reasons' that what Le Carré writes is accurate. Le Carré

introduced him to some intelligence chiefs, who did not correspond to his previous sartorial conception of them. He says that he met some men during the war whom he recognised as agents, and tells the story of how he encountered Graham Greene's nephew at a City lunch, soon after the nephew's return from Moscow. His uncle had asked him to look up Kim Philby, but the sometime spymaster had been away. However, on the morning of the lunch, the nephew had received a letter from Philby apologising for his absence and adding: 'Don't bother to let me know when you're coming again. I'll know'. Philby may, of course, have been having a joke, as he surely was when he described *The Old Country,* in which Guinness appeared as a

understood when you think of the notices *Crossroads* attracts) extends to those who talk of the curse of the Crossroads Motel'. During a nine-month period in 1976-77, five members of the cast and crew died. Noele Gordon denied that someone somewhere was sticking pins in wax models: 'The explanation is that we're a long-running programme'.

Her fans include Mary Wilson, wife of the former Prime Minister, and the Queen Mother. Mrs Wilson invited Noele Gordon to tea and apologised for her husband's lack of familiarity with the motel personnel. The Queen Mother asked to meet Noele Gordon when she visited ATV's studios. (She has also met Prince Philip and Princess Alexandra.) These encounters with the Royal Family are not the only reason that she is grateful to *Crossroads* – 'The series gives me more opportunities to act than any artist has had in the history of TV or the theatre'.

LARRY GRAYSON

Born: 1923, Banbury.

Like his close friend, Noele Gordon, Grayson (né William White) is unmarried. He lives with his foster parents' daughter, Fan, who brought him up after they died when he was six. She, too, has never married. Indeed, her fiancé left her when she refused to abandon the Grayson boy. They live with their poodle, Arthur Marshall, in a house called 'The Garlands' in Hinckley Road, Nuneaton. It is not far from the terraced cottage from which, at the age of five, he used to gaze at hoardings proclaiming the coming attractions at the Hippodrome.

William White was born out of wedlock to Ethel White, who was so scared of her parents' reaction, that she went to Banbury for the birth. She brought her baby back to Nuneaton, where he was fostered by friends of hers. Until he was about eight, he

had no idea that the Auntie Ethel who visited him regularly was really his mother. He never met his father, William Sully.

After a sickly childhood, he took to the stage as Billy Breen, female impersonator, when he was 14. For more than 30 years, he played summer seasons, tatty clubs, Moss Empires, works canteens. In 1971, when he was working in Paignton, he consulted a clairvoyant called Madame Credo (Mrs Helen Edden), who told him he would be a star before long. The following year, he got his series, *Shut That Door,* and was voted Show Business Personality of 1972.

One of his regrets at not achieving fame earlier is that he missed meeting some of his heroes, who include Noel Coward and Ivor Novello. Among the living great, he admires Danny La Rue, but is a bit diffident about Bruce Forsyth, who he succeeded on *The Generation Game*, and has met only once.

character based on him and which he had never seen, as 'rather silly'. This despite the fact – or because of it – that Guinness's portrayal was said to be very close indeed.

Not for nothing is Guinness peculiarly suited to impersonating those who inhabit the grey world of espionage. Kenneth Tynan once wrote of him: '"Slippery" sums him up. He looks unmemorable. Were he to commit a murder, I have no doubt that the number of false arrests following the circulation of his description would break all records'. He certainly does possess a most unactorish anonymity, as though he really is the ideal blank canvas onto which the marks of a character can be drawn, no less in 'real life' than on stage or set. During the war, for instance, he says that he impersonated a naval

officer and a gentleman. He possesses an uncanny gift for metamorphosis without the aid of make-up, false noses, etc.

He was brought up in London, Bournemouth and Eastbourne by his mother – his father had abandoned her when his son was a year old, and the last time that Sir Alec saw him was when he was eight. He received no particular encouragement as an actor when young, and became a copywriter when he left school. He was sacked from the agency for which he worked, when he ordered a photographic block 4ft rather than 4in square for an advertisement on the front page of the *Daily Mail.* He then attended Fay Compton's Acting School and was taken under the wing of John Gielgud, who had come along to present some awards. His

first part was as a Chinese coolie in the revue, *Queer Cargo* and, by the time he was called up, he had established himself at the Old Vic in a number of productions, including Gielgud's modern-dress *Hamlet.* After the war, he combined theatre with his startling film career, which began with *Great Expectations.* He adapted the novel for the screen and also did the adaptations of *The Horse's Mouth* and *The Brothers Karamazov.*

He has two homes, both apparently modest, at Petersfield and Westminster. He has been married for more than 40 years to the former actress, Merula Salaman, and has one son, the actor and writer, Matthew Guinness. He describes his art rather curiously as 'child's make-believe mixed with adult cunning'.

DAVID HAMILTON

Born: 1939, Surrey.

The lowbrow's Michael Aspel describes himself as 'a natural purveyor of happiness'. Like his namesake, the photographer of nymphets for Pirelli calendars, Hamilton (né Pilditch) is something of a ladies' man. He married at the age of 23: 'In those days there wasn't drugs and sex everywhere. We were all brainwashed into believing in getting married'. He was, he thinks, too young. However, he is on good terms with his ex-wife, Sheila, and a good chunk of his sizeable earnings goes on the education of his children — Jane, 15, and David junior, 13. He lived for some time with Kathy McKinnon, the daughter of the Old Bailey judge, Neil McKinnon, and they split up shortly before they were due to marry. His latest girl friend (well, at the time of going to press) is Penthouse Pets' football team captain, Hannah McCarthy, 21. She is apparently as keen on the game as he is, although she is not yet a director of Fulham Football Club.

This directorship is but one of Hamilton's many activities. He has always been an energetic man and, at the age of 15, was contributing an authoritative column to *Soccer World.* He got the sack when the editor discovered his age, which seems a bit unfair. Now, as well as radio and TV, he has his road show and a sideline in Diddy merchandise.

Standing 5ft 7in in his platform soles, Hamilton, whose hair is dyed, lives in a house overlooking Barnes Common, where he enjoys entertaining and reading his abundant fan mail. He owns a Silver Shadow and a Mini-GT. Unfortunately, the Rolls is a target for vandals when they spot him inside it.

ROBERT HARDY

Born: October 29, 1925

Hardy's passions are archery, in which he became interested when playing Henry V, and horses — fairly appropriate for an actor who fears that he is becoming too well-known as the quick-tempered vet in *Creatures Great and Small.* His first book, published three years ago, is called *Long Bow: A Social and Military History.* It tracks the history of the weapon from Neolithic times to the present, although the greater part of it is concerned with the Middle Ages, of course. The book is a mine of information to delight the magpie mind, and includes among much else some scholarly guesswork about the identity of Robin Hood.

At his farmhouse at Harpsden, near Henley, he keeps a number of horses. They are tended by his wife, Sally, and his daughters, the older of whom, Emma, has competed in the Horse of the Year Show. She has also, like her father, suffered serious injury in riding accidents. He describes himself as 'like Mill Reef', held together by 'three screws and a plate'. As well as riding and making films in which horses play a big part, Hardy has also eaten the flesh of one, although he says that he was betrayed into doing so by a wartime restaurateur who did not advise him of the provenance of the steak that he was offered. Among Hardy's friends is Donald Sinclair, the original of James Herriot's Siegfried Farnon. Hardy occasionally accompanies Sinclair on his rounds in Skildale.

BOB HARRIS

Born: 1946, Northampton.

Harris' brand of vibes 'n'-peace earnestness seems dated now, as does his all-denim outfit. He appears to be locked in some kind of sartorial and gestural time warp, circa 1970.

Harris started on *Old Grey Whistle Test* in 1972, replacing Richard Williams. Harris had previously been involved in 'underground' journalism and was one of the co-founders of *Time Out* magazine. Before that, he had followed his father's footsteps (very large) into the Police Force. He was a cadet for two years, but it is difficult to imagine the whisperer apprehending a villain.

He is a big man, 6ft 1in, and used to dream of playing rugby for England. He was, however, ordered to give up the game at the age of 19, after he had been concussed 25 times in one season. These injuries have, of course, had no long-term effect on him. He has produced records by groups called Druid and Wally.

Harris lives in a house in Putney with his wife and their two daughters.

ROLF HARRIS

Born: 1930, Perth, Western Australia.

It was meningitis that got Harris into show business. He was a teacher in a Perth suburb when he was struck down. After he had rested for a while, he decided to come to London, where he arrived in 1952, hoping to make use of his degree in table tennis studies. One of the first things he did was to attempt to get rid of his accent. It took him eight years to learn that he was trying to achieve the impossible. His grandfather was a Welsh painter, a Cardiff bohemian who made a good living from portraits. His Welsh wife, Alwena Hughes, is a sculptress who studied at the Royal College, and he himself has exhibited at the Royal Australian Academy. He still paints, as well as taking photographs, some of which have been shown at the Kodak Gallery. Much of his work done for TV shows he gives to charities for auction. His home in Sydenham is full of work by him and his wife.

RUSSELL HARTY

Born: September 5, 1934, Blackburn.
Educated: Blackburn Grammar School; Oxford.

The most gifted former Giggleswick master to present a chat show, Harty is also the most famous son of Blackburn to write a weekly column of autobiography. Let us recap. His parents, Fred and Myrtle, owned a vegetable stall in Blackburn market. The young Harty was scholarly and bookish and got a scholarship to Oxford, where he read English and where one of his contemporaries was David Hockney's literary twin, Alan Bennett. He taught at Giggleswick and The City University, New York, got a job as a BBC radio producer in the mid-'sixties and moved into TV with the arts programme, *Aquarius*. He made a film on Salvador Dali for it, which gained him an Emmy Award. The rest is, if not history, a modern something or other.

Harty is the man who met his Waterloo—or 'Emu' as he would have it—with The Who, complete with the late Keith Moon. He is also the man who asked David Bowie's wife if she still slept with him; the man with 'the manner of an escaped hairdresser', whom viewers wish to see take a tumble', and so on. For someone who makes a handsome living out of self-exposure and exposing others

(he believes his job to be to extract information from the famous on behalf of the ordinary Joe), he is a reticent fellow, who dislikes being prodded and pointed at by grubby punters in the street. In the service of anonymity, he tends to employ a large pair of sun-glasses which itself attracts attention, of course. He keeps the address of his shared Yorkshire farmhouse a secret. His co-owners are Madge Hindle (of *Coronation Street*), who is an old friend from Blackburn, and her husband, who is Harty's solicitor. Harty's chunk of the premises is a converted barn. His London nest is not a million miles from Marks and Spencer in Kensington.

Harty is a popular escort, who does not allow his gently spreading belly to deter him from gambolling in the capital's niteries. Indeed, the belly is the product of those same niteries, as well as of a sweet tooth, and a fondness for decent wine. He is not the sort of man who goes jogging.

NIGEL HAVERS

Born: 1949

Havers is the youngest son of Sir Michael Havers, Mrs Thatcher's Attorney-General and sometime counsel for Keith Richards. The affinities between advocacy and acting are obvious, and Havers junior concedes that 'lawyers are ham actors'. He describes his father as 'quite brilliant.'

While he is hardly an aristocrat—his father is not a Baronet and was knighted only seven years ago—Havers is certainly among the actors most capable of portraying young aristocrats and gentlemen of noble birth. This kind of actor is known to his fellows, fittingly enough, as a 'Nigel actor'. Other such actors are Jeremy Childs, James Villiers and Donald Pickering. Before he got the title role in *Nicholas Nickleby* three years ago, his career had been, well, stagnating. His greatest success until then had been two consecutive years as Billy Owen in *Mrs Dale's Diary*. For a while, he quit acting and worked in the wine trade. Then, through the offices of a friend who worked on the *Jimmy Young Show*, he secured a job as a researcher at the BBC. Once inside the dinosaur, he somehow found his way back to his original trade. Havers is married, and he and his wife, Carolyn, share a happy existence in Hammersmith with their two-year-old daughter.

DICKIE HENDERSON

Born: October 30, 1922, London.

Henderson's first dance teacher was Rita Hayworth's father. His mother had enrolled him at Signor Cansino's School for kiddy hoofers when the family arrived in Hollywood in the early 'thirties. Henderson senior was a vaudeville comedian. His son made his debut in the film of Noel Coward's *Cavalcade* in 1933, showing for the first time the knack of being in the right place at the right time – the film required a 10-year-old boy with an English accent, and young Henderson was there. His father wasn't keen on his pursuing a show business career, and he didn't make another appearance until his late teens, when he was back in Britain. This was the first performance that his father had witnessed, and it did nothing to convince him that his son was in the right trade. It was at the Glasgow Empire – the comic's graveyard – and the 18-year-old Henderson could get no response from the notoriously difficult audience. Exasperated, he turned to the band leader and said: 'It's like trying to get blood out of a stone, working for this lot'. Whereupon the audience did respond, with a traditional Glaswegian display of displeasure.

That experience taught him never to blame an audience, no matter how dreadful it might be, and to this day he is acutely aware of his duty towards the people paying his wages. He is also aware of his debt to the artists with whom he performed in his youth. He became an all-rounder by teaching, say, a juggler to dance, in return for juggling lessons. As a result, he can juggle, turn somersaults, and perform a variety of tricks which comics of a more recent generation are incapable of doing.

His opinion of such people is not high – and not merely because of their limited repertoires. He attributes his 'cleaner than clean' image to his Catholicism, and has no time for material of even the faintest blue hue. 'I don't believe people would accept this from me or from Max Bygraves. I sound like a vicar, don't I. But I stick to what I believe in'.

A keen golfer who plays in pro/am charity matches, Henderson lives with his second wife and his terrier in a large flat near Baker Street.

PAUL HENRY

Born: 1947, Birmingham. Educated: Birmingham School of Speech and Drama.

Crossroads' resident half-wit has lived in Birmingham all his life and he is now well-known around the city even, he says, by people who claim never to watch the show. His characterisation is so convincing, that the easily led presume

that he really is educationally sub-normal and ask him if he needs help. They also think that he must be rich, which he isn't. Before *Crossroads*, he was at Birmingham Rep for eight years, during and after its period of excellence under Peter Dews. He had found that his experience of Shakespeare tended to thwart his previous attempts to get parts in TV comedy shows, and he now reckons that

people are so familiar with him as Benny that they are deterred from casting him in the parts which he would like. He lives only 20 minutes from ATV's studios. He met his wife, Sheila, when he started at the rep. They have been married for almost 12 years. Their two children, Anthony, 6, and Justine, 8, are fairly indifferent to *Crossroads*, and only watch if they are unable to find anything better to do.

BERNARD HEPTON

*Born: October 19, 1925,
Bradford.*

Hepton has a face, or a series of faces, known to everyone who watches the box. He has been in *The Squirrels, Sadie It's Cold Outside, A Pin to See the Peep Show* and more recently *Colditz,* where he played the commandant. He was rewarded for his success in that part by being given the part of an unalloyed goodie in *Secret Army.* The mobility of his features, the range of his voice and his prowess with make-up render him unrecognisable from one role to the next.

He began his career in York soon after the war. Progressing to Birmingham, he took up directing for the first time, doing nothing else,

apart from producing, for some time afterwards; in the late 'fifties he was in charge of the Liverpool Playhouse,

where he achieved a number of critical successes and enjoyed several showdowns with the theatre's management. Eventually he was forced to resign, when the management cancelled one of his productions.

He moved to the BBC, not as an actor, but as a producer. Among his work was *Compact,* the splendid soap opera of life on a glossyish magazine. After a successful period working alongside such notable producers as James MacTaggart and Tony Garnet, he decided it was time to get in front of the cameras again. He found that many of his fellow producers were unwilling to employ him as an actor, but he was eventually assigned to the role of Wemmick in *Great Expectations.* He has recently returned to the stage.

BENNY HILL

*Born: January 21, 1925,
Southampton.
Educated: Taunton's School,
Southampton.*

Hill refers to himself as 'the only womanising poof in show business'. He is obsessed by the girls who pose on Page Three of *The Sun* and often wonders why some of them don't get in touch with him — with a view to furthering their careers, of course. The sort of girl who used to decorate his show is what he calls 'nice' — Pet Clarke, Anne Shelton, etc.

Alfred Hawthorne Hill was born in Shirley — which is an endless, dreary, faintly respectable western suburb of Southampton. His father owned a surgical goods store, and during his school days he was forever being ribbed because of it: 'Hillie's dad sells Frenchies'. He can still recall the smell of the shop, with its stock of leather trusses and anklestraps. His first job was as a milkman. He drove a

horse and cart round Southampton pretending it was Dodge City.

From the age of 13 he worked evenings in pubs, telling jokes. In those days his idol was Max Miller. He left Southampton at about the time the German Air Force was destroying the city, and came to London. He worked back stage on numerous revues, slept rough on Streatham Common and

then went into the Army as a driver. After the war, he went back to the theatre and was Reg Varney's straight man.

He has been on the box for 28 years now. He is also an avid watcher, and reckons to sit in front of his set for four hours each night taking notes. He lives alone in a large flat in Kensington, and his only luxury is foreign travel. He has no car, loves walking about London and goes by bus to Thames TV's studios at Teddington. His wanderlust is insatiable. Whenever he has a week to spare, he flies somewhere, sometimes alone, sometimes accompanied by a lady friend. When he arrives at his destination — as often as not Marseilles, where he puts up at the Splendide — he walks up to 20 miles a day. He returns from these trips full of ideas for future shows jotted down on the backs of receipts and envelopes. They go to an 'angel' at Thames TV, who types them, after which he decides on those he is most probably going to use.

JIMMY HILL

Born: July 22, 1928, Balham.
Educated: Local grammar school.

Known to some of his colleagues as 'The Chin', and to others as 'The Rabbi', Hill is almost alone among football commentators in commanding the respect of players. He owes this to having been one of them — he was first with Brentford and then a few miles downstream at Fulham, in the days when Johnny Haynes and Bedford Jezzard were the stars of Craven Cottage. He is the first to admit that he was not the world's greatest player, but it is not because of his feats on the pitch that he is remembered.

His career really took off in 1956, when he was elected Chairman of the Professional Footballers' Association. During the next four years he steered the Association through its lengthy and often acrimonious negotiations with the Football League, in pursuit of the abolition of the maximum wage for players. His rivals may claim that he took too much of the credit for this victory, but there can be little doubt that, without him, the era of the golden boot would have been longer in arriving. It is ironic that nowadays, in private at any rate, he makes no secret of his view that players are overpaid and that greed has weakened the game.

Then, as a manager, he took Coventry City from the Third into the First Division. He got into TV as adviser to the BBC's unintentionally comic footballing soap opera, *United*. A couple of years later, after resigning from Coventry, Hill was appointed head of sport at London Weekend Television. ITV's football coverage had previously been regarded as something of a joke. Hill got to work quickly and had soon created a worthwhile alternative to the BBC. Some indication of the resentment he aroused is given by the fight that broke out between rival camera crews during the 1969 Cup Final. A pointer to the reputation he had established for himself is the BBC's desperate eagerness to lure him over.

His fondness for exposure to the public is well-known. He turned down top executive posts at LWT in order to remain in front of the cameras, and he thrives on charity functions, public appearances and the like. He devotes as much time to his business interests as he does to broadcasting. Jimmy Hill Ltd is a 'sports consultancy', which tracks down talent for the football-crazy sheikhs of the Arabian Gulf and advises clubs on how to increase their revenue. Hill is also, as he often reminds his audience, Chairman of Coventry City FC.

GORDON HONEYCOMBE

Born: September 27, 1936, India.
Educated: Gordonstoun and Oxford.

The former newscaster's preoccupation with his forebears, around which he built his series, *Family History,* began when he noticed in a local paper that an Edinburgh girl had married a man from Jersey called Roy Honeycombe. That was in 1955, and during the intervening years he spent many frustrating and a few pleasurable hours travelling round Britain, searching through parish registers, old wills and deeds of houses.

He pursued his hobby while he was an actor with the Royal Shakespeare Company, while he was subsisting on £3.17.6d per week dole between acting jobs, and after he went to work for ITN. It has indirectly

THORA HIRD

Born: May 28, 1916, Morecambe.

Thora Hird was born next door to the Royalty Theatre, Morecambe, of which her father was manager. She made her stage debut at the age of eight weeks. Later, her father became manager of Morecambe Central Pier, which was known as the 'Taj Mahal of the North'. It was a delightful playground for Miss Hird and her brother, and she rues the day that it burnt down in 1933.

It was in her early twenties that she was spotted by George Thornby. She was playing a woman of 60, and he thought she would be good as his mother in a forthcoming film. Ealing Studios' casting director travelled to Morecambe to watch her and offered her a contract, although she never got to play the part for which she had been intended. She went on to play more charladies than any other British actress — appropriate really, since she is fanatically tidy. Her daughter, Jeanette Scott, introduces her as 'the compulsive cleaner'. Her house is full of keepsakes from theatres — brass handles, door knobs, etc. — which are extremely

given him the subject matter of one of his novels. He discovered that his great-grandfather, Samuel, had been the founder of the first fire brigade to serve North Fleet in Kent. This prompted his already strong interest in the work of the Fire Brigade, and soon afterwards he began to spend his spare time at Paddington fire station, gathering material for a book. It was called *Red Watch* and attracted much praise when published in 1976.

He had already decided to quit ITN to devote all his time to writing, when the firemen's strike took place the following year. He lent his support to the strike and, in a *Daily Mail* article, urged that the men's demands should be met. To his amazement, he was reprimanded by the editor of ITN and suspended from duty. He resigned that week.

During a year that he spent jobless before he worked at ITN he booked himself a passage to Australia. In his years as a newscaster (not news-reader), he received some 17,000 fan letters and was forever being addressed by strangers. His life now seems to be free of the problems of both penury and celebrity. Unmarried, he divides his time between a flat near Regent's Park and another in Bournemouth. He continues to write and dreams of making a comeback one day as an actor.

---

tiresome to maintain in reasonable nick.

She resisted many offers before coming back to TV in *In Loving Memory* this year, because she felt that she was simply being asked to repeat her role from the series *Meet the Wife*.

She enjoys spending all the time she can with her husband, Jimmy, to whom she has been married for a good 42 years.

W. G. HOSKINS

Born: May 22, 1908, Exeter.
Educated: Hele's School,
Exeter; University
College, Exeter.

Professor Hoskins is atypical of the people in this book. He has never played the Glasgow Empire, was never a cub reporter on the *Batley Advertiser,* nor a Red Coat at Pwllheli, and is fairly short on home-spun philosophy.

He has pursued a distinguished and unusually, varied academic career. During the 'thirties, he lectured in economics at Leicester University, returning there after the war (during which he served on the Central Price Regulation Committee) to a readership in local history. Then he took up

FRANKIE HOWERD

Born: 1922, York.
Educated: Shooters Hill
School, London.

In 1962 Howerd thought that he would jack in show business for good. His career had had its ups and downs, but none so far down as that. His final disappointment came when a BBC producer from whom he was trying to get

a place at Oxford as reader in economic history, before going back again to Leicester as Professor of English History. His numerous books reflect the breadth of his learning and interests, and three TV series on the genesis of English landscape are the works of a polymath with an admirably open mind. Now that he has retired, he has gone back to Exeter, with which city he has always maintained a close contact. Indeed, four of his books are about Devon and its history. His family had lived there for many years. His father was a master baker, like his father before him. He lives with his wife, Jane, in a Regency house, and his two children and four grandchildren live fairly close by.

---

work told him that he'd have to do an audition. To make his problems worse he was heavily in debt to the Inland Revenue. He was rescued by an improbable Galahad, Peter Cook, who offered him an engagement at the Establishment Club. Howerd was amazed that he should be wanted at such a place, but he went down well and was subsequently booked for *TW3*. Thus began his second career, which shows no sign of abating 17 years later. This year, he returned to cabaret at the Country Cousin in Chelsea. Howerd somehow became up market, earlier he had been clean and a bit low. Not that he is keen to be too blue, actually, Stilton, not the sky — that's the ticket. He says that he used to excise some of the cruder passages in *Up Pompey* scripts.

His first career began when R.A.D.A. declined to accept him. He went on the halls, into the Army (his father had been a tough sergeant-major) during the war, and eventually into radio, where he made his name on *Variety Band Box*.

ROY HUDD

Born: May 16, 1936, Croydon.

Hudd was brought up by his grandmother who fostered his interest in being a performer. She used to take him to the Croydon Empire, and it was there that he began to love the music hall. He is now something of an expert on the subject, and he sometimes thinks that he was born 50 or 60 years too late. He would have liked to perform alongside Dan Leno, and one of the projects closest to his heart is the refurbishment of Wilson's Music Hall in the East End. Though he is an unashamed Londoner, the London he loves has just disappeared. It had more or less gone before he was born, and the past few years have only served to put the last few nails in its coffin. He became so disenchanted with the city, that he and his wife, Ann, and their son, Max, moved out to Nettlebed, in Berkshire.

His greatest joy is talking to old people, especially those with memories of the music hall performers he idolises. He loved doing the *Sixty, Seventy, Eighty Show* and was upset when the BBC dropped it. There seems to be only a slim chance that he will be granted the sort of show he'd truly like to do—'A chat show talking to old timers who are mentally alert'.

NERYS HUGHES

Born: 1940, Rhyl.

For years, Nerys Hughes was 28. Then a woman whose motives must have been rather petty wrote to a newspaper announcing her real age, which she knew because her daughter had been at school with Nerys.

She has for a long time been a great campaigner on behalf of animals. She is a zealous opponent of vivisection, and has on two occasions handed in petitions at the House of Commons calling for a ban on the exploitation of animals by cosmetic companies. She has also been to the House to hand in a petition in support of the Spastic Society Save a Baby Campaign. She is married to the director of *Blue Peter*, and former film cameraman Patrick Turley. They have two children.

Nerys Hughes grew up in a strict, puritanical environment.

ROD HULL

Born: 1935, Isle of Sheppey.

Emu is violent, aggressive, liable to bite on sight. Hull is none of these things, nor does he think about Emu when he is off-stage: 'There's just the puppet in a box somewhere'.

Hull comes from a rather eccentric family. His father was a fanciful sort of man, who used to take jobs which he hadn't a chance in hell of holding down—master carpenter, insurance salesman, etc. He also had a bike bell in his car which he rang when overtaking cyclists. His son became an electrician when he left school. In 1958, he married a local hairdresser, Sandra, in Sheerness. They have since divorced and, last year, he married his Australian assistant, Cheryl Hilton, by whom he has since had a daughter, Amelia. He has two teenage daughters from his first marriage. When he finished his National Service in the RAF in 1961, he decided to emigrate to Australia. His father was already there, failing in business as a seller of graveyard plots. Hull got a job designing floodlighting layouts. His mother acquired an organ on which to play *Rock of Ages* while her husband flogged the plots, but she couldn't play, so the ploy rather sadly misfired.

GARETH HUNT

Born: 1943, Battersea.
Educated: Webber Douglas Drama School.

Hunt fears that he is in danger of becoming 'a screen sex object, but he modestly denies that he has ever looked on himself as a 'male sexual thing'. This is surprising, since his life is the stuff of which

Her parents were chapel—which meant attendance three times on Sundays, newspapers on Sundays, and no alcohol at all. She signed the pledge when she was eleven, and did not have a drink until she was 23. Her parents would hardly have countenanced her becoming an actress, so she went to a teacher training college. While there, she was awarded the BBC drama prize, and that is what drew her into the trade she has pursued ever since.

Hull went on to a job as a lighting engineer for Australian TV and then started doing children's show scripts. Later, he got a series of his own five-minute comedy slots, called *The Constable Clod Show*. He was Clod. Other performers began to use his material and, after a few years, he became an established writer and performer with a daily chat show. One of his fans sent him an emu egg. He put it on a radiator and showed it to the audience every day. Each time, it was bigger than on the previous day. Eventually, Rod moved the egg into his bed—he presented the programme from a bed because this, remember, was Australia. After three weeks, Emu hatched, the bird that we know and love. The bird that assaulted Michael Parkinson and impersonated a bus conductor lives in a cupboard at its master's Tudor house near Sittingbourne, in Kent.

JOHN HURT

Born: January 27, 1940, Chesterfield.
Educated: Lincoln School and R.A.D.A.

Hurt's version—it was not an impersonation—of Britain's most stylish man, Quentin Crisp, in *The Naked Civil Servant* remains one of the most memorable performances by any actor on the box during this decade. Yet he has hardly been offered further parts commensurate with his talent. Maybe it's because, as he says, he has no 'image'. He is so absorbed by the parts that he plays that he somehow becomes 'invisible'. You would think, then, that Hurt must be the ideal actor—a blank canvas, a kind of manipulable chameleon. This would appear to be far from the truth, however. He has the reputation of being an unpre-

tentious man with none of the usual actorish characteristics. This, doubtless, is why he's so good. His father was a mathematician who became a clergyman, and his brother was for a time a Catholic monk. The correspondences between acting and preaching are, of course, considerable. He went to St Martin's art school but dropped out and went to R.A.D.A. He still paints a bit, and plays cricket a lot. His team, for which he keeps wicket and bats when the slow bowlers are on—'a ball in the mouth could put me out of work for a year', is called 'The Gentlemen of Hampstead'—'There isn't a gentleman among us'. He lives in that leafy suburb with his girl friend, Marie-Lise Pierrot, who used to be a model. They have been together for 11 years and have no intention of marrying.

Since *Midnight Express,* for his performance in which he was nominated for an Oscar, the price which he can command has risen sharply. He can now afford to live in some style. It's small wonder that he once called himself 'the most often-discovered actor in London'. A year and a half ago, he lost £30,000 because the South African Government refused to give him a work permit so he had to withdraw from the film *Zulu Dawn.* His role in Michael Cimino's *Heaven's Gate* will probably bring him twice that sum.

other men's fantasies are made: 'Once I was lying on a secluded beach below a castle, when this beautiful blonde girl suddenly appeared in a white costume. It was like an apparition. She could hardly speak a word of English. We finished up making love on that beach. It was incredible. At times of stress I often think of that moment'.

Before he pursued his beef-cake career, he was a merchant sailor. He left school at 15 and went to sea for six years. For four years during which time he married—he has a son called Gareth, who is 11—he worked in a number of jobs, including representative of a shopfitting firm. After drama school, he was at the Bristol Old Vic and the National Theatre, before

getting a break in *Upstairs, Downstairs.* And *The Avengers* has led to a couple of films.

He has recently been living up to his *Avengers'* role, getting involved in a fight in a Hackney pub, which left him with some scars. His latest companion is Annette Walter-Lax, the former girl friend of Keith Moon, the drummer of The Who rock group, who died last year.

JOHN INMAN

*Born: June 28, 1936,
Preston.*

The gap-toothed bachelor isn't that keen on camp, but is grateful for the exposure that *Are You Being Served?* has given him and the opportunities it has brought. He has played Mother Goose for the last three Christmases and Charlie's Aunt once last summer at the Adelphi. He was proud to have been given that part, which such people as Arthur Askey, Norman Wisdom and Frankie Howerd have done in the past. He is steeped in show biz lore, having been brought up in Blackpool, where his mother kept a boarding-house. As a child he used to frequent the theatres, and one of his favourite performers was Frank Randle, to whom he has paid tribute on TV.

His family had given up its hairdressing business in Preston and moved to the seaside when he was a small child. He was a timid lad and remembers his father as 'a drinking man who used to knock my mother about'. He made his stage debut at the local rep when he was 13 and left school two years later. He was taken on as a dogsbody at the South Pier Pavilion. However, in order to get a living wage, he left and became a trainee window dresser. When he moved to London, he worked at Austin Reed in Regent Street. He used to pose in the window, trying to keep a straight face, with a sign attached to him saying: 'Available in other colours'. A resting actor told him about a job going in Crewe and Inman made his second start in the theatre. For years, he played old men in cloth caps and, with Barry Howard, was one of the country's top Ugly Sister acts.

Mr Humphries was the first camp part to come his way. His playing of the role has outraged many homosexuals, and his stage shows have been picketed by members of the Campaign for Homosexual Equality. He doesn't really endear himself to the campaign by announcing that his favourite pastime while at home in Maida Vale is sewing.

GORDON JACKSON

Born: 1923, Glasgow.

Jock o' the North says that he is a *Coronation Street* and *Crossroads* man. 'I've never appeared in either, but that is the kind of thing I like to be involved in — your bills and your mortgage are paid. I'm not one for stardom'. Nevertheless he is a star. To all America he's Hudson, the epitome of the English butler. The sort of steadfast integrity with which that character was associated has made Jackson's a trusted face, just the thing to sell insurance and biscuits in commercials. His role as the boss of the ultra-violent yobs, Doyle and Bodie, in *The Professionals* is the

HATTIE JACQUES

Born: September 7, 1924.

Hattie Jacques was a stage-struck child. Her ambition then was to be a ballerina, and she would dance for anyone in the garden of her parents' house. At the age of 15, she realised that the question of her size was insurmountable, so she decided to be an actress or a singer — she had long been a fan of the musical turns at the Players' Theatre in Covent Garden. During the war, she was variously a Red Cross nurse at King's Cross and a welder of Bailey bridges. After the war she auditioned for the Players' and was taken on, before moving into radio and ITMA, where she played the vamp and Sophie Tuck Shop. She continued her association with the Players' and produced pantomimes and variety there.

She met Eric Sykes when they were together in *Educating Archie* in the early 'fifties. By this time, she was married to John Le Mesurier, by whom she has two sons, both of them rock musicians.

latest in a career which has spanned more than 40 years.

He began acting as a schoolboy in Glasgow, under the tutelage of an English teacher who was keen on amateur dramatics. He did a few broadcasts in BBC radio in Scotland, and when he was 17 was offered a small role in a wartime propaganda film called *The Foreman Went to France*. He was an engineering apprentice at the time, and even after the film, had no intention of making his living as an actor. However, when another film part was offered to him, he decided that his aptitude for acting was greater than for engineering, and decided to make a go of it. He has made more than 50 films. 'Character men', he says, 'always get more work than stars'. His theatre work has been extensive and distinguished. He doesn't really mind what work he does. Even being 'Token Jimmy' is OK, so long as he has work. His two greatest fears are unemployment and forgetting his lines. He claims that he is still as nervous as he was when he started out.

Jackson's modesty is not false. He has called himself 'A hack. . . . a jobbing actor. . . . a well-known face, like Katie in the Oxo ads. . . .' His private life is quiet and eminently respectable. He has been married for 28 years to the actress, Rona Anderson, whom he met while they were making *Flood Tide*. He doesn't drink alcohol now, and can remember being drunk only once in his life. At home in Hampstead – he has two sons both in their late teens – he plays the piano, listens to Mozart, reads and 'just flops'.

One is among Rod Stewart's sidesmen. Her professional association with Sykes has endured longer than her marriage, which ended in 1965, though 'we all stay friends'. She and Sykes are mutually dependent: 'We're really orphans in the storm, needing each other. We'll never leave each other again'.

She has also worked with most of the other top comics of the past 25 years. Of them, Tony Hancock, is the one for whom, perhaps, she feels the greatest regret. 'An awful waste of brilliant talent'. She doesn't much like farce or very broad comedy, nor does she enjoy playing 'nagging wives or butch battle-axes'. Inside her, she says, 'is a little helpless kitten'.

DAVID JASON

Born: February 2, 1940, London.

Before he became a slapstick comedian and actor, Jason was an electrician with his own business. It failed because of the time he took off for amateur dramatic society rehearsals. Having turning professional, he became involved in a string of flops, and it wasn't until he took *A Sharp Intake of Breath* that he achieved the sort of acclaim that he had long felt he deserved.

5ft 6in tall and unmarried, he lives in a flat near the Post Office tower. He says he has no intention of marrying until he is in his mid-forties and quips wittily: 'I mean, who needs it. It's like throwing yourself in the river when you only wanted a drink in the first place'. He was briefly engaged when he was in his early twenties, and sometimes wonders what has become of his erstwhile fiancée. Perhaps in a couple of years, she should get in touch with him if she still fancies the prospect.

JIMMY JEWELL

Born: 1912, Sheffield.

'A legend in his own lunch-time' is what Dickie Henderson called Jewell at a Variety Club do to celebrate his first 50 years in show business. Henderson was evidently in good form that day. Referring to Jewell's second career, begun at the age of 54, he reminded the guests that 'a dramatic actor is a comedian who is not getting any laughs'. Like Max Wall, Jewell has shown that there is no one better to play an old failed comic than an old successful comic.

His partnership with his cousin, Ben Warriss, who was born in the same bed on a different day, lasted from 1934 until 1966. They began at the Palace Theatre, Walthamstow ('the kiss of death'), and, during their heyday in the late 'forties and early 'fifties, were the most highly paid entertainers in Britain. They were early regulars on TV, appeared on the *Ed Sullivan Show* and were making

£2,500 per week 30-odd years ago.

Their style of variety was well out of fashion by the mid-'sixties and, for some years before the act broke up, Jimmy Jewell had been working as a carpenter and carpet-layer for his own small property company in-between their increasingly rare bookings. Their last show together was at a pub in

Salford. Warriss went to live in Fleetwood, where he ran a pub and a restaurant, and worked as a consultant to a holiday camp chain. He also has business interests in Spain. For about a year and a half, Jimmy Jewell devoted himself entirely to his company. He had no intention of performing again, when Frank Muir offered him a part in a BBC play.

He said he was no actor, but his wife, Belle, and son, Kerry, convinced him that he had nothing to lose. He went on to such shows as *Spring and Autumn,* which topped the ratings, and achieved a notable success in Trevor Griffiths' *Comedians* at the Nottingham Playhouse and National Theatre.

Jimmy Jewell's father was in show business. He was variously a stage manager, an actor, a novelty artist and a comedian. His son, Kerry, is also in the business as an impressario and comedian. So, while much on *Funny Man* is fictitious, it has a root in the truth of its central character's life.

BRIAN JOHNSTON

Born: June 24, 1912.
Educated: Eton and New
College, Oxford.

'Johnners' (he addresses and refers to everyone in a similar way, calling Brian Redhead, for instance, 'Redders' and, presumably, Peter 'Dimmers' Dymock) actually retired from his post as BBC cricket correspondent seven years ago. However, that has not stopped him from continuing as part of the inimitable team of Arlott, Trueman, Frindall ('Oh bearded one'), Bailey, etc. which commentates on cricket for BBC radio. He is, of course, known to all those who watch cricket on the box, simply because half of them dispense with the sometimes

colourless and solemn commentaries provided by the telemen and relish the mixture of anecdote, reminiscence, jokes, analysis and acute observation that he and his colleagues provide. He is also known to people who cannot quite place him. In *It's a Funny Game,* he recalls being approached while waiting to change planes in the Middle East. 'Don't I know you?' 'Who do you think I am?' 'Didn't you drive a bus in Watford once?'

Johnston did not become a broadcaster until after the war. When he came down from Oxford, he joined his family coffee business. Commissioned in the Grenadier Guards, he encountered, just before the Normandy landings, the BBC reporter, Stewart MacPherson, who

suggested he try broadcasting when demobbed. As the presenter of *In Town Tonight,* Johnston was 'a participatory journalist' long before that ugly term was coined. He lay in a pit while the Golden Arrow raced above him; he spent a night alone among the effigies in Madame Tussaud's; he impersonated a down and out busker; he advertised for young ladies of adventure to meet him on the steps of the Criterion Restaurant, and caused a traffic jam in Lower Regent Street.

He lives just around the corner from Lord's. When he commentates there, one of his many admirers always turns up with a bottle of wine for him (contrary, though, to popular belief, the radio commentators work sober).

FREDDIE JONES

Born: 1927, Stoke-on-Trent.

Jones didn't start acting till he was nearly 30. After leaving school, he got what was considered a good job in the Potteries, 'where people's expectations are very low'. He was, in fact, a research assistant with a firm making exothermic ceramic products: 'It was driving me mad. It was frightening'.

For an actor who gets consistently good parts, he claims not to be very fussy about what work he does. He'd sooner live a life of reasonable luxury with his wife and three sons in Sussex, than starve for the sake of Shakespeare. In fact, last year, he turned down an offer from The Royal Shakespeare Company, whose actors are hardly on the breadline. He does not share the still common snobbery about television. He reckons that the medium has been rather good to him. 'What has the theatre ever done for me?'

He was thrilled to be offered a role in *Zulu Dawn* alongside Burt Lancaster and Peter O'Toole, and revels in the recognition that such an offer implies. It is also likely to keep the wolf from the door, at least for a while.

YOOTHA JOYCE

Born: 1927, Wandsworth.
Educated: R.A.D.A.

Yootha Joyce's family was musical. Her father was a baritone called Hurst Needham who, one day in 1927, was playing the Clapham ground. His pregnant wife, the former singer and concert pianist, Jessica Revitt, was with him and decided to go for a walk on Clapham Common. It was there that she went into labour and admitted herself to a nearby nursing home, which she found while looking for somewhere to phone for an ambulance. It was apparently an act that was typical of her.

Yootha Joyce's parents lived in Hampstead. Her father's career was erratic. Periods of affluence gave way to periods of impecuniousness. She claims that she learned from her father not to value security and never to put by money for a rainy day. Nevertheless, she owns a flat in Paddington, a house at Nerja, east of Malaga and has an interest in a ski shop not far away in the Sierra Nevada. She left school at the age of 15, after having been evacuated to Hampshire. She got into R.A.D.A., to which she

used to travel each day with Roger Moore, but left to tour with ENSA and was then a assistant stage manager at Croydon. She changed her name to Joyce, broadcast a lot and met Glyn Edwards, whom she was later to marry. Edwards recommended her to Joan Littlewood, whose Theatre Workshop at Stratford East was then in its heyday. It was there that she first worked with Brian Murphy, with whom she has enjoyed such success in *George and Mildred*.

Her marriage to Glyn Edwards broke up after 12 years in 1968. Eight years later, she was to form a music hall act with his second wife, Christine Pilgrim. She has also done some music hall with Brian Murphy.

Since her divorce, she has lived with Cyril Smith (a different, thinner one, who is a pop manager) and with Terry Lee Dickson, who is her own manager. She swears that she will never remarry: 'Even at the register office I knew I was making a mistake'.

She owes her name to her mother's indecision. She had no idea what to call the child, so the future Yootha's grandmother suggested that she be called after the next woman to walk through the door of the nursing home ward. This turned out to be Yootha Rose — a dancer on the same bill in Clapham as her father — bringing a bouquet on behalf of the show's chorus. She knows of only five other Yoothas. One of them is a horse in the New Zealand police force.

MIRIAM KARLIN

Born: June 23, 1925, London.
Educated: South Hampstead
High School and R.A.D.A.

Miriam Karlin's father was a barrister who specialised in trade union affairs, and she has been an indefatigable supporter of causes. People who feel that they need to be given guidance in political matters by theatre folk and football managers may be interested in and influenced by the fact that she is a prominent member of the Anti-Nazi League. However, she is quick to dissociate herself from certain of the groups which constitute the League. 'Vanessa Redgrave and Enoch Powell would make magnificent bedfellows', she says. She is a zealous petitioner on behalf of Soviet Jewry and is on the Council of Equity, the actors' trade union. She claims that she is something of an evangelist for whatever she believes in, for instance – yoga, abstention from tobacco or raw foods, etc.

In the 13 years between the end of the first *Rag Trade* series and its reappearance, she played in Shakespeare and Shaw, was in *Fiddler on the Roof,* and toured in her own one-woman show. This is based on the letters of Lisa Lotta, who was married to the homosexual brother of Louis XIV Philippe, Duc D'Orleans. It presents a harrowing picture of a young woman's introduction to the grossly corrupt beaumonde of Versailles – which is actually among the places where Miriam Karlin has presented it. She has also been seen in it in such diverse locations as Austria and Australia, where she was the subject of an impudent headline which asked: 'Was this ever the Sheila from *The Rag Trade?*' The answer is: Yes, Bruce, it was.

PENELOPE KEITH

Born: 1940, Sutton, Surrey.
Educated: Annecy Convent,
Seaford; Webber Douglas
School of Drama.

Since she married Detective-Constable Rodney Timson (her first, his third), the statuesque actress has cut down on her professional commitments in order to devote herself to home life. Not that this means that she has actually given up working. It's just that the busy detective constable ('I enjoy nicking villains') requires a lot of feeding. 'He eats huge meals. He loves my suet puddings and he loves bread and potatoes.

BARBARA KELLERMAN

Born: 1949, Manchester.

Miss Kellerman, who is married to the actor, Robin Scobey, and lives in North-East London, has an academic background. Her father lectures in physics at Leeds University; her French mother advised the Yorkshire Education Authority on language teaching; her sister is a doctor; her brother is a sociologist. She started professional life as a bunny girl, after giving up a teacher training course.

Before she became well-known in *General Hospital* and *Glittering Prizes*, she had made good use of her fluency

He's getting fat'. She spends a lot of time putting stuff into the deep freeze and shopping: 'I look a real slut in tatty jeans and old wellies'. Their home is a seventeenth-century manor house called Mousehill near Milford, in Surrey. Which seems appropriate enough for the star of *To the Manor Born.* This series was written especially for her, and one of its attractions was that it did not require her to do a version of her snooty *Good Life* character, Margot.

Before she married the detective-constable – he wears size 11 boots – Miss Keith was 'sort of engaged' twice. One of her earlier suitors was theatre carpenter Len Tucker, who met her during her first professional engagement at Chesterfield in 1959. In those days she played 'Cockney whores in courtroom dramas, for which I dyed my hair red because they couldn't afford the wigs'. She moved on through reps at Lincoln, Manchester and Salisbury before the Royal Shakespeare Company took her on. She started playing rich bitches in the late 'sixties in *Kate.*

in French and had obtained a major role in the film *Le Fils D'Amour Est Mort.* She also speaks fluent German.

Quatermass is not the first futuristic nightmare in which she has had a part. Two years ago, she was seen in the rather preposterous BBC series, *1990.* She is 5ft 8ins tall, and, rather curiously, has one blue and one brown eye.

FELICITY KENDAL

Born: 1947, India.

Miss Kendal's parents are Geoffrey and Laura Kendal, whose Shakespearian company toured India and was the subject of James Ivory's film, *Shakespeare Wallah*. She made her stage debut at the age of 9 months in *A Midsummer Night's Dream*. She first came to England when she was five, and it was at that age that her son, Charlie, first went to India. He saw his grandparents, he saw lots of people, but he didn't see any elephants. He made his acting debut at an even earlier age than his mother — six weeks, in *Dolly* — and has quite frequently appeared with her since. He it was who presented the Queen with a bouquet when she came to a recording session of *The Good Life*. His father is the actor, Drewe Henley. Miss Kendal and Henley were divorced earlier this year, after 11 years of marriage. He described himself as 'excessively emotional'. For a time, her name was linked with that of the playwright, Robert Bolt. She now lives with Charlie in a small house off Putney High Street, where she cooks lethally hot curries to recipes which she picked up on the Malabar coast.

This year, she has been enjoying a long run in Michael Frayn's highly acclaimed *Clouds* at the Duke of York's.

KENNETH KENDALL

Born: August 7, 1924.
Educated: Oxford.

The elegant news-reader — his clothes have been praised by *Tailor and Cutter* lives alone in North-West London. Like all gentlemen of his calling, he receives numerous proposals of marriage. He has also received a proposal of a different sort from Lord Weidenfeld. The ennobled publisher, realising that anything, but anything, written by a news-reader is an almost certain best seller, approached Kendall and asked him if there was anything he would like to write a book about. There really wasn't: 'I'm just not that

LUDOVIC KENNEDY

Born: November 3, 1919.
Educated: Eton, Christ Church, Oxford.

Kennedy is a Scottish separatist, a Whiggish man, who has drawn attention to injustices in a series of books that have not endeared him to certain members of the Scottish judicial establishment. His *10 Rillington Place* was instrumental in obtaining a posthumous pardon for Timothy Evans. Certain writers on crime, however, notably Rayner Heppenstall, thought that Kennedy's case was misguided. Either way Evans is dead. *A Presumption of Innocence* helped to earn a pardon for Patrick Meeham, who had been convicted of the murder of a bingo hall-owner in Ayr. It also resulted in the blackballing of Kennedy's application for membership of the Honourable Company of Edinburgh Golfers. This happened despite the fact that Kennedy had the support of two former captains and that his maternal grandfather had been the historian of the Muir

sort of person'.

He is well-known as a perfectionist and still gets nervous before he goes on the air. He hates watching himself and doesn't actually much like watching anything else. 'I am a great theatre goer and I quite like musicals. And I read a lot, especially when on holiday.'

He has a nightmare about showing some reaction towards an item of news that he has read — sobbing, or laughing, or betraying anger. The fact that he manages to keep a poker face and do his job with such total professionalism is doubtless what caused Anna Ford to praise him as 'the newscaster's newscaster', a strange-sounding beast.

Fields Club. At about the same time, he was also rejected for membership of the New Club. He appears to have enemies among top Scots. He may well make more with the book on which he is currently at work. Its subject is the imprisonment of two men nine years ago for the murder of a sub-post-master in the course of an armed robbery at Luton.

He has also written extensively on the naval history of World War II and made several films about it. (His father lost his life in 1939, while commanding the merchant cruiser, *Rawalpindi*, against Scharnhorst and Gneisenau off the Faroes.) Like his peer, Robin Day, his only active big-time political involvement has been as a Liberal. He contested Rochdale at a by-election in 1958 and at the General Election in 1959, and lost both times.

His wife is the former ballerina, Moira Shearer. They have three daughters and one son, and divide their time between the cities of London and Edinburgh.

CHERYL LADD

Born: July 21, 1951, Huron, South Dakota.

Cheryl Stoppelmoor's movie career began with lots of 30-second walk-ons in swimsuits. 'My biggest handicap was my body', she says thoughtfully. 'Finally, I said: "If they can't see me as something more than a body I quit"'. She had arrived in Hollywood almost by chance. At the age of 16, she joined a group called The Music Shop Band in her sleepy home town, where her father was an engineer with the Chicago North Western Railroad and her mother a waitress. The reputation of the band spread, and it was eventually offered an engagement in Las Vegas. While there, two of its members were injured in a car crash, so the booking was prematurely terminated. Cheryl trekked across the desert to Los Angeles, equipped with nothing but that body, those teeth and an unshakable belief in herself. She sang commercial jingles, wore out swimsuits and eventually got a part in a film called *Jamaica Reef.* On this film, she met David Ladd, the younger son of Alan Ladd and

JIM LAKER

Born: February 9, 1922, Shipley, Yorkshire.

Everyone can probably remember where they were when they heard of Jim Laker's extraordinary feat in the fourth Test at Old Trafford in 1956. In that game, he took 19 wickets for 90 Australian runs. Among those he dismissed twice was Richie Benaud, his fellow commentator. That same season, he also took all 10 Australian wickets for Surrey at the Oval. The records he set that year (most wickets in a match, most wickets — 46 — in an Ashes rubber) still stand, and may well do so for ever.

In the Manchester test that year, the one wicket Laker didn't get was taken by Tony Lock, with whom he spun Surrey to seven successive county championships during the 'fifties.

When he retired from professional cricket at the end of 1959, he caused something of a stir with his book *Over to Me,* which included criticism of the Surrey and England captain Peter May, of the sometime MCC manager, Freddie Brown, and of various other players and officials. Both the MCC and Surrey CC withdrew Laker's membership. He has since, quite properly, been reinstated. He spent a couple of seasons as an amateur with Essex and, before becoming a commentator, was a director of a knitwear firm and a public relations consultancy.

Cricket-mad from boyhood he used to forego family holidays at the seaside in order to practise. When he was 15, he went to Herbert Sutcliffe's indoor school and was guided by the old Yorkshire player, Benny Wilson. He worked with Barclays Bank until he was called up into the army. While serving in the Middle East, he met and was coached by Hedley Verity, the great Yorkshire spinner who was shortly afterwards to lose his life.

DINSDALE LANDEN

Born: September 4, 1932, Margate.
Educated: Kings School, Rochester.

Landen denies that he is rakish, smooth, suave, lecherous, a rotter — all the things that he portrays with such finesse. He is, he says, simply a fairly successful actor who has been happily married (to the actress Jennifer Daniel) for almost 20 years and who nearly became a clergyman. Actually, he only got as far as being an acolyte.

He owes his name to his father's whimsicality. He is a twin — his brother, Dalby, is a Reading solicitor — and his father was so shocked to find that he had two sons that he went away for a week to recover. During that week, he read an article about the Wesleyan minister, Dinsdale Young, by Barrington Dalby; hence the names he bestowed on his two sons. The young Landen was encouraged, when he left the RAF and became a professional actor, to change his name to something like Dale Land. (His name is actually a source of pleasure to those who enjoy anagrams.) He found work

himself an actor and former child star. At that time, David was divorcing his first wife and was rather badly off – he doesn't get anything from his father's estate until he is 35.

After the birth of their daughter, Jordan, he wanted Cheryl to quit acting and become a housewife. She had different ideas, however, and went on to parts in such shows as *Policewoman, Police Story, Happy Days,* etc., before taking over from Farrah Fawcett Majors. She says that *Charlies' Angels* 'is waving a flag for women. It shows us working effectively in a man's world'. She now

has as many fans as her predecessor, and is constantly pursued by them and by manufacturers anxious for her to sponsor their products.

She would like to have another child and then, perhaps, 'adopt one or two'. Her family life is known to be extremely happy, and she enjoys the Sundays spent with David's mother, Sue Carol, who holds court for her four children and nine grandchildren. Her ambition is to star in a Broadway musical, and to this end she keeps up her dancing and singing. Some time last year she released her first album.

BOB LANGLEY

Born: August 28, 1939, Newcastle.

'Craggy, husky, rugged, handsome' – even if you have never seen the man, you know him now. Langley, of course, denies cultivating the image of a sort of telly Hemingway (a species of big bear sucking a lollipop) and says simply: 'If there was a film to be made on top of a mountain, I'd be the one they'd pick'. What he has done is to profit from his fondness for outdoor pursuits. One of the several books that he has published in the last few years is called *Walking the Scottish Border.* Another is *Lobo.* This is an account of three years he spent in the USA, Canada and Mexico during his early twenties. Before National Service, he had worked as an insurance clerk, but was determined not to return to that way of life, so when he was discharged, he crossed the Atlantic. He worked as a fruit-picker and in tobacco fields, as a lumberjack and a labourer. He rode freight trains and lived the sort of life immortalised in a thousand folk songs.

When he returned to his native North-East, he became a script writer and news reader with Tyne Tees TV before joining the BBC in London. He has now returned to the North and commutes to Birmingham, where he introduces *Saturday Night at the Mill* from a cottage near Keswick. He says that he and his wife, Pat, lead a simple life and that he spends most of his time walking or writing. As well as his two non-fiction volumes, he is the author of three thrillers. One of them is about the kidnapping of the BBC director-general, and another is set in his beloved Lake District. He intends to write two or three more.

hard to come by at first, for this was in the days when it was practically *de rigeur* for a young actor to come from Salford or Heckmondwyke and have an unreconstituted tripe and clogs accent. Landen had lived until then in Sittingborne and Brighton, so he had no chance at all.

It was while doing his first TV part, Pip, in *Great Expectations,* that he met his wife. Soon after that, he became a founder-member of the Royal Shakespeare Company, having met Peter Hall several years before in Worthing, where he advised

the cultural commissar of the future to start at the top – advice that Hall evidently heeded. He has maintained his connection with Hall, and is one of the better reasons for visiting our National Theatre.

He and Miss Daniel live in Putney. They have no family, and this lack of responsibilities enables them both to be fairly choosy about the work they accept. Landen's only failure in a long TV career, which has included such diverse shows as *Mask of Janus* and *Glittering Prizes,* was a series called *Mickey Dunne,* a dozen or so years ago.

SUE LAWLEY

*Born: 1946, Wolverhampton.
Educated: Dudley Girls' High
School; Bristol University.*

At Bristol University, which
has a strong tradition of
drama, Sue Lawley wanted to
be an actress. She was only
dissuaded by her mother, who
convinced her that she
wouldn't enjoy the travelling

involved. Earlier on, she had
fostered what now seems an
even more improbable ambition—she wanted to be a
singer in the tradition of Ella
Fitzgerald. To this end, as a
16-year-old, she sang with a
dance band at halls in the
grim West Midlands—at
Wolverhampton, Willenhall
and Dudley (where, not so
long ago, a couple of maniacs
slit the necks of the kangaroos

EDDIE LARGE

Born: June 25, 1942, Glasgow.

Eddie McGuinness' first
ambition was to be a
professional footballer—a sort
of joke, considering that he is
over 15 stone, almost twice
the weight of his partner. He
claims, though, to have been
useful in midfield. He arrived
in Manchester at the age of 10
and thought it was some sort
of paradise after Glasgow.
When he met Syd, he was an
electrician who had learnt to
make jokes in order to deter
the bullies anxious to put one
over on him because he was a
Scot.

His football prospects came
to an end at the age of 17,
when he was run over by a
bus. Soon after he and Syd
were offered their first TV
engagement, they were
involved in another accident.
On the way home at night
from a club in Sunderland
they were in a collision that left
Syd trapped in the wreckage
of their car.

Since then, the greatest
threat to life and limb that he
has suffered is a perforated
appendix. The result of this is
that, for a while, he went down
to a mere 14 stone. He
spends as much time as he
can at home eating, while his
wife, Sandra, washes the
mounds of dirty laundry he
accumulates during a week
away at work. They live in
Bury and have two daughters,
Alison and Samantha.

JOHN LE MESURIER

Born: April 5, 1912, Bedford.

Le Mesurier divides his time
between homes in Baron's
Court and Ramsgate, which
may not be Walmington, but
is at least on the sea. He used
to be a well-known figure
around London, rather dandily
got up in a brown bowler and
a three-quarter length camel
coat with a liver-colour collar.
Regrettably, it was his liver that
got the best of him. A few
years ago, he suffered a bout
of hepatitis, with the result that
he now tends to limit himself
to the occasional glass of
beer. He is liberal on the
question of intoxicants and
showed a touchingly paternal
reaction, when his guitarist
son, Robin, was arrested for
possessing cannabis: 'I am
proud of my son. His conviction doesn't worry me a
scrap'. Just as he is properly
contemptuous of silly laws, so
is he unimpressed by pomp
and its trappings.

In one of the rare public
utterances by an actor that is

actually of interest, Le
Mesurier let it be known what
he thought of Harold Wilson's
Retirement Honours List—all
rag traders and self-seekers in
show biz. 'When I think of
the Order of the British
Empire awards made to
people like certain actors and
singers, I am appalled. They're
being made respectable, like
White House servants who
have collected their gongs, in
the same way as other people
get a clock'. Nor does he have
much time for the civic dignitories of Ramsgate, which he
describes as a 'rather
decaying seaport'.

Le Mesurier was brought up
in Bury St Edmunds, where
his father was a solicitor, and
he trained for the stage at Fay
Compton's School. He and
Alec Guinness were the only
men among 30 girls. He
made his first TV appearance
in 1938 and his first film in
1946. In between, he served
as a captain in the Royal
Armour Corps on the North-
West Frontier. His face was
undoubtedly familiar to the
nation long before his name
was. He was a ubiquitous
character player throughout
the 'fifties and 'sixties. In 1971,
he was named television actor
of the year for his part in
Traitor, and a couple of years
ago he embarked on a career
as a recording artist. His first
record was made with Annie
Ross and Allen Clare: 'I don't
exactly sing. I just talk through
the songs.' Another instance
of his refreshing frankness.

in the zoo. This, a wag in a Dudley pub remarked, 'will put Dudley on the map'.)

The second daughter of a dairy farmer and his wife, who owned a dress shop, she left Bristol with a third in modern languages and a new accent. She had shared digs with a girl who spoke in Home Counties standard English, and had determined to lose her Black Country twang. Her first job was on the *South Wales Echo* in Cardiff. She moved from there to BBC Plymouth and thence to *Nationwide* and, for a time, *Tonight.*

She and her husband, David Ashby, who is a solicitor, met when he was doing the conveyancing for a house she was buying in Putney. They still live in that suburb, in a larger Victorian place, and have a son called Thomas, who is pushing three. She had not intended to work for some time after his birth, but found herself getting restless and could not resist the smell of the crowd. Her life is necessarily fairly hectic, but she finds time to compete in local tennis tournaments with her husband, and to cook to a standard that emphasises her general competence.

TONY LEWIS

Born: 1938, Neath.
Educated: Neath Grammar School; Christ's College, Cambridge.

The man in the velvet jacket who presents *Saturday Night at the Mill* is also a sports journalist and columnist (on the *Sunday Telegraph*); a former cricketer who captained Cambridge, Glamorgan (for whom he made his debut at 17) and England; a former rugby player who represented Gloucester, Neath and Cambridge, and a proficient violinist who was a member of the Welsh National Youth Orchestra. On his first appearance on the Mill show, as a guest, he played a Handel sonata.

He was, rather unusually, appointed captain of England (for the 1972-73 tour of India and Pakistan) when still uncapped. He was the second Welshman to captain England — the first, Cyril Walters, was also a former pupil of Neath Grammar School. In his first Test at Delhi, he led England to their first victory in India for 20 years. The match was a personal triumph for Lewis who, after getting a duck in the first innings, scored 70 in the second in a 101 stand with Tony Greig. This clinched a six-wicket victory. Although England eventually lost the rubber and drew the three Tests in Pakistan, the tour was remembered by old hands like Knott and Underwood as one of the happiest they had made, and Lewis's sportsmanship and refusal to employ the 'professional' tactics that have become the norm since his retirement, met with nothing but praise.

He announced his retirement from the Glamorgan captaincy during that tour (he is now on the county committee) and missed most of the following domestic season due to a cartilage injury. He quit the game the next season in order to concentrate on journalism — he had for some years written regularly on Welsh rugby and had appeared frequently on local TV. Test appearances apart, he had played more than 300 first class matches, had captained Glamorgan to the county championship in 1969 and had scored more than 15,000 runs, his highest individual score being 223.

He lives with his wife, Joan, and their two daughters outside Cardiff.

MAUREEN LIPMAN

Born: May 10, 1946, Hull.

The ill-starred counsellor of *Agony,* who has such problems with her unspeakable psychiatrist husband, is actually married to the playwright and scriptwriter Jack Rosenthal, who did *The Evacuees* and *Bar Mitzvah Boy,* among much else.

She first attracted attention in *Up The Junction* — the film, not the TV play or, for that matter the song. Though many might disagree, she reckons that *Agony* is the best thing that has come her way and feels very close to the character she plays. She says that she is 'everybody's left ear. I just seem to stand there and someone starts telling me a great long tale of woe'. Equally, she finds that she can just stand there and tell her husband a great long tale of woe: 'Sometimes I think I am married to a saint. He is always there to support me and talk to me'. She says that they both share the same sense of humour which, as all those who have seen Rosenthal's stuff know, is considerable and painful. She defines Jewish humour thus: 'It comes from having to joke your way out of a dangerous situation'. The couple live with their two small children in Muswell Hill, North London.

SYD LITTLE

Born: December 19, 1942,
Wythenshaw, Manchester.
Educated: Yew Tree Secondary
Modern School, Wythenshawe.

Cyril Mead was an interior decorator who played guitar and sang in pubs around Manchester dressed in a drape, bootlace tie, crepe soles, etc. One night, when he was dying his usual death and being heckled to boot, he invited his loud-mouthed antagonist on stage to see if he could do better. It turned out to be a lad called Eddie McGuiness. That was the inauspicious beginning of the now famous double act, Little and Large. For the next ten years, they played the club circuit, changing their names along the way and perfecting their act.

Syd has had to take a lot of stick. He knows that many people advised Eddie to go solo, and the knowledgeable, experienced voice of Bernie Winters still opines that 'The straight man should do more. It should be 50/50, it's more like 85/15'. Les Dawson also reckons that Syd needs to 'develop'. However, it is Syd who has been the driving force behind the act. He it was who resolved that they should

turn professional. Around that time, in the clubs where they played, they were competing against such great talents as Mike Yarwood and Jimmy Tarbuck. Their then lack of success had the effect of breaking up Syd's marriage to a girl he had met in Manchester. They have two children, Paul and Donna. He is now remarried to a former dancer

called Sheree, with whom he lives in Atherton, a small suburb on the outskirts of Manchester.

His great regret is that his father did not live to see his name in lights. 'He died with a pint in his hand after a fishing trip. I always reckon he is looking down on us at this moment saying, "Well done, lads, keep it up"'.

JACK LORD

Born: December 30, 1930,
New York.
Educated: New York
University.

Lord, who was born John Ryan, is possibly ten years older than the above date of birth suggests. It depends what you want to believe. If you want to believe that the humorless cop of *Hawaii Five 0* was a war hero who spent 16 hours in a lifeboat when his merchant ship was torpedoed off East Africa in 1944, then you have to accept that he is

older than he looks. His sartorial style is a young man's. His wife is called Marie De Narde. She is American-born of French parents. One thing that *is* certain is that Lord is a millionaire. He has a stake in *Hawaii Five 0*, is president of Lord and Lady Enterprises, owns real estate and property in Los Angeles, Australia, and Hawaii. Lord and his wife, who is actively involved in his businesses, live about 20 minutes' drive away from Honolulu, near the Kahala Hilton. He has no intention of moving back to mainland America.

Before he became an actor, Lord was a car salesman. That's one story. Another is that he was a painter. The latter, improbably, is the more likely. He certainly took a degree in fine arts and he certainly has works in an impressive selection of American and European galleries, including The Metropolitan Museum of Art and the Brooklyn Museum. He has also exhibited in London, Paris and Washington. His other interests include marketing jewellery designs, writing about Hawaii, flying and photography.

ARTHUR LOWE

Born: September 22, 1915,
Hayfield, Derbyshire.

Lowe didn't become an actor until he was 30, and it was a long time thereafter that he achieved the sort of celebrity that he enjoys today. This, no doubt, is why he has little time for many young actors: 'They think they are Marlon Brando after one TV appearance. Give them something tricky to do and they couldn't act their way out of a paper bag. Some of them don't exactly have good manners, either'.

War and boredom contrived to turn him into an actor. Brought up in Manchester, he had originally intended to go into the merchant navy but failed the eyesight test. Instead, he got a job at Fairey Aviation as 'a sort of time and motion man called a production chaser'. He was a sergeant-major serving in Gaza, when he decided that life might be brighter if some diversions were organised, so he and some other soldiers put on impromptu shows and one-act plays. He returned to Manchester where, in those days, there were numerous theatres, including five in one street. It was in rep in the city that he met his wife, Joan

Cooper. They now live in Little Venice, and she has returned to the stage, now that her two sons—one of them by an earlier marriage—have grown up and left home. (The elder is a music master at Stowe. The younger has achieved his father's thwarted ambition and become a merchant navy officer.) They have a 180-foot

schooner, built in 1885 and thought by Lloyd's to be the oldest private yacht in commission in Europe. They found it decrepit in Chiswick, and have spent a small fortune renovating it.

It was the part of Leonard Swindley in *Coronation Street* that made Lowe a national figure. Like many other members of the early *Coronation Street* cast, he had, of course, no idea what he was letting himself in for. He says that he couldn't care less whether he went on playing the part, so long as every time he asked for a rise, it was granted. Eventually Swindley was given his own show, *Pardon The Expression.* That was in 1965 and, three years later, he began his long-running impersonation of Captain Mainwaring in *Dad's Army,* 'a military extension of Swindley, prudish and pompous'.

Away from the box in the past few years, he has acted in a number of films and plays, including a revival of Priestley's *Laburnum Grove,* which was his idea. He says that he prefers working to holidays and can think of nothing better than being on tour with his wife. He only regrets that there are so few provincial theatres left at which to alight.

JOANNA LUMLEY

Born: May 1, 1946, Kashmir.

Joanna Lumley, whose latest effort has been in *Sapphire and Steel* with David McCallum, was a model before she was an actress. Before that, she was a schoolgirl who once asked Diana Rigg (whom she succeeded in *The Avengers*) for her autograph. A sometime squatter in most of the nation's gossip columns, she has recently been too busy working to attract the attention of the inky-fingered.

Formerly, she was associated with a diverse bunch of gents, including Patrick Lichfield, Rod Stewart and Michael Kitchen. She was also briefly married to Jeremy Lloyd, the actor turned script writer who is responsible for *Are You Being Served.*

The face that launched a hundred thousand haircuts—a national paper even ran a look-alike competition a few years ago—now hides below something shaggier than the basin coiffure of yore. Its owner lives with her 12-year-old son, Jamie, in the Holland Park area.

DAVID McCALLUM

Born: September 19, 1933, Glasgow.
Educated: R.A.D.A.

McCallum is one of the numerous actors (others included Drewe Henley) who was going to be the British James Dean. Of his performance in an early film called *Violent Playground,* a critic wrote: 'He plays as if he had to emulate James Dean or die'. McCallum became a teenyboppers' heart throb in the mid-'sixties when he played Napoleon Solo in *The Man from Uncle.* In 1965 6,000 American teenage girls polled by a magazine named him as their favourite film and TV star. When, in one episode of that show, he kissed a girl, 2,000 pupils of Wellesley Girls' College threatened to blow up the studio. On another occasion, mounted police had to intervene when he was mobbed on 5th Avenue.

McCallum comes from a musical family. His father was first violin with the London Philharmonic and had met his mother in an orchestra pit. He himself plays oboe, piano and violin. At the height of his success, his record titled *Music . . . A Part of Me* sold well. He spent his National Service as a lieutenant in the Royal West African Frontier Force before going into rep for six years.

He met his first wife, Jill Ireland (by whom he had three sons), when he was under contract to the Rank Organisation. He first went to Hollywood in 1962, to play Judas in *The Greatest Story Ever Told* and has lived in America almost permanently ever since. His marriage to Jill Ireland, who is now the wife of the egregious Charles Bronson, ended in 1967, and soon afterwards, he married the ex-model Katherine Carpenter, of the 'socially prominent Long Island family .

McCallum's present home is New York, and though he sometimes now plays Americans, he has retained his British passport. He is not really quite sure why. He admits to no particular feeling for Scotland and abhores Caledonian societies. In the last couple of years he has had a lot of work in Britain — *Kidnapped,* as well as *Sapphire and Steel* — but that's the only reason he has been here. 'I believe that being a citizen of the planet earth is what's important'.

ROBERT McKENZIE

Born: September 11, 1917, Canada.
Educated: King Edward High School, Vancouver, University of British Columbia and L.S.E.

The psephologist has for the past 15 years been Professor of Political Sociology at the London School of Economics, where he has taught since 1949 and where he mediated between administration and protest-kids during the occupation of the school in 1969. He has been associated with the LSE since he came here to do his doctorate after serving in the army during the war. He has written extensively on British politics and is the author of *British Political Parties,* which is the standard work on that murky subject. With Allan Silver, he is co-author of a study of working-class conservatism entitled

Angels in Marble.

His greatest admiration would appear to be for Harold MacMillan. Even so, he was mildly critical of the old wizard at the time of the Night of the Long Knives in the Cabinet. A long-time friend of Pierre Trudeau, he was able to obtain the first overseas interview with the former Prime Minister. McKenzie lives in Knightsbridge, and describes his broadcasting and journalistic activities as recreations.

LEO McKERN

Born: March 16, 1920, Sydney.
Educated: Sydney Technical High School.

Rumpole of the Bailey occupies a singular place in British TV as the only situation comedy which is neither by nor for the educationally subnormal. Rumpole is based partly on his creator, John Mortimer, QC — a self-deprecating portrait painted both with tongue in cheek and with a sigh of 'There, but for the grace of God' — and partly on a friend of John Mortimer's father. McKern, who impersonates the old boy with such style, is from a very different background. Nothing literary or legal there, my old darlings.

His father is an engineer, and that is what the young McKern set out to be. While he was serving his apprentice-

TREVOR McDONALD

*Born: August 16, 1939,
Trinidad.*

McDonald became Britain's first black TV reporter when he was hired by ITN in 1973. When he wrote to the editor of ITN asking for a job, he made it clear that he was a black West Indian. He says that he has been much more aware of his colour since he arrived in England in 1969 to work for the BBC's overseas service. His wife, whom he met while she was working for Tate & Lyle in Trinidad, is English. The difference in their colours did not, he says, occur to him until they decided to marry and a friend asked him if he was sure he knew what he was doing. He feels more conscientiously West Indian than he ever did before, but then, it is the invariable lot of expatriates to be acutely conscious of their nationality. He has no particular desire to

go back and work in Trinidad, although his 13-year-old son Timothy yearns to return to the country he can hardly remember. The life that McDonald, his wife and family (he also has an eight-year-old daughter) lead puts them in 'a cushioned position' he feels. It is evident that class prejudice is more firmly entrenched than colour prejudice.

His background was materially poor. His father was a refinery engineer who was also a smallholder and cobbler. McDonald began in radio, which was run by whites, when he was 20 and then moved into TV before coming to London. He now commutes to Wells Street from a house in Farnham. Sport is not simply a professional interest. He is a passionate spectator of cricket, tennis and football. He is also an avid reader, his preference being for West Indian literature, particularly poetry.

ship, he lost an eye in an industrial accident. It appears not to worry him. After all, he can still see. Then he became in turn a squinting commercial artist and an actor. He arrived in England in pursuit of the Australian actress, Jane Holland, whom he subsequently married. Determined not to be saddled with playing Australians, he struggled hard to lose an accent which, he recalls, 'you could cut with a knife'. During his early years in this country, he continued to work as a commercial artist and was a bacon porter. He was so poor that in the ghastly winter of 1946-1947, he was forced to sell his only source of heat, a gas fire, and wear three pairs of long johns.

Despite a distinguished career in films, he much prefers TV or theatre. He made £40,000 after tax from *Ryan's Daughter,* but still can't

help considering it a year wasted, and finished up profoundly depressed. He sold his house at Kew, his yacht, his Rolls, his collection of porcelain, etc., and bought a Volkswagen caravan. He shoved his wife and children inside, drove overland to Australia, and settled near the sub-tropical tourist resort of Cairns, in Queensland, where he spent the best part of two years cutting down grass and putting up fences. When he returned to England in 1972, he found that the house that he had sold for next to nothing had gone for £80,000. He has no regrets, about what he did, though: 'I am choosy, but I am not a winner'. Since he was last seen as Rumpole, he has been in Ronald Harwood's *Dresser,* at the Manchester Royal Exchange, in a role based on Donald Wolfitt, to whom he bears a passing resemblance.

BILL McLAREN

*Born: 1923, Hawick.
Educated: Hawick High
School and Aberdeen
University.*

A colleague reckons that McLaren would exchange all the delights and responsibilities of commentating on rugby for the chance to have played for Scotland at flank forward. It was at that position that he was selected for the final trial of 1952. He did not play, however, having been told that he had TB. 'Psychologically, I was shattered'. He had apparently contracted the germ of the disease during his year as a soldier in Italy towards the end of the war – he had served as a captain in the artillery. Though the drug streptomycin cured him, his rugby career was over. During it he played for Hawick, the South of Scotland, and a Scottish 15 against the Army. No caps were awarded for that game, which wasn't a full international.

Apart from the war, his longest spell away from his native border town was when he studied physical education at Aberdeen. When he returned, he was unable to get a job as a teacher and joined the *Hawick Express,* where he reported funerals, flower shows and WI meetings, and edited the sports page. Before getting a job as a teacher (he is now in charge of PE at five schools in and around Hawick and has resisted all offers to become a full-time broadcaster), he was given an audition with BBC radio in Scotland. He took over from Peter West as the televoice in the mid-'sixties.

When he is not teaching or commentating, he is, as often as not, playing golf or coaching young rugby enthusiasts. He is proud of the 100-year-old tradition of good rugby on the border.

PATRICK MACNEE

Born: February 6, 1922,
Berkshire.
Educated: Eton.

The son of a racehorse trainer and a cousin of David Niven, Macnee began acting at Eton (playing Queen Victoria), where his contemporaries included Michael Bentine and Humphrey Lyttleton. When he left school, he worked on a farm for six months, making his film debut in Michael Powell's *The Life and Death of Colonel Blimp.* His progress was far from startling. For a long while, he lived the life of a beach bum at Malibu, drawing unemployment pay in order to keep his two children at school in England. Between spells on the dole, he took any acting job he could find, even playing a sheriff in *Rawhide.* During his time in America, he also worked as a barman in a strip club, where he fell for one of the artistes.

Gareth Hunt was recruited to join Macnee and the fourth *Avengers* girl, Joanna Lumley, because it was felt that Steed,

in his mid-fifties, might be getting a bit past it. Macnee, however, claims that he is as fit as a fiddle: 'Most of my friends in my age group are dead—heart attacks. Jack Hawkins, a close friend and a great actor, always had a glass of gin in one hand and a cigarette in the other. Nobody was surprised when he came along and said that he had had his throat out'. Macnee had treatment from a psychologist to rid himself of his four packets a day cigarette habit and has had a

course of 'vaccinations against old age' from the Harley Street gerontologist, Peter Stephan. He claims that he feels 20 years younger. This eagerness for rejuvenation is not, he protests, connected with his fondness for romance—those days are gone. He says: 'I definitely don't want a dolly bird. I've got more chums with young blonds and heart pace-makers than I have had hot dinners'.

Macnee lives alone in Buckinghamshire. He has been married twice and divorced twice. He left his first wife and their two children to become a Canadian TV actor in 1952. Now that his first wife's second husband is dead, he once again supports her, regretful that he left her in the first place. His second marriage, to Catherine Wood-ville, lasted less than a year. Macnee attributes this to the difference of 16 years in their ages. Both of his children now live in North America. His son makes documentaries in Toronto, and his daughter is a cook in Los Angeles.

MAGNUS MAGNUSSON

Born: October 10, 1929,
Iceland.
Educated: Edinburgh Academy
and Jesus College, Oxford.

A former Pipe Man of the Year (in the shag-reeking wake of Harold Wilson and Freddie Trueman) and former rector of Edinburgh University (where he was kidnapped and held to ransom for charity), Magnus Magnusson is certainly the best-known Icelander in Britain. He arrived in Scotland at the age of nine months with his parents. His father was a businessman who was to become Icelandic Consul. His name was Sigursteinn, and had Magnusson lived in Iceland, he would, in accordance with normal practice, have called himself Sigursteinnsson. However, he preferred to take his grandfather's given name, Magnus, and add 'son' to that. It means, of course, Great, Son of Great.

He won a scholarship to Oxford and intended to pursue an academic career. While he was researching for his thesis on Old Norse litera-

ture, he began to freelance for the *Scottish Daily Express* and was eventually offered a job on the staff. Then he moved on to ITV and eventually came to London to join the BBC's *Tonight* programme. He and his family still live in a large house in Glasgow. His wife, Mamie, is a former journalist, and he has three daughters and a son. The entire family is musical and play together as often as they can.

Magnus Magnusson has written several books of a more or less archaeological bent, and is currently preparing a TV series on the Vikings. Among his other publications are several translations of Norse sagas. He has also recently been appointed to the editorship of Popular Archaeology.

LEE MAJORS

Born: April 23, 1940,
Wyandotte, Michigan.
Educated: Eastern Kentucky
State College.

The husband of F.F.M. and former Bionic Man got himself a new nose last year. His previous one had been broken three times playing football (he had offers to turn professional from St Louis, Kentucky, among others) and twice in accidents. It will evidently be a help to him as he tries to put behind him the role of Steve Austin. It may also be a boon to his breathing, but that's another story.

When Majors was about 13, he went up into the attic on a rainy day and was looking through a trunk, when he came across a few newspaper cuttings which reported that a Mrs Majors had been run over by a drunk and killed, and that her husband had died a couple of years previously in a steel mill accident. He also read that their son was to be adopted by relatives in Kentucky. This was the first

that he knew of his real background. He says that his determination to succeed in life was prompted by the sense of guilt he felt when he reflected on the generosity of his adoptive parents.

The back injury which ended his football career came shortly after his first marriage, by which he has one son, Lee junior. He was introduced to Rock Hudson, who encouraged him to become an actor, and he started working his way

towards stardom via the usual route of bit parts and more bit parts. He is now said to be worth more than $6 million, and has properties at Bel Air, Malibu and Arizona.

He evidently has something of a charmed life. Having escaped all those accidents and having often done his own stunts, he watched a year ago as a stunt man working with him on the film, *Steel,* fell to his death. Not long ago, F.F.M. and Lee Majors agreed to a trial separation.

BERNARD MANNING

Born: 1930, Ancoats,
Manchester.

The adipose gagman trades frequent insults with other gentlemen of his calling. Freddy Starr and Tommy Trinder are among those who have felt the rough edge of his tongue. It is of course standard practice among comedians to pass comment on each other's shortcomings, but few, surely, enter into the spirit of this show biz convention with *his* robust earthiness, which manifests itself further in his taste for strong jokes.

When he isn't slagging off his fellow comedians, Manning runs a club called The

Embassy in Harpurhey, Manchester, in a converted Nissen hut. His wife and mother work in the place taking money at the door and making sandwiches, and his son, Bernard, is on the management side of the establishment. He lives not far from the club and drives there in his one and only Rolls (1 BJM) or his one and only Cadillac (1 LAF), heaving his 18-stone body in and out with difficulty. His first job was selling flowers and vegetables from his father's old Ford van. Though he did school concerts, he never thought of being anything but a greengrocer until he was in the army doing National Service. He started singing with a regimental dance band and continued when he was

back in Civvy Street, working in local pubs. Apart from a spell with Oscar Rabin's band in London (with which he was to have made his first broadcast, cancelled when King George VI died) his life has been centred on Ancoats. A trip to Rochdale or Oldham is quite an event. Las Vegas, where he played a couple of years ago, was a treat for him. 'Everything is enormous there'. He says he owes everything to the Granada TV producer, Johnny Hamp, who put him in *The Comedians* and *Wheel Tappers.* He describes his act as aggressive and dislikes the puritanism which proscribes jokes about Irishmen, Scotsmen or Pakistanis, though he says that people of all races regularly visit his club.

M

DAN MASKELL

Born: 1908, Fulham.

The voice of tennis and of Robinson's Lemon Barley Water began life as a ball boy at Queen's Club in Fulham and was, for 16 years, British professional champion. He was coach to the All England Club from 1929 to 1955 and from then till his retirement in

1973 was training manager of the Lawn Tennis Association. During the war, which interrupted his championships, he served in the RAF and rose to the rank of squadron leader. Each year during Wimbledon, he is heard in 17 countries, and Arthur Ashe wrote: 'It wouldn't sound right if I heard a different voice'.

Dan Maskell has been broadcasting since 1937 and

BILL MAYNARD

Born: October 8, 1928, Farnham.

The 18-stone actor ('I am the best actor in Britain. I am the finest actor I know. I am the actor I am today because I have slept in waiting rooms and have had nothing to eat) used to be a fairly thin comic and variety performer. In the 'fifties, he was the partner of Terry Scott in a long running TV show called *Great Scott—It's Maynard*. He wore a huge, sloppy pullover and the spikey haircut of a skiffle performer. In fact he had a hit in 1958 with a song called *Hey Leli Lo*. His partnership with Scott began when they both worked at Bucklands, Skegness, in 1951. As little

Billy Williams (his real name is Walter Williams) he had been doing the rounds of working men's clubs since the age of nine, playing guitar, doing impressions, tap dancing and so on. Like Tommy Steele, he had learnt guitar while in hospital. By the age of 13 he was making more than his father, who worked as gardener to the Bishop of Leicester and had unwittingly encouraged his son by taking him to see the variety turns at South Wigston Working Men's Club.

When he left school, he tried to become a professional footballer and was signed by Kettering Town. An injury put paid to that career. While he sought more work as an entertainer he was a salesman, a tea boy and a

coal heaver. His success in the 'fifties made him behave like 'a demented pools winner', he says. He also had a desire to quit variety and become a straight actor, so he went into Rep. It proved to be a costly mistake at the time. His earnings plummeted from about £1,000 per week to less than £50 and he was clobbered by the Inland Revenue and eventually declared bankrupt. Then came a gruelling round of cabaret performances, small film parts and decent, but rather badly paid, theatrical engagements.

His 15 years of penury ended when he began to get dramatic roles on TV, and these led to Selwyn Froggitt— a character based on a man Maynard had actually known

CLIFF MICHELMORE

Born: December 11, 1919, Isle of Wight.
Educated: Cowes Senior School.

In the autumn of their days old telly personalities—that is to say, first-generation telly figures who, in the 'fifties, gaped from tiny bakelite frames, whither they migrated after careers in forces broadcasting—tend to turn up. Michelmore is a case in point. Famous for his watertight, indisputable statement: 'And the next *Tonight* is tomorrow night', he is just the sort of

wholesome figure, untouched by scandal, which that show requires. He is a former Congregationalist and used to

preach in chapel ('Christianity is a seven days a week job'.) The only ripple on the millpond of his personal life was when he and his wife, Jean Metcalfe, were the victims of unfoundedly malicious gossip in Reigate: 'I want everyone to know that I and Cliff are very much in love and always have been', said the veteran of countless editions of *Family Favourites*. It was that programme that brought them together. Miss Metcalfe introduced it from London and Michelmore from Hamburg. They did not meet until they had been on the air together for six months.

In the 'fifties, Michelmore

has been commentating on TV since 1951. He is still as keen as ever: 'When I lose my enthusiasm for Wimbledon, I'll know I've lost my enthusiasm for life.' He hasn't missed a day of the championship since 1929; since his life has revolved around the place, it is hardly surprising that he and his wife live in a house only a mile or so away in the Merton Park area.

and about whom he had talked to the writer, Allan Plater. The main problem of recent years has been obesity. The strain of his stomach was more than his back could bear, and he suffered a badly slipped disc not so long ago. He was eventually healed by the Brighton spiritualist, Tom Pilgrim, and was able to dispense with the steel corset that he had until then been forced to wear.

Married for 30 years, Maynard and his wife, Muriel, live in the Leicestershire village of Sapcote, where he devotes much time to playing cheese skittles, on which he has commentated for the Indoor League. His son is the actor and singer, Maynard Williams, and he also has a daughter called Jane.

was perhaps the best-known face on the box. His non-appearances on *Tonight* were rare and matters of national concern. His hernia operation in 1959 made the papers. So, too, did his collapse from exhaustion a couple of years later. His schedule was gruelling. He introduced *Tonight* and its successor, *Twenty-Four Hours*, for 11 years, after which he left in order to pursue his burgeoning career and to spend some time with his family. Since then, he has worked on a variety of programmes, devoted some time to his post as editorial director of *Barclay Card Magazine*.

JONATHAN MILLER

Born: 1935, London.
Educated: St Paul's;
Cambridge; University College
Hospital.

'Satirist', doctor, medical journalist (hardly an adequate handle), actor, film-maker, theatre and opera director, and many other things besides, Miller has temporarily forsaken the screen to head the BBC's so far meagre production of the entire Shakespeare canon.

The Body in Question caused him to be described as a 'corduroy vulture' and a 'cannabilistic charcutier' and to be compared with the liver. This is an organ of which he is inordinately fond, to the extent of calling himself 'a hepatic rhapsodist' and one which is as capable as the rhapsodist of fulfilling a wide range of functions.

For the best part of 20 years, he has combined medicine and show business (the arts, if you like). He made his name in 1961 with *Beyond the Fringe*, and still lives in the Camden Town house he bought with the proceeds of that show. Alan Bennett is

reputed to live in a corner of the kitchen.

Miller's father was a military psychiatrist. His great-great-uncle was the philosopher, Henri Bergson. As a child he was always on the move. As an adult he has displayed an extraordinary restlessness. All that is outwardly constant about him is attire, which is vague early 'sixties Ivy League. Nothing short of a book twice the length of this one would do him justice. Suffice it to say that he is very sensitive to criticism and does not much enjoy having fun made of him; that he is a tireless devotee of anachronism in the setting and interpretation of classical works (prescient fans are looking forward to his hospital Hamlet—Claudius as a bent ear specialist, Hamlet as a student of psychiatry, grave diggers as mortuary attendants, etc.); that his wife Rachael, by whom he has two teenage children, is a GP; that he says he has kept up his doctoring out of a spirit of curiosity; that he wants to make some films about painting, the tricks and legerdemain of artists and the way in which our eyes are able to 'read' them.

SPIKE MILLIGAN

Born: April 16, 1918,
Ahmednagar, India.
Educated: Poona, Rangoon,
South-East London
Polytechnic.

'A late starter, a successful failure driven up the wall by fear of the bank manager' — Milligan on himself. The comic was a war hero before he was a comic: see *Rommel, Gunner Who, Monty: My Part in His Victory* and *Adolf Hitler, My Part in His Downfall.* In those days, he was lance-bombadier Terence Milligan, trumpeter. During the war, he met Harry Secombe and shortly after it, Peter Sellers, in a public house in Victoria. Years later, he attacked Sellers with a kitchen knife: 'I tried to kill him. Either that, or I just wanted to peel him'. He is not habitually a violent man. He

has campaigned against the culling of seals and the slaughter of whales for profit. Some of the animal preservation groups with which he was associated took a dim view of his statement a few years ago that he kept an air rifle to shoot 'up the arse' cats which went near his nesting boxes. The question of the rifle was raised when he appeared in court after having taken a pot-shot at a yob who was trespassing in his garden.

Milligan's other antipathies include the exhibition of pornography and the smoking of tobacco. His admirations include his former secretary, Shelagh Sinclair, who has been his companion since the death of his wife, Paddy, a couple of years ago; the Royal Family; archaeology, and travel. He has establishments in Bayswater and Whetstone.

JOHN MILLS

Born: February 22, 1908,
Felixstowe.
Educated: Evesham and
Norwich.

Before he went on the stage Sir John was a salesman of lavatory paper and disinfectant for Sanitas, and a grain merchant. His first part was in

the chorus of a revue *Five O'Clock Girl* at the London Hippodrome in 1929. A year or so later, he was spotted by Noel Coward working as a song and dance man with a concert party called *The Quaints* in Singapore. The Master arranged auditions when he got back to London and recommended him to Cochran and that, he says, is how it all began. He has been in more than 100 films, including the late Robert Hamer's marvellous *The Long Memory; The History of Mr Polly; Mr Denning Drives North,* and *Ryan's Daughter* (for which he got an Oscar). His favourite is *Tunes of Glory.*

Quatermass is not his first TV series, but is certainly the most notable, if only for the amount of interest that it has generated. Just as he has not been lucky with TV roles, so with some of the parts which he was to have played at the Old Vic. These were grabbed from him by the outbreak of war — and included Hamlet,

Richard II and Henry V.

Briefly married when a young man to Aileen Raymond (the mother of Ian Ogilvy), he has now been married for almost 30 years to Mary Hayley Bell. It is a source of some chagrin and no little puzzlement to them that the first marriages of all their children — Juliet, Hayley and Jonathan — have broken down. Lady Mills says: 'They fell in love with the wrong people, and too soon'. They brought up their children at a gorgeous house called 'The Wick' on Richmond Hill. After they sold it, they found they missed it so much, that they bought it back. Then they sold it again — to Ronnie Wood of the Rolling Stones. A year later, they approached the hirsute millionaire with an offer to repurchase it, but he didn't want to sell. When eventually it came on the market, its price had soared and Sir John said that he could only afford to buy it if he owned an oil well. They now live at Denham.

BOB MONKHOUSE

Born: June 1, 1928, Beckenham.
Educated: Dulwich College.

With his partner, Denis Goodwin, whom he met at a party in 1948, Monkhouse was one of the most prolific writers of comedy scripts in the 'fifties, and was also a frequent performer—both of his own material and of others'. Even then, he was called 'a smart alec', 'the man with the phoniest grin in the business', 'too brash', 'too smooth', 'too slick'. His first success on the box was *Fast and Loose*. He subsequently had numerous shows of his own and became a widely used compère.

Even as a schoolboy, he had a sure eye for the main chance and used to sell tadpoles, frogs and anything else he could convince his friends were the things to have. He rescued a little girl from drowning in Kelsey Park, Beckenham—he couldn't actually swim—and was subsequently awarded a medal for bravery at the Penge Empire. Instead of making the usual noises of thanks after the presentation, he launched into a 15-minute comedy act.

It wasn't as if he was fighting his way out of the gutter. His father was a prosperous Methodist businessman who owned a custard firm called Monk and Glass, and he always regarded the information that 'one day the company will be yours' as a threat.

At the age of 12, he showed a precocious talent as a strip cartoonist and began to contribute to national comics. When he left Dulwich, he joined Gaumont British Films to train as an animator. Called up into the RAF, he organised troop shows, and when he was demobbed he joined the BBC as, of all things, a 'trainee comedian'. During this period, he married for the first time.

The notion that all comedians must experience a full quota of misfortune is no doubt a sad truism to Monkhouse. He and his wife lost four children who were born prematurely, and his elder son, Gary, is a spastic. He says that it was not until his son was 11 years old, that he learned to understand how the boy must see the world, as a series of disconnected gestures.

In 1965, Monkhouse and Goodwin ended their partnership. They had frequently rejected lavish offers from America, and eventually Goodwin decided it was time to go. They had been turning out up to seven shows a week, working up to 16 hours a day. 'Muir and Norden were the Fortnum and Mason of script writing. We were the Tesco'. Monkhouse's career as an actor (he later called himself 'unimpressive') had already begun to flourish, although neither the films nor the plays and pantos in which

he appeared enjoyed the popularity of the then novel *Candid Camera,* of which he became the first compère in 1961.

From early on in his career he had acquired old films, on which he is an acknowledged expert, and as long ago as 1965 his collection of the work of such silent stars as Buster Keaton and the Keystone Cops was valued at more than £30,000. From this he developed his *Mad Movies* series. In the late 'sixties, he began to devote an increasing amount of time to his 11 companies, and it was about then that his marriage broke up. In 1973, a group of men from whom he had bought copies of films were jailed for defrauding film companies by selling 'junked' prints. It was Monkhouse's suspicions which led to their arrest. Leading the case for the Crown was Michael Worsley, who this year prosecuted Monkhouse when he was cleared of similar charges.

BRIAN MOORE

Born: February 28, 1932,
Benenden, Kent.
Educated: Cranbrook School.

A year ago, it looked as if Moore might be about to quit ITV for the BBC. His contract with LWT ran out in March, and for some months before, the tales of secret assignations with would-be poachers from the Beeb and less secret 'clear the air' meetings with worried ITV executives were commonplace. It seems that it was only his employers who failed to recognise that he is now indisputably the top soccer commentator in the country, and so in a position to dictate his own terms.

These, when he eventually signed a new contract, included a guarantee of the commentary on every England match for the next five years (which cannot have delighted Hugh 'Christian-names-terms with the lads' Johns) and a series of documentaries on top sportsmen and women: 'Basically I want to look for the gladiators. I am fascinated by how a top star lives, what sort of house he has got, whether he visits his mum regularly. I would like to see myself as a sort of sporting Alan Whicker'. He feels that sports coverage is too restricted, that it concentrates on the action to the exclusion of background material.

Moore's father was a farm worker, and it was the young Moore's good fortune that he was able to win a scholarship to Cranbrook, where he became captain of cricket and hockey and managed to set up a soccer team, even though the school's game was rugby. He was a good enough cricketer to play for Kent Young Amateurs in a year when the team was captained by Colin Cowdrey.

He became a journalist after National Service working on a magazine called *World Sports*, moved to an agency specialising in sports news, and went from there to *The Times* as a sub-editor. He did his first radio commentary in 1963 at Fratton Park, where Portsmouth was entertaining Bolton Wanderers. He remembers it as 'the greatest moment of my career' – not on account of the quality of his commentary, but because he sat next to his hero, Raymond Glendenning. He became a full-time radio man on *Sports Report* and was recruited by LWT in 1968.

Moore and his wife, Betty, live near Orpington.

PATRICK MOORE

Born: March 4, 1923.
Educated: Privately.

'I am morally sure that, at this very moment, on a planet orbiting another star in our galaxy, a speaker is saying very much the same thing as me'. Are we to assume that the speaker is a professional odd-ball who, if he didn't exist, would be unlikely to be invented? Despite observations of this sort, Moore insists that he is not a prophet. He is, rather, a scientist—and a self-trained one at that. He became interested in the galaxies at the age of six, and got his first good telescope when he was 11. He still has it, standing in the hall of his house near Selsey, where he lives with his 93-year-old mother (who calls him 'Moore'

or 'chum') and their house-keeper, Mrs Woodward.

He was a sickly child, suffered from heart trouble and was, perforce, lonely. He taught himself astronomy and could type well by the time he was seven. He had to fiddle his medical to get into the RAF, where he served as a navigator with Bomber Command. When he left the RAF, he became a teacher at a boys' prep school. He still looks like the quintessential prep school master, all leather elbows and Varsity Shag. He once illustrated the constellations for his pupils by positioning them in appropriate places on a cricket pitch. He began writing science fiction stories for boys, and got into TV in 1957: 'Just happened to be around'. The author of some 60 books (which provide him with an income far larger than his TV earnings), his most recent enterprise has been to found a political party. The United Country Party is not greatly different from numerous other manifestations of Right-wing individualism. It is dedicated to fighting 'global Communism', and cutting immigration and taxes. It has seven members, one of whom, Lieutenant-

ERIC MORECAMBE

*Born: May 14, Morecambe.
Educated: Euston Road
Elementary School,
Morecambe.*

'Historically', says Ernie Wise, 'it is the comic who dies first. Eric is the comic'.

'I don't want to do a Sid James and die during a performance', says Morecambe.

All this is prompted by the sad fact of Morecambe's second heart attack (which necessitated a 7-hour open-heart operation in June), and the possibility that Britain's top double act may be forced into retirement. If they do split, Morecambe fancies a spot of acting. Not going to the National, like Jimmy Jewell, but a radio sitcom, maybe. He also has a novel about show biz under way, but has been advised not to work too hard on it. One thing he has been doing during his convalescence is growing a moustache, which seems to suit him rather well.

M and W took 38 years to reach their extraordinary position as clownish king-makers—the invitation to appear on one of their Christmas shows is apparently the most sought-after accolade in a certain stratum of the entertainment world. Old music hall turns like Harold Wilson and Angela Rippon have appeared; coming stars like Prince Charles, Anna Ford and Roddy Llewellyn have declined. Charles said: 'Our position makes it impossible'.

John Eric Bartholomew and Ernie Wiseman met as young music hall artists. Then a singer, Morecambe had been entering talent contests since childhood and was eventually 'spotted' by Bryan Michie, who ran a discovery show.

Morecambe lives with his wife near Harpenden, where the locals don't pester him. When he wants to be pestered, he drives into Luton. The Morecambes have a son, Gary, an adopted son Steven, and a daughter.

Colonel Edmund Iremonger, fought Chichester in the General Election. Iremonger expresses his views thus: 'The Tories are sort of wet. Mrs Thatcher is the only man among a lot of women'.

Moore is quite pleased that everyone reckons him to be an eccentric boffin: 'All scientists are mad'. Politics apart, Moore's other activities include composing operas— his *Perseus and Andromeda* was successfully performed at Brighton five years ago; playing cricket—leg breaks a speciality—he is a Lord's Taverner; playing chess and tennis; driving his ancient Ford Prefect, 'the Ark'. He also crops up in unlikely places, such as the BBC musical, *Curriculee Curricula,* which starred Chris Farlowe, who owns a German militaria store in Islington, North London.

JOHN MOTSON

Born: 1945, Salford.

Motson's greatest moment came at the end of the 1977 Cup Final, which he must have been praying that Manchester United, captained by Martin Buchan, would win, so that he could say: 'How fitting that a man called Buchan should be the first to ascend the 39 steps to the Royal Box'. Had the keen young commentator been out there counting the steps? Or did he simply know how many there were from the massive filing system that Mrs Anne Motson slaves over at home in St Albans?

Motson was brought up in South London, where his father was a Methodist minister. He began in journalism at Barnet and then got a job on the *Sheffield Telegraph.* A keen footballer, he qualified as an FA preliminary coach and attracted the attention of the paper's sports editor, who gave him his introduction to Radio Sheffield where he began his commentatorial career.

Motson keeps up his football with the commentators' eleven, which plays charity matches. He is also keen on squash and table tennis. His memory of the games he has seen is prodigious. Ask him about, say, Southampton versus Birmingham at the Dell in 1973-1974, and he'll not only give you the score, scorers, bookings, etc., but describe in detail Peter Osgood's perm, the jagged landscape to be seen in Kenny Burns' mouth and the pattern made by a set of studs on a shin.

PATRICK MOWER

Born: September 12, 1940, Oxford.
Educated: R.A.D.A.

'Looks like a hairdresser pretending to be a mercenary'— one estimate of the preposterously violent cop, Hackett, whom Mower played for two series of *Target* before the BBC decided that enough groins had been kicked and that it was time to call it a day. He is probably not too sorry to see the end of it, since he has the actors' habitual fear of being known as the character he plays. He recalls seeing people come up to Edward Woodward and say: 'Can I have your autograph Mr Callan'. He insisted on being written out of Callan, killed off after 13 episodes. Thames TV's switchboard was jammed as a result.

Mower was brought up in Oxford, whither his father, a Welsh miner, had migrated when unable to get work in the pits during the depression. Mower was accepted at R.A.D.A. at the age of 16, but

his father insisted that he should have something 'to fall back on', so he trained as an engineering draughtsman at BMC's Cowley plant, got his HNC and then reapplied to R.A.D.A., having gained much experience with amateur groups.

He married his childhood sweetheart, Audrey, and she worked as a secretary and model to help him through drama school. They have two children: Simon, 15, and Claudia, 11. (Mower now lives with Suzanne Davis, star of *Carry on Emanuelle* and a former dancer from Ilford.) His first TV part was as a wide boy in the excellent soap opera of local corruption *Swizzlewick*, which was taken off following protests from various dignitories in a town not too far away from where John Poulson practised as an architect. Mower has tended since to be associated with tough-guy roles. By coincidence, he took over from another actor associated with similar roles, John Thaw, in Stoppard's *Night and Day* earlier this year. The part is

FRANK MUIR

Born: February 5, 1920, Broadstairs.
Educated: Chatham House School and Leyton County High School

Wordsmith, punster, anthologist, script writer, sometime (short time) telly executive— these are all the things that

those unfortunate enough to know Muir only from panel games and commercials ('Fruit and nut case') have missed. They should have listened to radio.

Muir was brought up in fairly strict circumstances. His father was a New Zealand ship's engineer who stayed on in this country. At Chatham House School he was a fellow pupil of another author, Edward Heath. It was evidently, then, not the environment of that establishment which made Muir such a consummately funny man. Muir wrote his first piece for a parish magazine, which later went broke. When his father died, he was not yet 15, but he went to work for his father's employers as a salesman, a post he did not much like,

though it taught him to live on his wits and brought him into contact with all human life.

During the war he was— one look at him will tell you this— in the RAF, a cameraless photographer in Iceland, a writer of sketches for Forces Radio, a parachutist. He met Denis Norden at Ted Kavanagh's agency for comic writers, to which he had applied upon leaving the RAF. It was a marriage of opposites which worked marvellously. There has never been a funnier radio programme than *Take It From Here*. They also did other Jimmy Edwards shows, including *Whack-O*. When they split up in 1963, Muir went into telly administration, first with the BBC and then with LWT—a squarish peg in a

that of a hard-bitten Australian journalist, and it was as a hard-bitten Australian rogue that he played opposite Thaw in *The Sweeney*. He is rare among actors in not making apologetic noises about the violence in shows like *Special Branch*, and opines that since murders, muggings, and the like have occurred since the beginning of time, TV is unlikely to make a lot of difference. He says this despite an unsavoury experience, when a man threatened him in a pub. He thought nothing of it—a common enough occurrence and one to be ignored. The fellow persisted: 'My girl friend thinks you're marvellous, but I think you're a great poof'. Mower didn't retaliate, and his adversary stuck a broken bottle into his stomach. He has a two-inch scar as a souvenir of that encounter. It can doubtless be seen somewhere beneath the heavy jewellery that Mower slings over his bare chest.

He rates himself as 'the fifth best actor in England, above Gielgud and Richardson'.

ARTHUR MULLARD

Born: 1912, Islington.

Mullard still lives in Islington, near Highbury Fields in a council maisonnette. He spends most of his time in local pubs, where he is a well-known figure. He reckons to spend about £50 a week on drink which, he says, is his main pleasure. He started drinking after the shock of his wife's death almost 20 years ago. He has not remarried, although he says that he is often lonely. Not that he is ever short of companionship; it is friendship that he wants.

Arfur's teachers told him he was a born actor. When he left school, he became a butcher's boy. He was a professional boxer before he got into films as cauliflower-ear colour in East End scenes.

A couple of years ago, he published his autobiography, because 'I bin a cult figure for years' and thought the public would be glad to know his story and views. What he likes, apart from booze and birds, isn't clear. What he dislikes is actors 'poncin' off the dole', acting schools, and travel. He rarely goes further than Southend save when working. He also hates going on stage.

He has three children and five grandchildren. One of his sons, Johnny, is a professional comedian, though his father has refused to help him, saying that he has seen too many of his colleagues push their children and see them flop.

roundish hole. He left after a year or so, and has been writing and performing ever since. *You Can't Have Your Kayak And Heat It* is a compilation of punningly punch-lined stories told by Muir and Norden on *My Word!* The *Frank Muir Book* is a bizarre and fastidious anthology.

Muir married in 1949. He and his wife, Collie, have two children: Jamie, who works as a researcher for LWT, and Sally, who works for a publisher. His home is a Victorian house at Egham, near the A30. He collects rare editions of Fielding, Smollett and Dr Johnson (he is a former president of the Johnson Society); he likes snuff and bow ties, and hates jokes. He is 6ft 6in tall.

BRIAN MURPHY

Born: September 25, 1933, Ventnor.
Educated: R.A.D.A.

Murphy is happily married and lives in Highgate. He and his wife, Carol, have two sons: Trevor and Kevin, both in their early 20s. They have also fostered a number of other children over the years. He is forever being accosted by half-wits who assume that George Roper's problems are his own, and has regretfully learnt to stay away from various pubs that he used to frequent.

Murphy met both his wife and Yootha Joyce at Joan Littlewood's Theatre Work-shop in the mid-'fifties. He moved to London with his parents, who were in the restaurant trade, when he was a child, and became a keen amateur actor. After National Service he auditioned for R.A.D.A. However, he was unable to get a grant, so when the money that he had saved during his years in the RAF ran out, he was forced to leave and work at odd jobs. The only sort of odd job he has to do now is to make records (his first was called *Jogging*) and to decide whether to accept the many offers of stage work with which he is inundated. The theatre is his main enthusiasm. He has played *Hamlet* (in Warsaw), *Iago*, *Falstaff*, etc., in his time, and he is grateful that he is now able to accept fairly meagrely paid jobs without impairing his family's security.

IAN NAIRN

Born: 1930, Bedford.

Nairn's telly journeys (often as not made in an ancient Morris 1000 convertible in which, to judge by his famous rumpled suit, he has slept) comprise but a tiny portion of his prodigious output. An architectural journalist since the middle 'fifties when he came out of the RAF, he quickly established a reputation as a vehement opponent of the shoddy excesses of the town planners and architects who were defacing Britain and have continued to do so. Of course, the lay public supported him. Of course, the architectural profession, with its endemic smugness and insularity, dismissed him.

His criticism in *The Observer* throughout the 'sixties was notable both for its quality and because it reached a wide audience without speaking down to it. Since he joined the *Sunday Times*, he has tended to write more as a guide. His numerous books actually include two fine guides — one to London and its suburbs, the other to Paris. They are admirable anthologies of the unexpected, the quirkish and the grand — and they are, in a way, accurate mirrors of their begetter.

Buildings and travel apart, his great love is beer and the various places in which it is to be found.

ARTHUR NEGUS

Born March 29, 1903, Reading. Educated: Reading School.

The Cheltonian sage became a telly wallah at the age of 62. He was brought up in Reading, where his father was both a cabinet-maker and an antique dealer. He was also, of course, the man who encouraged the young Negus in his acquisition of an apparently boundless knowledge of the trade. At 17, Negus inherited the shop and proceeded, he recalls, to make every mistake in the business: buying dear and selling cheap, acquiring objects which it would take seven years to clear, etc. He eventually tired of working by himself, sold the shop and joined Reading Fine Arts as a buyer. During the war, in which he served as an air-raid warden, Reading Fine Arts's premises were bombed. On duty at a police station one

DEREK NIMMO

Born: September 19, 1932, Liverpool.
Educated: Quarry School (A.k.a. 'a good fee paying school.')

The popular 'silly ass' was educated at the same school as half of the Beatles (Lennon and McCartney's earliest group was called the Quarrymen). At the age of 17, he was running a dance hall in Penny Lane. It was there that he met his wife, Pat: 'We had our first date in the shelter mentioned in the song'. She introduced him to amateur dramatics and, after a few years, he decided to give up his job as a paint salesman and turn professional. He started at Bolton, and when he arrived in London four years later, he and Pat and their first child Timothy (who is now a mini-impressario in Hong Kong)

night, he came across an advertisement for a cataloguer with the Gloucester auctioneers, Bruton, Knowles. He joined them in 1946, although it wasn't until 1972 that he became a partner.

The producer of *Going For a Song* read an article which referred to Negus' expertise as a valuer when the programme was in its planning stages. Initially Arthur was not keen on the idea but, as everyone knows, took to the box like a fish to chips. He rather wishes

lived in a caravan. They toured in it, dragging it along behind an old Buick, and had a car park off the Edgware Road as their base. Between his rare jobs as an actor, Nimmo worked as an assistant to Lord Grade — who was then merely Lew and an agent — as a road manager for Al Martino, and as a 'publicist'. To publicise *See You Later, Alligator,* he walked about wearing an alligator's head, and to publicise a panto, he wandered along Oxford St dressed as a cat: 'The police make you walk in the gutter when you do that'. He was also a ventriloquist, straight man to Arthur Haynes and part of a roller-skating act, as well as a stall-holder in Petticoat Lane, hot dog salesman, etc. With some understatement, he says: 'My career has been unplanned'.

His constant stage and television appearances here and in Australia, the Middle

it had happened earlier, but nevertheless enjoys the popularity it has brought him.

He lives with his wife, Irene, who is also passionately interested in antiques, in Cheltenham. Their home is not, perhaps surprisingly, one of that beautiful town's Regency houses, but a modern flat discreetly furnished with 'just a few good pieces'. They have been married for more than 50 years and have two daughters—one lives in Malaysia and the other in South Africa—and five grandchildren. Though he is, of course, not fond of the sharp practices which have got auctioneers and antique dealers such a bad name, he has a measure of admiration for the dedicated faker: 'If he takes enough trouble, he is worth his money'.

Known as 'a middle-class folk hero' and 'Lord Clark with price tags on', he is the author of several books and an energetic lecturer.

DENIS NORDEN

Born: February 6, 1922, Hackney.
Educated: City of London School.

Frank Muir's long time partner and the presenter of LWT's compilations of studio gaffes and of that company's *Looks Familiar* used more often than not to win the story competition on *My Word*. This, considering that he always disclaimed the ability to do anything but write dialogue, is either surprising or just a sign of his diffidence.

After he left school, where he was a contemporary of Kingsley Amis, he took his first step towards academe by becoming a boiler-man's assistant. Then he went into the theatre as a stage-hand and, at the age of 17, became a theatre manager. He spent the war in the RAF. During his 17 years with Muir and for some time afterwards, he

worked in a sixth-floor room high over Regent Street. His solo stuff has included the screen plays of such films as *The Best House in London*. Despite his flirtation with films and TV, his true medium is surely steam radio. He and Muir shared the Variety Club award as top radio personalities of 1977. His daughter, Maggie, who does educational programmes for Capital Radio, won the Independent Radio Personality of the Year Award the following year.

East and America, have enabled him to lead a life of some style. His house in Kensington, which was robbed in the summer, was a repository of numerous paintings, objets de vertu, pieces of good furniture and porcelain. He enjoys posing there for photographers, wearing a dressing gown. Jeremy Thorpe is a close friend. So is Clement Freud. Nimmo's attitude to dogs is unknown. Like Thorpe, he is a dandy, and like Freud, he is an epicure. He is also a Liberal and, it was rumoured (incorrectly, he says), had Mr Thorpe been unable to get his trial postponed until after the General Election, he was among the eager no-hopers anxious to present North Devon to the Tories.

The Nimmos' two younger children are Amanda, 20, and Piers, 12. The name Nimmo is his own: It is Scottish.

BARRY NORMAN

Born: August 21, 1933.
Educated: Highgate School.

The son of the film producer, Les Norman, who was responsible for *The Cruel Sea* and for numerous Australian projects, Norman junior was a journalist in South Africa and on the *Daily Mail* before he exposed himself to the nation seven years ago. He was made redundant when the *Mail* swallowed the *Daily Sketch* and, after a period of writing occasional pieces, was taken up by Late Night Line-Up.

As the only person on TV who seems capable of talking about films and film stars without resort to jargon, he is someone to be thankful for. As the bags beneath his eyes have developed into pendulous sacks, so has his prose become ever pithier. So, too,

have his activities broadened. He has written several novels, including a thriller and an entertainingly accurate picture of newspaper life.

He lives with his wife, Diana, in a Hertfordshire village, plays cricket, has two daughters, and receives a great deal of admiring mail.

JOHN OAKSEY

Born: March 21, 1929.
Educated: Eton; New College,
Oxford.

In addition to his TV duties, the 2nd Baron Oaksey and 4th Baron Trevethin is the racing correspondent of the *Sunday Telegraph* and the author of a history of steeplechasing and *The Story of Mill Reef.* He was, until four years ago, when he retired on doctor's advice after the last in a series of bad falls, a leading National Hunt jockey. During a 21-year career, he had ridden more than 200 winners. He was twice champion amateur, and his victories included the Hennessy Gold Cup, the Whitbread Gold Cup, the Foxhunters' Chases at Liverpool and Cheltenham, the Imperial Cup, etc. Success in the Grand National eluded him. In 1963, on Carrickbeg (his favourite mount), he was leading at the last fence, but was beaten to the post by Ayala.

His father was a senior judge at the Nuremburg trials and a sometime KC to the Jockey Club, and his grandfather was Lord Chief Justice. He, too, read for the Bar, but at the age of 28 gave in to his fondness for racing and began to write for the *Daily Telegraph.* Lord Oaksey is married with two children, a son and a daughter.

DES O'CONNOR

Born: 1932, Stepney.

In Anahuac, Texas, there lives a family called Heard, which has collected every one of O'Connor's records. The family saved for seven years so that they could come to England to shake hands with their idol. Such devotion is, apparently, not unusual. Nor is absolute loathing, but that's another matter. O'Connor is well aware that not everyone warms to him. He calls himself 'the most hated man since Hitler'.

The fact of the matter is that O'Connor is liked for the same reasons that he is loathed, that is, for his, well, ordinariness. He gives hopes to all those who sing while washing their armpits. That should be his last worry. His first record, *Careless Hands,* sold a million, and his total sales to date are well over 10 million.

O'Connor reckons that one advantage of watching him on the box is that you can get up and make a cup of tea, knowing that you'll miss nothing crucial.

The son of a milkman, he started performing in RAF talent shows and later became a Redcoat at Filey, before going on to make his first professional appearance at the Newcastle Palace in 1953, after Butlins had tired of his rather strong jokes. Nowadays he is only too anxious not to offend anyone with his material.

He has been married twice. The daughter of his first marriage, Karin, is the girlfriend of punk idol Billy Idol. She herself is in a group called 'Charlie's Devils'. O'Connor comments on this liaison, which Mr Idol (not his real name) describes as 'an arrangement'. 'Punk is part of the music business, like Beethoven or Debussy'.

BILL ODDIE

Born: July 7, 1941, Rochdale.

The hairiest Goodie is really a closet Robert Dougall. He spends his holidays in the Shetlands or the Scillies, birdwatching, and has augmented the British list with a sighting of Pallas's Reed Bunting, which is a native of Siberia. His other pursuits include football. He plays for the Top Ten Eleven, and is a sort of honorary pro, having had a cartilage operation a while ago.

As an antidote to his Goodies record ('We were getting like human Wombles'), he has performed with a group called 'Pacific Eardrum', which tried to introduce some sort of humour into pop music. Nothing has been heard of it for some time, which doubtless shows that the music business is as humorless as ever.

His two daughters, they are 8 and 11, didn't watch *Saturday Banana* (né *Bonanza*), but provided their old father with a source of material for it. He is of the opinion that too many children's programmes treat their audiences as idiots, and is anxious to rectify that.

IAN OGILVY

Born: 1943.
Educated: Eton and R.A.D.A.

Saint Ogilvy says that he would not mind following his predecessor Roger Moore into James Bond's buckskin loafers. This, no doubt, is why his Simon Templar looks for all the world like an impersonation of Mr Moore. The Bobby Vee hairdo and the voice are ringers for Moore's. All that is different is the car (Jaguar instead of Volvo) and the fact that Templar no longer smokes. This is because his creator, Leslie Charteris, has given up tobacco and rather quaintly

stipulates that Templar abstain too. Ogilvy himself is a heavy smoker and, it follows perhaps, less of an athlete than Templar. His most vigorous pursuit is riding motor cycles. When he left Eton, his father, a sometime actor, ad man and the brother of David Ogilvy (*Confessions of an Advertising Man*) wrote to his house-master complaining: 'I have spent a large sum of money sending my son to supposedly the best school in the world . . . he has come out with an extensive knowledge of motor cycles'.

Eton is not a place, says Ogilvy, that an actor should mention he has had acquaintance with: 'Nobody takes you

seriously unless you shut up about it'.

Nor did the school do much to encourage the fledgling actor. When Ogilvy left, he spent a lot of time 'dashing about on a bike'. Then he went to R.A.D.A. and, after the usual period in rep, made his name in films like *Witch Finder General* and TV series like *Upstairs Downstairs,* in which he played Elizabeth Bellamy's impotent husband.

Ogilvy met his wife, Diane, a former model, when they were both *en route* to Rome to audition for parts that they didn't get. They live with their son, Titus, who is 10, and Diane's daughter by a previous marriage, Emma.

PETER O'SULLEVAN

Born: March 3, 1918.
Educated: Charterhouse and Collège Alpin, Switzerland.

The extraordinarily popular horse wallah is not to be confused with the perhaps equally popular but nowadays less famous horse wallah Bernard O'Sullevan, who founded *Race Form.* Peter O'S is also, of course, Irish, the son of a

soldier and magistrate from Killarney.

He was in publishing before he put to profitable use his fondness for the turf. He joined the Press Association after spending the war with Chelsea Rescue Service, and became racing correspondent of the *Daily Express* in 1950. He first broadcast in 1946 and became TV's permanent mouth in 1953. Since then he has gabbled through several

thousand races, none more exciting for him than those in which his nags, Be Friendly and Attivo, have run. They were trained at Epsom by Philip Miller, and Attivo gave him particular pleasure when it won, fittingly, the Daily Express Triumph Hurdle and the Chester Cup 5 years ago. O'Sullevan is married, wears tinted spectacles, lives in Chelsea, enjoys food, wine and travel.

RICHARD O'SULLIVAN

Born: 1944, London.

O'Sullivan was one of Britain's most constantly employed child actors in the '50s. (He was, for instance, the BBC's Little Lord Fauntleroy. The '60s treated him less favourably. He worked as a petrol pump attendant and mini-cab driver, and even thought of joining a kibbutz. In those days, he used to frequent pubs in West London in the company of such other former child actors as Denis Waterman and Jeremy Bulloch. They all shared a passionate enthusiasm for

football and played often. After he became well-known in the *Doctor* series, O'Sullivan turned out regularly for show biz teams, but age and a couple of broken legs have forced him to give up the game. In his day he is said to have combined the ball-playing skill of Norman Hunter with the fierce commitment in the

tackle of Trevor Brooking or Duncan McKenzie.

In 1971, he wed Diana Terry, but the marriage lasted less than a year. His name has more than once been linked with that of his *Robin's Nest* co-star, Tessa Wyatt. He is reticent on the subject of women. All that he will say on the subject is along the lines of: 'I am not a monk . . . the only female in my life is Dick Turpin's horse Black Bess'. Black Bess is played by Fury who is a stallion.

Now that he has quit football, his preferred sport is pool. He also enjoys cooking, and is willing to prepare a complicated dish which requires some attention, even if he is eating alone.

MICHAEL PALIN

Born: 1943, Sheffield.
Educated: Shrewsbury and
Brasenose College, Oxford.

Palin was not brought up within sight of a steel works. He cannot remember the day when his father dragged home a bath across the cobbles and said to his young son, who suffered from TB and rickets: ''Appen lad, summat to put coal in'. His background was wonderfully middle-class— Birkdale Prep School and the promise of a career like his father's as a captain of industry.

In the months before he went up to Brasenose ('a railway waiting room, anyone can go in'), he joined an amateur theatrical group called 'Bright Side and Car-brook Co-operative Players'. At Oxford, he acted a bit and, with Robert Hewison formed a comic double act known as 'Seedy Entertainers'.

After Oxford, he trod the familiar path of radio comedy, *Do Not Adjust Your Set, Monty Python's*, etc. He lives in a rather obscure part of Hampstead with his wife and three children.

LEONARD PARKIN

Born: June 2, 1929, Yorkshire.

Among Parkin's numerous correspondents is a lady in Cardiff who is convinced that the news bulletins he reads contain coded messages for her. Another wrote to him apologising for having watched him while wearing curlers in her hair.

Parkin worked as a journalist on local papers before he joined the BBC in 1954. He became a foreign correspondent and was the Corporation's man in Washington during and after John Kennedy's Presidency. He joined ITN upon his return to England, and has been with the company for 12 years. He is married, and has a son of 21. He is a non-smoker and is a keen fisherman who enjoys both the rigours of deep sea fishing and the more subtle pleasures of casting a fly while, miles away in Wells Street, someone else tells the nation why camels are wearing pith helmets this year.

MICHAEL PARKINSON

Born: 1936, Barnsley.

'Parkie is quite as capable of doing it as the next man', says Russell Harty, who knows. Parkie endorses his rival's opinion: 'I can interview anybody'. All this and much more was said when the Barnsley favourite son looked like getting a five-nights-a-week 'current affairs' programme, which was to have been on the air this autumn. The BBC scotched the project, but not before a number of people with typewriters had expressed their misgivings. While no one, of course, questioned his ability to get knocked over by Emu, tell the world that Boycott's the best, enchant us all with another vasectomy yarn, or ask searching questions of Jimmy Tarbuck, Parkinson, despite his experience on *Tonight*, was not thought of as a political inquisitor.

His progress from folkloric journalist to fully fledged show biz personality has been rapid. Parkinson's Law states that when in doubt (a) grin, (b) wrinkle your face into a cartographic representation of the Ganges Delta, (c) say Barnsley and/or parkin (which is a disgusting sweet-meat eaten in the North).

Parkinson began life as a junior reporter on a local paper, did his National Service in the army, and met his wife, Mary, who was then a school teacher and is now a telly presenter, on a bus. He told her he liked her figure. They married in Doncaster and began life together in a run-down flat in Manchester, where he was by now working on *The Guardian*. He came to London with a job on the *Express*, worked on a couple of defunct magazines, *Town* and *Topic,* and moved into TV. His critics, whom he

NICHOLAS PARSONS

*Born: October 10, 1928,
Grantham.
Educated: St Paul's School
and Glasgow University.*

Parsons, son of a Lincolnshire
doctor, may actually be five
years older than the date of
birth given above indicates.
He is a coy as an actress
about his age and says: 'I have
not worked it out. A person is
as old as he bloody feels.
Anything between 40 and 60'.
Either way, he is a contemporary of his home town's
most famous daughter,
Margaret Thatcher. If they
romped together as brats, the
event is not recorded.

He was a late developer. He
couldn't talk until he was 2½,
and when he did he had a
dreadful stutter, which he
didn't get rid of until, at the
age of 15, he found that with a
script in front of him he could
speak with confidence. He
had moved to Hampstead
(where he still lives), when his
father bought a practice there,
and made his stage debut with
a group called the 'Stock
Exchange Players' at the
Cripplegate Theatre near
Liverpool Street.

At the age of 16, he left
school to take up an
engineering apprenticeship in
Glasgow, where he became
known as 'Big Nick'. He joined
concert parties as an
impersonator and comedian
and was spotted by Carroll
Levis, for whom he did his first
broadcast as *The Radio
Deceiver.*

Back in London, he worked
as a comedian at various
clubs and got a residency at
the Windmill, after which he
joined the BBC's Drama
Repertory Company. Here he
first met Denise Bryer, whom
he married a few years later.
He established himself during
the early years of ITV as
straight man to the late
Arthur Haynes.

describes as envious,
seem to reckon that his early
performances on *Cinema*
were at least free of the
enthusiastic reverence which
he has sometimes displayed
since. A certain softening-up
almost inevitably accompanies
the transformation of a critic
into an interviewer.

Films apart, Parkinson's
other great enthusiasm is
sport and big sports stars. He
wrote George Best's 'autobiography' and the number of
articles he has written about
the quaint goings on at cricket
matches played in places with
quaint names is legion.

He plays cricket himself in
the show biz ghetto outside
Maidenhead, where he and
his wife live with their three
children. His opinions on
cricket have sometimes met
with less than total acclaim
from some of the game's more
notable practitioners, Lord
Ted Dexter for one.

Parkinson's pronouncements
are, however, not confined to
the proclamation of opinions
of sports and dipsomaniac
stars. The widely broadcast
news of his vasectomy
provoked some harsh critics into
accusing him of trying to
encourage other men to
follow his course.

SUSAN PENHALIGON

Born: 1950, St. Ives.

Described by her admirer,
Sean Day Lewis, as 'eternally
nubile', Miss Penhaligon has
spent four years living down
the reputation she got in
Bouquet of Barbed Wire as
'Bitch of the Year'. This year
she will be seen on the box in
YTV's Dick Francis racing
thrillers. She has also recently
had parts in several films,
including *Soldier of the Queen*
and *Leopard in the Snow.*

She was brought up all over
the place by her itinerant
parents. (Her father worked
for Shell and her mother was
an actress during the war,
entertaining the troops.) At
drama school, she married a
fellow student called Nicholas
Loukes. He died soon after
they were divorced, from
swine fever contracted in
Canada. She is now married
to the film director David
Munro, with whom she lives in
Chiswick, where she houses a
collection of paintings
acquired in St Ives and on her
travels. She drives a Morris
1000 convertible, enjoys
home decoration and likes
cats. She is only distantly
related to the Liberal energy
spokesman, the Cornwall MP,
David Penhaligon.

P

JON PERTWEE

Born: July 7, 1919, Chelsea.
Educated: Sherborne, Fresham
Heights and R.A.D.A.

The son of one playwright, Roland, and the brother of another, Michael, Pertwee became known as a comic (a description he loathes) on radio programmes like *Waterlog Spa, Up the Pole* and, later, *The Navy Lark*. His earliest TV appearances were not notably successful, and his looks inevitably led to his being considered a sort of English Danny Kaye. He used to point out, somewhat unconvincingly, that, at 6ft 2ins, he was five inches taller than the American. He was also a flashier dresser.

He became the third *Dr Who* in 1970 (after William Hartnell and Patrick Troughton) and established himself as a kiddies' favourite.
No matter that his earliest fans are now pushing 20 and have probably forsaken such diversions, he has found a new generation with *Worzel Gummidge,* though he is most gratified by the approbation of his contemporaries, like William Franklyn: 'To have a favourable reaction from other professionals means more to me than anything'.

A gay (in the old sense) bachelor in his young days, he first married at the age of 35. His wife was Jean Marsh (the creator and co-star of *Upstairs Downstairs*), who was then beginning her career and was unwilling to sacrifice it for marriage. He remarried in 1960. Ingeborg Rhosea is the daughter of a former Bonn politician whose interests are literary as well as theatrical. Her first novel (which she wrote in England) was about an actor, his mistress, and his mistress's daughter. The Pertwees have a son, Sean, who wants to be an actor, and a daughter who is training as a designer.

RON PICKERING

Born: May 4, 1930, London.

As well as being a commentator and occasional compère, the BBC's athletics man is a sports consultant and a coach of great repute. His speciality was the long jump, which he gave up when his girl friend, Jean Desforges, constantly beat him. He began coaching her, and she ended up as captain of the British Women's Team, 1954 European Champion and his wife. His most famous pupil was Lynn Davies, who was under his tutelage during his years as AAA National Coach.

PAT PHOENIX

Born: 1925, Manchester.

Miss Phoenix married Alan Browning in 1974. They have since separated five times, and earlier this year, she announced her intention of filing divorce papers. She met Browning when he was cast as her fancy man and, subsequently, husband on the *Street*. He was a veteran of *The Newcomers* and has since moved on to another soap opera, *The Cedar Tree.*

Pat Phoenix was born illegitimate, though she didn't know it, nor did her mother, until she was eight. It was then that her father was involved in an accident, and a policeman arrived at the house to tell her mother that he was in hospital — with his wife. This woman turned out to be one with whom he had gone to live after leaving home. The accident was reported in the paper, and a previous wife emerged from the past. This episode was sad enough, but it was followed by her mother's remarriage to a decorator whom the young Pat disliked.

As a teenager, she often broadcast on *Children's Hour,* and when she left school to work in the gas department at Manchester Town Hall, she spent her evenings at an amateur dramatic society. She turned professional when offered a job with a touring company, and when she was 26 married an actor called Peter Marsh, whom she met in rep. The marriage lasted for a year. Nine years later, she was recruited to *Coronation Street.* The show has afforded her considerable celebrity, a house which was formerly no fewer than 3 cottages, and all sorts of unwelcome publicity.

She is extremely generous to her friends, even to the extent of selling them at a loss houses she has bought. She coughs a lot, smokes 60 cigarettes a day, but doesn't drink much. Miss Phoenix is an immensely popular figure in the north-west, as indeed throughout the whole of Britain.

ANDRE PREVIN

Born: April 6, 1929, Berlin.
Educated: Berlin and Paris
Conservatories.

The man about music (and about TV, TV commercials and the boards) was separated earlier this year from his third wife, Mia Farrow, by whom he has had three children (two of them twins) and with whom he had adopted two Vietnamese babies.

His parents fled Germany, where he had already begun to display musical talent, when he was nine, and settled in Los Angeles. He played the piano for silent movies in an art house and, at the age of 16, made a jazz record which sold 200,000 copies. It was as a jazz pianist that he became known in Britain during the 'fifties. His first marriage was to the jazz singer, Betty Bennett. The two daughters of that marriage are now in their early twenties.

He was, meanwhile, making a big reputation and more money as a composer of film scores. He got Oscars for *Irma La Douce, Gigi, Porgy and Bess* and *My Fair Lady.* Other films on which he worked included such classics as *Bad Day at Black Rock* and *Silk Stockings.* He later said that he spent too long in Hollywood, considering that it wasn't what he really wanted to do: 'But then it was seductive — the glamour, the parties, the chorus girls'. When he left Hollywood, many of his friends, in the words of the director Norman Jewison, 'were convinced he was wrong He was the most successful, most sought-after composer-arranger in Hollywood'.

It was his second wife, the song-writer and singer, Dory, who encouraged his ambitions to become an orchestral conductor. He trekked about America conducting a number of different orchestras and

establishing a serious reputation. In 1968, he was appointed musical director of the Houston Symphony Orchestra, and a year later was offered the job that he gave up this August — principal conductor of the LSO. For some time, he commuted between London and Houston, before abandoning the latter.

His promotion of the orchestra has been financially most successful. It has appeared with him on his TV shows and has become the most recorded in the country. His showmanship has been astute — getting Edward Heath to conduct, getting Julie Andrews to sing carols, etc. *Every Good Boy Deserves a Favour,* shown on the box this autumn, was conceived with Tom Stoppard and the LSO for a one-off performance and despite — or because of — being eccentrically described as 'anti-Soviet agitprop', is a remarkable piece of theatre.

MAGNUS PYKE

Born: December 29, 1908,
Paddington.
Educated: St Pauls School,
McGill University, Montreal,
and University College, London.

Dr Pyke was for most of his life a nutritionist employed by the scientific civil service and by the Distillers Company. He didn't take to the box until he had retired at the age of 65 from the directorship of the Glenochil Research Station in Scotland. He is the author of some 20 publications, about two-thirds of which are concerned with nutrition. The others are mostly concerned with the social applications and implications of science.

He has been described as, among many other things, 'a marionette on dexedrine', 'our most popular living scientist', 'the archetypal mad boffin'. Magnus Pyke himself likes to

think of himself as 'the Bernard Levin of science', ie, someone who is understood by all yet still respected — more or less — by his peers. The trouble, of course, is that he has courted the animosity of his peers by his swift and often less than tactful refutations of their opinions and theories. Even at the age of 70, he still entertains the happy illusion that science can somehow improve man's lot. He believes in the ability of science to provide finite answers to problems.

The history of science might be thought to put the boot into this notion and leave stud marks all over it. Some of his suggestions, though, are absolutely admirable. During the war, when he was working in the Ministry of Food, he proposed to Lord Woolton (he of the Pie) that the nation's dogs should be fed to chickens, who would in turn

lay more eggs to be fed to pregnant mothers. The idea met with little favour.

Dr Pyke's first intention was to be an actuary. However, he found work in an insurance company uncongenial, and sailed from Britain to Canada on Grand National Day, 1927, aboard the *Montcalm.* During his seven years in Canada he put himself through university, where he studied agriculture, and worked on farms and on cattle boats. He subsequently did research at London University into the effects of Vitamin B2 on the lenses of rats' eyes.

His broadcasting career grew out of his books ('I determined to write a page a day'), and he was the first person to talk on radio about chlorophyll. He admits — it is obvious, is it not? — that he is no gastronome and no cook. He lives with his wife in Hammersmith.

ESTHER RANTZEN

Born: 1941, London.
Educated: North London
Collegiate School and
Somerville College, Oxford.

Breast freeder, scourge of the mail order spiv, champion of the downtrodden and the half-witted consumer, La Rantzen is TV's first lady and Britain's third. All this in spite of teeth to which she has had 'everything done'. All this despite the sort of selflessness which, as a customer, prevents her from complaining. 'I haven't the energy or the time', she says.

She has been with the BBC all her working life. Her father was one of the Corporation's senior engineers. After Oxford, where she was the contemporary of Melvyn Bragg, she did a secretarial course at Mrs Hoster's ('I have never hated anything more'), and then became a studio manager, which she also hated. Ned Sherrin gave her a job on *BBC3* and then she filed photographs for *24 Hours.* The man who gave her a break was Bernard Braden—'Anything good I do I owe to him'. His producer put her on screen in *Braden Week* 11 years ago, and she has been there ever since, carving out a little niche which has grown into an empire. It's an empire which has been encouraged by her friendship with, and subsequent marriage to, Desmond Wilcox, head of the BBC's General Features Department, under whose aegis *That's Life* is produced.

Emily Alice Wilcox, born on January 26, 1978, is now the nation's best-known baby. She and her parents live in Chiswick. Her mother, who is expecting another baby in January, has fought for creche facilities for her at the BBC and has since become a sort of professional mother. Her latest project is characteristically worthy. It is an organisation called 'Mama', which is intended to advise women suffering from post-natal depression.

Meanwhile, back at work, Miss Rantzen receives £25 dress allowance and sometimes wears Petula Clark's cast-offs.

She is said to be motivated by a fear of the fate which befell Simon Dee. As well as *That's Life,* she has produced and presented a number of other programmes, such as the film series *The Big Time.* She has, surprisingly, only rarely been sued by firms and persons whose activities *That's Life* has investigated.

BRIAN REDHEAD

Born: 1930, Newcastle.
Educated: Royal Grammar
School, Newcastle; Downing
College, Cambridge.

'I am not often lost for words'. Every morning he gabs a wad of them at a waking nation. Sometimes we get the face as well as the voice, bearded and bonhomous and undeniably keen.

Redhead began his successful journalistic career after taking a first in history and doing National Service in Malaya. He worked on the *Seaside Chronicle* in Whitley Bay and on a paper in Newcastle before joining *The Guardian* in 1954. With the exception of a year of working full-time on *Tonight,* he was with Guardian Newspapers for 21 years.

In 1969, he became editor

of its sister paper, the *Manchester Evening News,* which he left in 1975 when he failed to obtain the editorship of *The Guardian* itself. Since then, he has been a more or less full-time broadcaster, though he is rumoured to have ambitions of an academic life. It was doubtless to this end that he contributed a long essay on James Callaghan to a volume on British Prime Ministers edited by the late Scottish MP John MacIntosh.

His other professional activities include a visiting fellowship at Manchester Business School and active participation in the Cancer Education Campaign, for which he has written a widely distributed primer.

He lives with his wife and four children just outside Manchester, in the Cheshire town of Cheadle.

ANGELA RIPPON

Born: October 18, 1944.
Educated: Plymouth Grammar
School.

Miss Rippon is, of course, more interesting to much of her audience than the news she reads. A few months after she made her celebrated appearance on the Morecambe and Wise Christmas show three years ago, she was banned from speaking to the press by the BBC. The Corporation likes to pretend that its news readers are good Cubs and Brownies, and Miss R's activities, though in the best possible taste, etc., were thought to be *de trop*. Not, of course, that the ban prevented her from going on making the news—the brief career as a jockey; the new 'younger' hairdo; the lunch on the Royal yacht; the freedom of the City of London; her narration of *Peter and the Wolf*; her election as Show Business Personality of the Year; the admirer who was bound over after bursting into her office and who later claimed that he was simply trying 'to get into TV'; her announcement that 'one day in future' she would quit reading the news, and so on and on.

The daughter of a marine, she left school at 17 and joined the *Western Morning News* as a photographic assistant, moved to the *Sunday Independent,* joined BBC local radio in Plymouth, worked for Westward TV, where she was editor of women's programmes and introduced a show for children. Then she got the call to London.

In 1967, she married Christopher Dare, who has what he describes as a 'car body spares' business near Tavistock and whom she met at a YMCA dance when she was celebrating her seventeenth birthday. In those days, he was working in Devonport dockyard, and during the six years of their courtship, he spent some time away at sea in the merchant navy. He says that their common interests are cars and food, but that otherwise they are dissimilar: 'She was educated. I wasn't. Ange likes drama and the arts. I couldn't give a monkey's for them'.

She has great admiration for her husband's business prowess and for his calming influence on her—'He soaks up everything'. Their life on Dartmoor is ideal as an antidote to the strains of London, and the long-distance commuting is a small price to pay. Devon is still the centre of her world, and the fact that she is outdoorsy and sporty is increasingly reflected in her non-newsreading commitments. Her new contract with the BBC allows her 8 months a year in which to make documentaries at BBC Bristol (which is about 2 hours' quick drive from her home) and to introduce such Bristol-based programmes as *Country Game* and *The Antiques Road Show.* Referring to this contract, Mr Bill Cotton, Controller of BBC1, said: 'She drove a hard bargain. You should see the scars'.

Last year, she was voted Head of the Year. This, apparently is a hairdressers' award and should do wonders for Plymouth crimper, where she goes for a weekly set. She has never commented on those predictions which have her as the BBC's first woman Director General but she undoubtedly has the correct Thatcher-esque appeal and authority. Mrs. T., though, never had Miss Esther Rantzen to contend with.

ROBERT ROBINSON

Born: December 17, 1927, Liverpool.
Educated: Raynes Park Grammar School; Exeter College, Oxford.

'The compulsively garrulous chairman of numerous radio and television programmes'. Robinson could hardly argue with that. He is prolix, he is to be found everywhere, he does have a *bon mot* for every occasion, he is a glutton for pun. He is also not that keen on a lot of the broadcasting work that comes his way. As a follow who is known to read books and to have written a couple, he is rather dismissive of the bulging magpie minds which are merely good at quizzes: 'These programmes are conducted with people who suffer from an inability to shed miscellaneous information. I regard this as a kind of disease'. Of course he does, because he *can* shed 'miscellaneous information', whatever that means or—to put it another way—he can't retain it. Perhaps he thinks that the brain has a finite carrying capacity and that, if it stores all the scores that Keith Miller made in Sheffield Shield Matches, then it just won't have room for important stuff like the titles of his novels (*Landscape with Dead Dons, The Conspiracy*) and where the really eager fan can find them, or the titles of the half-dozen or so shows with which he is usually involved.

He was a happy child, he says, brought up in a suburb close to the Kingston By-Pass.

The headmaster of his school had literary pretensions and used to invite the likes of Auden to come and meet the boys. It was this headmaster who also taught Robinson that there was a horizon beyond the By-Pass. Glimpsed on the horizon were spires—he edited *Isis*—and bars—he began on Fleet Street as a film and theatre columnist. (Between Oxford and Grub Street he had done National Service in Africa.) He was first spotted on *Picture Parade* in the late 'fifties. It was, though, on *Points Of Views* that he established the clever, lofty, sometimes disdainful persona that we have all come to know and love. When Kenneth Robinson cropped up a couple of years later with a coarser version of the same manner, the nation wondered if the two Wisenheimers were brothers. They weren't and aren't. RR is an only child. He himself has three and one wife, Josephine. They have homes in Chelsea and Somerset. Robert Robinson has two false teeth but the bald pate, believe it or not, is real.

TED ROGERS

Born: 1934, Kennington.

Rogers began in show business as an entrant in Butlin's Talent competitions, doing impersonations of Danny Kaye. He branched out into other impersonations—Frankie Laine and Johnny Ray—and was heard on a radio talent show which got him his first theatrical engagement. While he was doing his National Service, he realised that he could make a living in show business so, when he was discharged, he asked at the Labour Exchange for something appropriate. He was sent to work for a ticket agent. By this time, rock and roll had arrived, so Rogers started to imitate the first generation of rock stars. He had not yet even begun to think of developing a line in one-line gags.

That came some years later, when he was invited to compère a Shirley Bassey show at the Palladium. He went on to introduce the last few weeks of *Sunday Night at the Palladium,* which led to spots on a Royal Variety Show and as compère of such visiting American stars as Perry Como and Bing Crosby. Crosby invited him to the States, and some of his cracks there about former President Richard Nixon's daughter Tricia—'Richard Nixon was the only President who was lying in state while in office'

and ' Kissinger's nightmare— to wake up and find the world at peace'. Similarly, he himself is grateful to strikers. 'Keep on striking, or I'll be out of a job'. Domestic objections have been raised to his tilts at miners ('I'd bury them underground for demanding £135 per week'), the Labour Party, Arabs, etc., etc. Most of his material is written in conjunction with Wally Malston, who is apparently known as 'King of the One-Liners', and says that Rogers is 'a barometer of what the public is thinking'.

So be it, but he is hardly a barometer of what the public is doing. His passion is polo— he has four ponies and plays at Cowdray Park, which is also a regular haunt of Prince Charles.

LEONARD ROSSITER

Born: 1928, Liverpool.
Educated: Liverpool Collegiate
School.

Rossiter wouldn't be where he is today had he not, in his early twenties, had a girl friend called Ida, for whom he used to wait outside the hall where she rehearsed with an amateur theatrical society. One night, he tired of waiting, entered the hall and watched the proceedings. Realising that he could probably do as well as anyone there, he joined a similar group and began to take elocution lessons in order to get rid of his thick Liverpool accent.

His only previous theatrical connection had been his father's occasional games of golf with George Formby, Senior, and Frank Randle. When he left school towards the end of the war, he failed to get into Oxford ('Latin wasn't good enough') and might anyway have had to turn down a place since his father, a barber and bookie, had been killed whilst on ambulance duty during an air raid. When he came out of the Army Education Corp as a sergeant ('You couldn't be less than a sergeant in that outfit'), he declined a place at Liverpool University to read modern languages. Instead, he joined an insurance company as a clerk and supported his mother. He was rather frustrated, he says, during the seven years he spent there. He took his exams ('I'm very thorough'), even though he knew that sooner or later he would quit. At the age of 26, he exchanged his £9 a week post as a claims assessor for a £4.10s a week job as a bit player at Preston Rep, which had guaranteed him two weeks' work. A few months later, he was unemployed and thinking that the Commercial Union hadn't been such a

terrible place after all. He went on to Wolverhampton and Salisbury before he arrived at the Bristol Old Vic. It was there that he made his name, and he turned down numerous offers of work in London in order to keep playing leading roles—'Never leave a pond until you're the biggest fish'. Though he is known, somewhat to his displeasure, as a comic actor on account of R. Perrin and Rigsby, he devotes only about two months each year to TV. The rest of the time he is on stage and, earlier this year, co-directed and starred in a revival of David Turner's *Semi-Detached* at Greenwich. He had originally played the role (a manic insurance man) in the play's first production at Coventry in the early 'sixties. Then, when it transferred to London, Laurence Olivier took over the part. Now Rossiter can, of course, himself pack a theatre and have his name above the title, etc.

He lives within jeering distance of Chelsea football ground with his second wife, Gillian Raine (who played opposite him at Greenwich), and their seven-year old daughter, Camilla.

WILLIAM RUSHTON

Born: August 18, 1937,
Chelsea.
Educated: Shrewsbury.

The very all-round entertainer is not merely a permanent embellishment of *Celebrity Squares,* but a cartoonist, author, librettist, actor and sometime columnist. He has been quoted as saying: 'I'll do anything. I'll drop my trousers at the drop of a hat'.

The son of a publisher and grandson of the philanthropic Lord Leverhulme's lawyer, he was one of the co-founders of *Private Eye* in the early 'sixties. His former headmaster attributed this aberration to the fact that he and his colleagues, having been brought up during the war, 'had had no nannies'. And, says Rushton, 'the old bugger meant it'.

In the good old days (1963), he stood as an independent candidate in the Kinross and West Perthshire by-election in opposition to Sir Alec Douglas-Home and Ian Smith (a different one, who owned a garage). The toothy Prime Minister made the usual noises about Rushton's 'debasing our political currency'. At the polls forty-five voters disagreed with Home.

After *TW3,* Rushton appeared briefly on a show called *Stars and Garters,* then spent some time in Australia, where he married the singer and dancer, Arlene Dorgan, in 1968. They now live in South Kensington with their son, Toby.

Rushton's books include entertainments for children and a work called *Super Pig* which he wrote with a photograph of Shirley Conran (Super Woman) pinned on the wall before him. 'Rather as Monty used to keep Rommel tacked to the wall of his caravan'.

ANDREW SACHS

Bern: April 7, 1930, Berlin.

The man who was Manuel from Bath-a-loner tried to persuade John Cleese to turn the role into that of a German but, famously, failed. An 'overnight success after 20 years in the business', Sachs was voted Most Promising Artist by the Variety Club after the first series.

His parents fled Nazi Germany and arrived in this country when he was seven. At the age of 16, he decided to make a career in the theatre, 'because I wanted to sign autographs'. The horrible irony is that no one is likely to waylay him in the street, so heavily disguised was he in his most famous part. He served a long apprenticeship in rep, and after that toured for years with Brian Rix's farce machine. During this time, he began to write, and his singular radio play, *The Revenge,* written in 1964, was broadcast a year and a half ago and has since been repeated. It owes nothing to the sort of play in which he has made his living. It has, in fact, no 'characters' and is the representation—by a staggering gamut of sound effects—of a man escaping from an asylum or prison, murdering someone, and giving himself up. He is now at work on a further play which is only partly contrived in such a way. Another piece, called *Maid in Heaven,* was presented at Chichester a few years ago.

Sachs is married to the actress, Melody Lane, and has two grown-up sons and a teenage daughter.

LEONARD SACHS

Born: September 26, 1909, South Africa.

The Chairman of *The Good Old Days* is an actor whose connections with music hall began in 1936, when he and a friend took over a club on what had been the premises of the celebrated—and notorious—Evans Song and Supper Rooms in Covent Garden, in order to found the Players Theatre. To placate the place's ghosts, they put on a show of Victorian entertainments and, so successful was it, turned the theatre into the Mecca of music hall revival. Sachs was in the chair there for more than a decade and was the only choice of *The Good Old Days* producer, Barney Colehan, when the show began in 1953.

Although he is worried that the public fails to realise that the part of the Chairman is a role played by an actor, he has not encountered much difficulty in finding other work

over the years. He began in South Africa at the age of 17 (he says that he could never go back), arrived almost penniless in Britain when he was 19, and made his London debut a year later in *The Chalk Circle.* He is married to the comedienne, Fleanor Summerfield, and has two sons—Robin, who is an actor, and Toby, who is an ad man. He lives in Bayswater.

JIMMY SAVILE

Born: 1926, Leeds.

Is this, as has been suggested, the face of big brother? Savile is populist, evangelical, proletarian, indefatigably philanthropic. The causes to which he has lent himself and in which he has participated are legion. Here are some of them: Environment Improvement Week (he cleaned up litter in a London park); The Hand of Peace (a campaign against football terrace violence); The Royal Association for Disability and Rehabilitation; the *Sunday People* Transplant Olympic, etc. He also works regularly as a porter at Leeds Infirmary, Stoke Mandeville Hospital and Broadmoor. This work has earned him all sorts of plaudits, including a Variety Club lunch in his honour, an occasion he regarded with some embarrassment. The last reason he does all he does is to win pats on the back. He does it, it appears, out of a mixture of genuine altruism and a conviction that he has much to be thankful for or, if you like, that, but for the grace of God, he, too, might have suffered like the people he helps. As a Bevin boy during the war, he worked down the mines, often lying on his back all day in a temperature of a 100°. A pit accident at Waterloo Colliery, near Leeds, effectively made him change his life. He was in a steel corset for three years, which forced him to lie down when the pain got bad—anywhere, in buses or department stores. He had originally been told, soon after the accident, that he would never walk again and would consequently be unable to lead a normal life.

It was, of course, his determination that saw him through. One day, he spotted an old man hobbling towards him and realised that it was his own reflection in a shop window. He resolved that he would throw away his crutches and steel corset, stuck a picture of a Rolls-Royce on his bedroom wall and threw himself into life with the frenetic enthusiasm of a man trying to break down a brick wall with his head. The remarkable thing is that he succeeded. His success has endowed him with a real fearlessness, the belief that even the most apparently insuperable odds can be overcome.

He did his first gig as a disc jockey in a room hired from a body called The Order of Ancient Shepherds above a café in Otley, where a fellow worker in a baby-clothing factory was celebrating her 21st birthday. He joined Mecca in the early 'fifties, when dance halls were doing well. Then he moved to Salford, where he lived in a more or less derelict house, with his impressive assortment of cars lined up outside. Salford Council gave him a flat, since he was giving the place a bad name, always being photographed outside a slum. Nowadays, he has more houses than cars. He keeps places in Bournemouth (where he is consultant to a leisure complex called Maison Royale); London; Scarborough; Teignmouth; Aylesbury; Windsor; Leeds and Dorset. A member of MENSA and the eldest of seven children— his beloved mother, whom he called 'The Duchess', died about six years ago – Savile has never married. He says though that he is 'no saint'. The nearest he has come to marriage was with the singer, Polly Brown, who broke off their relationship, saying that she 'wasn't ready to settle down'. It need hardly be said that Savile bore this misfortune with his usual chirpy stoicism.

PRUNELLA SCALES

Born: June 22, 1932,
Sutton Abinger, Surrey.
Educated: Old Vic School.

Prunella Scales is also Mrs Timothy West, which means that her life is complicated. Mr West's work with the Prospect Company and on TV means that they sometimes don't see each other for weeks on end. Mr West is, however, an inspired and regular writer of massive letters, so when he is away, his wife is kept apprised of what is going on at the other end of Britain or the world. Although she worked with Prospect for a while, the couple have only rarely performed together. John Cleese offered to write a part for Mr West in *Fawlty Towers,* but he was unable to make the time for a recording. Mr and Mrs West did meet through their work, though. They were both together in a TV play which was never transmitted.

They refer to themselves as 'the Lunts of radio'. The amount of work they get through is extraordinary, and the pressure is sometimes such that Miss Scales is forced to hire a hotel room in which

to learn her lines in peace, away from husband and two sons, who are 13 and 10.

As well as TV (it was *Marriage Lines* that first brought her to prominence) and theatre, Miss Scales takes an active part in other areas of her profession. She is on the General Council of the actors' union, Equity, and sits on an Arts Council board.

BROUGH SCOTT

Born: 1943.

As a jump jockey, Scott rode 99 winners. He also won one flat race and broke most of the bones in his body, neck, back (three times), arms, legs, collar, fingers and ribs. He lost a couple of teeth too. He claims to be rather embarrassed by any reference to the injuries he sustained, because 'they were nothing compared to so many other jockeys. I have only one pinned joint in me'. It was on one of his many stretcher journeys that he decided to call it a day. All he rides now around town is his Yamaha moped.

In addition to commentating on horses and dogs (he is part-owner of two White City greyhounds) he is also racing correspondent of the *Sunday Times* and a former Horse Race Writers' Association Writer of the Year. He began broadcasting after Julian Wilson had given him an introduction to the BBC. He had been with the Corporation less than two weeks, when ITV signed him up on a permanent basis. One of the numerous appeals that racing holds for him is that 'it provides a common interest among people from all groups of society'.

S

TERRY SCOTT

Born: 1927, Watford.

Scott describes his partnership with June Whitfield in *Happy Ever After* as the happiest of his career. She points out that Bill Maynard and Hugh Lloyd were men. Scott has never flourished without a partner, but unlike, say, Tony Hancock, he has always swallowed his pride and gone back to working on equal terms with another actor.

The son of a postman who retired to run a corner shop, he served in the navy. At the age of 21, he successfully auditioned for the BBC, worked briefly and unsuccessfully on radio with Bob Monkhouse, and then went off to learn his trade on piers and in clubs. His first job was at Clacton, at the foot of a bill topped by Hancock. During the 'fifties, as well as becoming a TV favourite with Bill Maynard, he did more radio with such performers as

Charlie Chester and Frankie Howerd. It took a few years before he re-established

himself in *Hugh and I.* Since then, he has worked extensively in films and the theatre, notably with Brian Rix.

Scott is a lay preacher, a rather fundamentalist Christian who believes in self-help and South Africa and the presence of Communists in high places in Britain. He once brought misery to the nation by threatening to emigrate to South Africa. Married for the second time to a former ballet dancer turned choreographer, by whom he has four daughters, he lives at Whitley, near Godalming. He is very houseproud ('nothing I like better than to clean the sitting room from top to bottom') and breeds tropical fish and exotic birds—budgies, parakeets, parrots, cockatoos—and, more mundanely, chickens. His menagerie also includes dogs and guinea pigs. As is evident, he enjoys food. Less obviously, he is a fan of Watford and Aldershot football clubs, and an enthusiastic gardener.

PETER SEABROOK

Born: 1936, Essex.
Educated: Chelmsford Grammar School; Writtle Agricultural College.

The tirelessly enthusiastic gardener prefers the handle 'professional horticulturist', though he really regards himself as 'a salesman'. He grew up on his grandparents' farm near Chelmsford (where he still lives with his wife and two children in a house whose garden is very similar to those around it). His father, who worked in a local factory, encouraged his interest in gardening, as opposed to farming. During his teens, Seabrook spent his weekends with a local firm of nurserymen and entered gardening contests, winning prizes for his sweet peas. At 16, he left school to work full-

time for this firm of nurserymen, and then went on to agricultural college and National Service in the Horse Guards, who allowed him to go to night school forestry classes. He went back to the firm with whom he had started, Cramphorn, and was responsible for a number of innovations which are now taken for granted. They include a means of packing roses for transportation, and a method of growing plants in individual containers so that they can be transferred to the garden at any time of the year. His other responsibilities included the production of catalogues, the organisation of shows and the answering of queries from his firm's many shops.

He next joined the Irish Peat Board as a salesman. Soon afterwards, he set up his own horticultural advisory service

and started to do some gardening journalism. He made his radio debut on *In Your Garden,* having introduced himself by his normal method of pointing out to the producer the programme's shortcomings. After a season of television appearances on *Dig This* and *Pebble Mill At One,* he was invited to replace Percy Thrower, who had fallen foul of the BBC by endorsing products on ITV commercials. Seabrook says: 'I would never consider doing commercials. I must be seen to be truly independent'. In his four years on *Gardener's World,* he has 'popularised' the series by getting rid of Latin names and cutting down the number of visits to grand houses. He has also been described as more 'male model than gardener'. A curious view that Seabrook would find amusing.

JACK SHEPHERD

Born, October 29, 1940.
Educated: Roundhay School,
Leeds; Newcastle University;
Drama Centre.

One of the most consistently employed actors in British TV, Shepherd is also a stage director and playwright. His *Underdog,* which was seen on BBC 2 earlier this year, is a splendidly complicated joke about two Whitehall civil servants. It certainly deserves to be repeated, though the fact that its producer, Stephen Gilbert, has been suspended by the BBC (for jumping the queue in the Pebble Mill canteen, or some similarly grave offence) may jeopardize its chances. Shepherd read art at university, taught for a brief, unhappy period, and then trained for the stage. He was taken on by The Royal Court and understudied 16 roles in his first season there. The next year, 1966, he played Mère Ubu opposite

Max Wall's Ubu in a celebrated production designed by David Hockney. This was the first of a series of notable performances at that theatre, which included the title role in *The Restoration of Arnold Middleton.*

The role which has brought him the widest recognition was that of Bill Brand in Trevor Griffiths' saga of a Tribune Group idealist finding out that politics is rarely pure, never simple. When that series was being transmitted and

attracting a great deal of attention, Shepherd was frequently asked if he shared Brand's (and Griffiths') more or less Marxist views. His answers revealed him to be an apolitical creature, despite the fact that his father, a cabinet-maker who had to turn to factory work with the introduction of machine-made furniture, was a keen trade unionist. He says that his parents' 'castrated ambitions were channelled into me'. He was also, as an only child, the buffer between his parents, 'who couldn't forgive themselves for what they had done to each other. Once I got over my grief at their deaths I felt liberated. It was no accident that within a year of my mother's dying, I separated from my first wife'.

He has remarried, and he and his wife, Ann, have twin girls—he had a boy by his first wife. This year, Jack Shepherd has been playing the part of Michael Herr in the National Theatre's adaptation of Herr's *Dispatches.*

DONALD SINDEN

Born: 1923, Plymouth.

Sinden's career has been notable for all sorts of reasons, not least for the sheer variety of genres in which he has enjoyed success — Shakespearean tragedy; TV sitcom; war films; doctor films; low farce; Restoration comedy. 'I've never sat around waiting for the right thing. I'm a great believer in taking whatever comes next'. The only part he has ever actually hoped for, he didn't get—Henry V. But he has played Lear, Henry VIII and Foppington and, this year, essayed Othello at Stratford in Ronald Eyre's production. It was at Stratford that he met his wife, Diana, in 1947. He had joined the company a year earlier, after spending the war with Mobile Entertainments

for the Southern Area—he had been turned down for the forces because of asthma.

Throughout the 'fifties, he was a highly paid and pretty ubiquitous film star, one degree less raffish than Leslie

Philips, and has recently become something of an institution as Robert the butler in *Two's Company.* But his first love is the theatre, and he is Chairman of the Theatre Museum Council. The Museum will open in the former flower market of Covent Garden next year. As you might expect of a man who has such an abundance of style, Sinden is devoted to style in all things—notably clothes, actors (he is a great admirer of the late Donald Wolfitt) and architecture. He is Vice-Chairman of the London Appreciation Society and abhors all that has happened to the city over the past 25 years.

He lives in a relatively unspoilt area on the edge of Hampstead Garden suburb. Both his sons are actors, and the elder, Jeremy, was seen in *Danger UXB.*

VALERIE SINGLETON

Born: April 9, 1937, Hitchin.
Educated: R.A.D.A.

The wholesome Auntie to the nation's kiddies on *Blue Peter* for 13 years (during which she accompanied her friend, Princess Anne, to East Africa) has, since her transfer from *Nationwide* to *Tonight,* become rather stern, both in appearance and manner. She began her connection with the BBC as an actress, and was taken on as an announcer before she got her *Blue Peter* job. As an actress, she has done lots of work in commercials and has played repertory seasons at Bromley, Bath and Cheltenham. Light comedy was her forte.

In the late 'sixties and early 'seventies, she was engaged to the old-time disc jockey, Pete Murray (himself a some-time actor, who also trained at R.A D.A.), but they didn't marry after the relationship had turned into what Mr Murray described as a 'stalement situation'. He has since married Tricia Crabb, a barrister. Miss Singleton remains single and lives in Earl's Court, where she takes an extremely active part in community affairs.

DELIA SMITH

Born: 1939, London.
Educated: Bexley Heath.

Delia Smith says that she owes her career to her agent, Debbie Owen—the wife of a sometime Foreign Secretary. It was Mrs Owen who got Miss Smith her first cookery column on the now defunct *Daily Mirror Magazine* nine years ago. Before that, she had been a professional cook preparing dinner parties and cooking dishes for spreads in magazines and advertisements.

She never trained at a catering college. Before she

started cooking, she was a hairdresser. Then she went to work as a washer-up in a restaurant called 'The Singing Chef' near Marble Arch, and ended up as an assistant to

DAVID SOUL

Born: August 28, 1943, Chicago
Educated: Augustana College, Sioux Falls; University of Minnesota; University of Mexico City.

Before he was an actor, Soul was a singer. In New York in the mid-'sixties, he worked in night clubs with a paper bag over his head. When he took it off, he was just like any other folk singer and thought it was

time to move on, to Hollywood. He was a bit player in numerous cinema and TV films before he became Hutch in *Starsky and Hutch.*

He was brought up all over the world. His father, Dr. Richard Soulberg, was a Lutheran minister and adviser on religious affairs to the US State Department. The eldest of five children, Soul lived in Germany, Mexico and Minnesota before he married for the first time at the age of

the chef. At the *Mirror Magazine*, she met and married Michael Wynn-Jones, the Deputy Editor, with whom she now lives near Stowmarket, in Suffolk.

Her first TV series, *Family Fair*, was in 1973, when tele fodder was mostly gimmicky and was prepared with charming gimmickry by the egregious Galloping Gourmet, Graham Kerr (who was converted to Christianity in a hotel room and now spreads the word, as well as writing books of frugal recipes). Miss Smith is by comparison straightforward and unaffected, keen on inexpensive ingredients.

19. His son by that marriage is now 14. In Hollywood, he married again. His second wife, Karen Carlson, is a former Miss Arkansas and actress: 'David loves me so much, that he wanted to spare me what he is going through now'. What he is going through now is 'women literally throwing themselves at him'. Soul now lives with another actress, Lynne Marta, and has no plans to remarry.

Now that *Starsky and Hutch* has been killed off, Soul has no regrets about having been associated with it for so long, though he is thankful that he has kissed it goodbye: 'All good things should come to an end'. Last year, his acting career almost came to an end when he was paralysed in a skiing accident. However, a five-hour operation was successful and, six weeks later, he had recovered sufficiently to begin work anew.

Jealous of his reputation, Soul has in the past couple of years sued *The Sun* (for publishing an unauthorised photograph of him); DPC Publishing (which marketed a magazine called *David Soul*) and a record company (which was going to release some records he made in the 'sixties).

JACLYN SMITH

Born: October 26, 1946, Houston.
Educated: Trinity University, San Antonio

The longest serving of *Charlie's Angels* and, possibly, the oldest (this depends on what age Barbara Bach is claiming now). Jaclyn Smith is the only one of the current crop who has no children: 'When I was married for the first time, I desperately wanted to have children. This time I'm sure there will be children'. Her first husband was Roger Davis, and her second, whom she

FREDDIE STARR

Born: 1944, Liverpool.
Educated: Huyton Secondary Modern School.

Starr is an inveterate joker. When stopped for speeding on the M1, he did an impersonation of Kermit the frog for the policeman. Later, in court, he claimed that he had not actually been driving. His friend, Adrian Fuller, who is 'World Champion Hairdresser', had been at the wheel. When the magistrates asked how long he had owned his XJS, he replied: 'I have no idea. I swop cars like I swop my wife'. His wife, Sandie, was at home at the time with their daughter, Donna. Home is a house in Windsor called 'My Way'. He has been married before and

married a year ago, is Dennis Cole. Both men are actors, and she met Cole when he was a supporting player in an episode of *Charlie's Angels*. He was previously the star of *Felony Squad* and *Bracken's World*.

Before she was an actress, she was a model, and before she was a model she was a student of drama and psychology. She still maintains a model's regime— lots of 'protein powder' and low-calorie salads. She goes to bed early so that 'calories don't stick around', and exercises with an imaginary skipping rope.

has a 12-year-old son called Carl.

A former bricklayer and boxer, Starr enjoys living life to the full. He was conditionally discharged for jumping from his Rolls and punching another driver; was accused of 'sacrilege' in a show he did at Chelmsford Prison chapel (he has since claimed a 'conversion' to Christianity); punched a singer who was in a show with him at Margate and put him out of the show for two days); was accused of throwing dozens of deck chairs on to a barbecue fire, etc., etc.

The son of a bricklayer and the youngest of five children ('we were really poor'), he won a talent contest impersonating Ruby Murray and Al Jolson when he was still at school, and had a small part in the David McCallum film, *Violent Playground*, when he was in his early teens. Then he played with a group called Howie Casey and the Seniors, before going solo as an impersonator and winning *Opportunity Knocks*. His first great success was in a Royal Variety Show, since when he has barely looked back, having starred in *Who Do You Do* and a string of his own, highly popular shows.

TOMMY STEELE

Born: December 17, 1936, Bermondsey.

British rock and roll always had more than a touch of music hall about it—Ray Davies and the Kinks, The Bonzo Dog Band, Screaming Lord Sutch and the first of the lot, Thomas Hicks. A sometime merchant seaman, he learnt to play guitar while laid up in hospital, sang at the Two I's in Soho, was 'discovered' by Larry Parnes and John Kennedy, and set out on a career that has seen him make a transformation from gauche kid with sequins down his drainpipes to *the* British song and dance man. It is a transformation from unwilling rebel to the pillar of the show biz establishment. He outraged all generations but his own, when he appeared on *Six Five Special*. Of course, countless

rock stars, from Jagger to Rotten, have done the same since, but in those days— 1956 and 1957—provoked incredulity as well as shock. By the time he was 22, he had starred in his cinematic biography, *The Tommy Steel Story* and in *The Duke Wore Jeans,* and by the time he was 24, he had done what all the callow rockers of those years said they would—become an 'all-round entertainer'.

Tony Lumpkin at the Old Vic, *Half a Sixpence* (which opened just as the Fab Four were beginning to make a noise outside The Cavern), and so on into the *Happiest Millionaire, Finnegan's Rainbow, Hans Andersen,* and a succession of TV spectaculars, of which he is not only the principal attraction, but is also—in the tradition of, say—Charlie Chaplin—the writer, choreographer, designer, etc.

As a rocker he has a head start on most of his British contemporaries, simply because as a steward on transatlantic liners, he had heard the new sounds coming out of America long before they reached these shores. Nowadays, though, he has little contact with rock and roll, and can sit in judgement like a youthful old statesman: 'The Rolling Stones are the Shadows plus 2,000 decibels. And I never did think much of the Shadows'.

In 1960, he married his long-time girl friend, Ann Donoghue, and they have a 10-year old daughter, Emma. He is a teetotaller and non-smoker, a keen squash player, a hard worker and hard taskmaster. He will not appear on TV unless he has total control over the show, and is fortunate enough to have found in Thames TV a company which will agree to his stipulations. *Quincy's Quest,* his latest musical, will be seen this Christmas.

RICHARD STILGOE

Born: 1943.
Educated: Cambridge.

Stilgoe is a small man who, like other small men before him, played the clown in order to avoid getting thumped—a sort of protective camouflage really. 'Nobody executes the jester', he says, though lie was given to this assertion by Scottish Nationalists and, indeed, most Scots would have clearly liked to make Stilgoe the one-man peace-keeping force on a Saturday night in Sauchiehall Street after an Old Firm match. Stilgoe, the best thing on *Nationwide* for years, had incensed that sensitive race with various remarks made during the referendum campaign earlier this year.

The sort of show he did in *And Now The Good News* is what he's been up to for years, ever since he performed with *Cambridge Footlights* in 1961. He played clubs and arts festivals all over the country, and eventually got a slot on the *Today* programme on Radio 4, which led to *Nationwide,* which led to fame, swimming pools full of Cointreau, huge houses and rounds of golf with Max Bygraves.

He describes himself as 'a more masculine Joyce Grenfell' or a 'second-rate Lehrer'. Actually, he seems a fairly original sort of performer.

JANET STREET-PORTER

Born: 1947, Fulham.
Educated: Grammar school and the Architectural Association.

Six feet tall, with famously 'tombstone' teeth, hair that is sometimes magenta and sometimes tartan, an over-developed Cockney twang and a marked lack of shyness, Janet Street-Porter (née Bull) trades on these attributes, which make her among the most instantly recognizable of current performers.

Like, among others, two members of Pink Floyd and her chum, the painter, Duggie Field, she dropped out of architecture school after she married fellow student, Tim Street-Porter. He became a photographer and she a journalist, and together they concentrated on fashion, fads of taste (they were rather

bitchily referred to as 'taste freaks') and their friends in the rag trade. Such well-known designers as Xandra Rhodes owe more than a little to the Street-Porters' promotion of them.

Janet worked on all sorts of papers and magazines, from *Honey* to the *Daily Mail* to the *Evening Standard,* where she was a notable success as fashion editor. However, her stay was brief, because of 'professional disagreements'. After splitting up with her husband, she became roman-tically entangled with the boyish entrepreneur and pub-lisher of *Time Out,* Tony Elliott. The besotted captain of industry created an editorial post for her, thereby incurring the wrath of his notoriously headstrong staff. Undeterred, he launched a magazine for her to edit. It was called *Sell Out* and was not quite the success that had been hoped. Janet did a stint on local radio and was spotted by

London Weekend Television producer Andy Mayer. She was signed up to host 'The London Weekend Show'. She is also, together with Russell Harty and Clive James, one of the presenters of the same company's 'Saturday Night People', a chat show for and about celebrities.

Her interests are related to her professional life or, rather, she makes a profession of her interests. For instance, fascinated by teapots, she wrote a (unpublished) book on their history and organized a complementary exhibition at Camden Arts Centre. Her Thameside house in Narrow Street, Wapping (where she is a neighbour of the glamorous Devonport MP, Dr David Owen), is a repository of borax and jazz, modern and 'fifties objects. Now divorced from Tony Elliott, she lives there with the film-maker, Frank Cvitanovich, who, besides making brilliant films, is obsessed by horses.

ELAINE STRITCH

Born: February 5, 1927, Detroit.
Educated: Actors' Studio.

The anglophile comedienne lives with her husband, John Bay, at the Savoy, shops at Fortnums (where she was asked where the butler was), drives a Rover and loves walking about London, for which she has the kind of fondness that is not uncommon among expatriates living here. Life at the Savoy is not, perhaps, as expensive as one might imag-ine. She gets a special rate and, of course, has no house-hold expenses ('I can afford it — I clean the sixth and seventh floors'). Nor does she have the tiresome worries associated with running a house, worries which she thinks would detract from her work. It was her great friend,

Noel Coward, who introduced her to the Savoy, when she first came to England in 1962 to appear in his musical *Sail Away.* Coward told the manager: 'I want her to stay at the Savoy, because she has no class and you can give her some'.

Before her arrival in Eng-land — she has been here on and off ever since — she had been on Broadway in musicals like *Pal Joey* and *Call Me Madam.* In New York, she knew everyone, dined with the Kennedys and turned

down offers of marriage from Ben Gazzara and the late Gig Young (who shot himself and his fifth wife), because both men had been divorced and she is a staunch Catholic, a relation of Cardinal Stritch of Chicago. During her early days in New York, she achieved the extraordinary feat of living in a convent (on the instructions of her father) and dating Marlon Brando, who was one of her fellow students. When she revisits her native country, she goes by QE2, on which she works her passage in cabaret.

Two years ago, in the nick of time, she was diagnosed as diabetic: 'I was 24 hours this side of coma, which might be a great title for a movie'. She now has to inject herself with insulin twice a day: 'I just say I'm going to the ladies' room to shoot up. Am I going to have the last laugh when they call the drug squad'.

MOLLIE SUGDEN

Born: 1925. Keighley.

Mollie Sugden spent so many years playing supporting roles that she doesn't fear getting into a rut with Mrs Slocombe in *Are You Being Served?* Besides, over the last year, she has also done her regular stuff in *The Liver Birds* and in her own series, *Come Back Mrs Noah.*

For many years, she was in rep, and it was in Swansea that she met her husband, William Moore. He has played her screen husband, the hapless Mr Hutchinson, in *The Liver Birds*, and has also appeared with her in *Coronation Street*, where she was once the rival landlady to Annie Walker. They have twin sons, and their life at home in East Horsley, in Surrey is often so hectic, that she says: I regard coming to the TV studios to work as a rest.

She reckons that being recognised as Mrs Slocombe means that she gets good service, since shopkeepers think she really is a battleaxe. Being recognised has its pitfalls, too. Once, when she was in a fitting cubicle trying on a dress, a woman marched in and demanded her autograph.

ERIC SYKES

Born: 1923. Oldham.

Like most of the comedians of his generation, Sykes started in troop shows during the war. Before he was called up, he had worked in a cotton mill, a sawmill and a grocery shop. His only experience of entertaining had been as a drummer in a dance band. Though he did well and topped the bill in numerous services shows, his early years as a pro on civvy street were none too happy. He wrote scripts for Bill Fraser, whom he had known in the Army, was sacked from Oldham Rep for demanding a rise from £3 to £4 a week, and toured the halls. It was Frankie Howerd who advised him to concentrate on scripts, and he made his name writing *Educating Archie* for three years. His first TV appearances in the late 'fifties were bizarre, anarchic affairs, with Sykes as the put-upon compère of a show in which nothing went right, props disappeared, etc. His partnership with Hattie Jacques began in 1960 and made him the most popular comedian on the box, eclipsing even Hancock, who was then just past his prime.

In the early 'sixties, at the height of his popularity, news of his severely impaired hearing was published for the first time. He had been almost entirely deaf in his right ear since a mastoid operation in 1952 and, in 1963, had to undergo further surgery at the London Clinic, in order to preserve the hearing in his left ear.

During the seven years that he and Hattie Jacques pursued solo careers, Sykes made a few films and began a career as a stage actor. This career was most publicised when he and Jimmy Edwards took their show, *Big Bad Mouse*, to Rhodesia, despite Equity's objections. Sykes had a few meetings with Ian Smith, though he declined to discuss the subject of their talks.

Golf is his greatest enthusiasm. He is a member of several leading clubs and was recently elected to membership of The Royal and Ancient, whose tie is a prized possession. Rather different from the days when St George's Hill Golf Club blackballed him, even though his house backed onto the course. He and his Canadian wife and four children simply moved to another house in a different part of Weybridge, similarly adjacent to a course.

JIMMY TARBUCK

Born: 1940, Liverpool.

One of many people who were known as the fifth Beatle — others included Brian Epstein, Dorothy Squires and Billy Shears, Tarbuck made his name at an age when most comics haven't even begun. However, he denies that he was really a comic: 'Just a cheeky personality'. He thinks that his timing is now much better than when he used to introduce the Palladium Show, and attributes his comparative lack of success as a pure comic on TV to inexperience and the fact that he thrives on working in theatres. Although he'd like to do something along the lines of, say, *The Two Ronnies* (The Two Jimmys?) he is content for the moment to restrict his work as a comedian to summer shows and to restrict his TV appearances to *Winner Takes All*. He is, in fact, an apparently contented man altogether. His house at Kingston-on-Thames is not far from Coombe Hill Golf Course. He spends much of his time on the course, and says that he is far from being the stereotypical sad man behind the clown. He is a very happy man with a great family, wife Pauline, two daughters and a son.

A milkman before he started entertaining at Butlin's in North Wales, his teenage ambition was to be a footballer, and he had two trials at Anfield. He still follows Liverpool, gambles on them frequently (which must make him richer still) and strongly believes that football hooligans deserve the birch.

SHAW TAYLOR

Born: October 26, 1924, Hackney.

Taylor is actually called Eric, though he is more frequently called 'Whispering Grass' or 'The Shoppers' Guide'. Crime has done him proud now for almost 18 years. In 1962, he was a quiz master and compère, when the programme controller of Associated Rediffusion asked him to introduce a five-minute filler. Scotland Yard was initially suspicious of the idea, but once the then Commissioner, Sir Joseph Simpson, was told that the police would have control, *Police Five* was on the road. It has been a notable success, so far as the Met is concerned. Unofficial estimates for the arrest/crime ratio are one to five. In one in three of the cases spotlighted on *Police Five*, an arrest is made following the programme. One of the pleasures Taylor derives from the show is the fact that he is accepted 'as part of the Police team'.

As well as *Police Five*, Taylor also presents *Drive In*, and he is currently training a new generation of crime-spotters in the series, *Junior Police Five*.

JOHN THAW

Born: January 3, 1942, Manchester.
Educated: R.A.D.A.

Thaw — that really is his date of birth above ('I was born looking fifty'), is married to Sheila Hancock. He was once described as 'brown ale' to her 'champagne', and it seems pretty apt. The son of a lorry driver, he is a former fruit market porter and baker's apprentice and, like Patrick Mower — who replaced him in *Night and Day* this summer — he has invariably been associated with tough roles — Regan in *The Sweeney*, a military policeman in *Red Cap*, a hard squaddie in *The Bofors Gun*. It was his own decision to quit as Regan, just as Dennis Waterman had had enough of Carter. But Thaw knows that it was that role which enabled him to go back to the theatre as a star: 'Television makes you. I'd never underrate it'.

Like his wife, Thaw is an opera-lover and a regular patron of Covent Garden and Glyndbourne and, again like his wife he is a Labour Party campaigner in Brentford and Isleworth — their home is actually in Chiswick Village. They first met years ago, then re-encountered each other soon after Miss Hancock's husband, the actor, Alec Ross, had died. They both have daughters from their earlier marriages, and now have another, Joanna, who is five and very pretty.

CHRISTOPHER TIMOTHY

Born: 1940, Wales.
Educated: Central School of Speech and Drama.

The nation's favourite vet lives with the nation's favourite vet's wife, Carol Drinkwater, who says of herself: 'I was usually cast as a whore before I got the part of Helen in *All Creatures*'.

Timothy got the part of James Herriott after John Alderton and the late Richard Beckinsale had turned it down. He was previously best known as the man who sold *The Sun* in endless commercials. He had also made a good living from voice overs. His career began on, of all places, Broadway, where he went straight from drama school with a production of *Chips With Everything*. He was subsequently in rep in Worthing and an understudy (27 parts at once) at the National, where he left for a part in *Here We Go Round the Mulberry Bush*. For the next ten years, he worked constantly on TV, in films and in the theatre. He was only just able to enjoy the success of the first series of *All Creatures* since a couple of days before transmission of the opening episode, he was run over in a country lane and remained unconscious for a week.

HILARY TINDALL

Born: August 14, 1940. Manchester.

Miss Tindall has this year been seen in *Tropic*, though she is best remembered as the unutterably bitchy and deceitful Ann Hammond in the grim transport saga, *The Brothers*. Before that she has appeared in such series as *The Troubleshooters* and *Z Cars*. She says that she found it hard to live down her image as a 'bitch and scarlet woman'. She found herself being eyed up and down at parties and in hotels, unwilling prey for any wolf who might be lurking.

She is in fact married to the literary and theatrical agent, Robin Lowe, and has two children, Kate and Julian. They live in a Regency house, in a road frequented by top scientific civil servants, not far from Twickenham Green. She decorated the place herself with great enthusiasm.

ROGER TONGE

Born: 1946.

The cripple of *Crossroads* is not a well man in real life. He was operated on for a blood disorder some years ago and was subsequently discovered to be suffering from Hodgkin's Disease, which afflicts the lymphatic glands and enlarges them. The disease provokes anaemia, and the only treatment is radio therapy, which Tonge undergoes regularly.

He has been in *Crossroads* since it began in 1964, when he was 18 and playing the character of Sandie, aged 14. The character broke his back in a car crash, and Tonge says that 'people are surprised if they see me in the street actually walking. Sometimes they even seem a bit disappointed'. It is, of course, improbable that Sandie will ever walk again. Tonge seems to think that this is the result of a dreadful mistake: 'I believe Sandie was intended to get better. But the injury that was written into the script was so severe that there was no way the writers could get round it'. He receives many invitations to meet and talk to the handicapped.

Tonge is unmarried and lives in Birmingham with his parents. Although Sandie in *Crossroads* was the first part he ever played, he has had enough time off from the programme to appear in such shows as *Nearest and Dearest* and *Z Cars*. He has also worked on stage, notably at Coventry. He is not oblivious of the press's opinion of *Crossroads*, although he does not let it worry him. He says: 'being a national monument is a bit like being a Nelson's Column. The critics do to us what the pigeons do to poor old Nelson. Frankly, I turn a blind eye'.

114

JAMES VILLIERS

Born: September 29, 1933.
Educated: Wellington College
and R.A.D.A.

Britain's leading 'Nigel' actor and one of the very few who can play a toff with a nob's assurance, or vice versa, Villiers (pronounced 'Villers', like a group of houses in the suburbs) is a member of the family of the Earls of Clarendon and a descendant of Charles II's good friend, Barbara Villiers.

His appearances on TV are all too infrequent. Theatre and films occupy most of his time. He was one of the better things in *The Passion of Dracula* at The Queen's Theatre last winter.

DAVID VINE

Born: January 3, 1935, Devon.

The Vine file is to be found between those of Gene Vincent, the crippled, leather-clad rock singer who died of a perforated ulcer, and Leonardo da Vinci, the painter, mathematician, scientist, and scholar. Vine is none of these things, though he speaks better English than Leonardo did and knows more about the sharp end of Clive James' Sheaffer Krait than the rock singer did.

Vine worked on regional TV in the south-west before he was let loose on an unsuspecting and wondering nation as the BBC's man for very obscure sports like ski-flying.

ANTHONY VALENTINE

Born: August 17, 1939, Blackburn.

Having played bastards, cads and rogues (*Colditz, Raffles,* etc.) for most of his TV career, Blackburn's second favourite son this year hung up his knuckle-duster and his sword stick, and appeared in *The Dancing Years,* Ivor Novello's escapist wartime musical. Though he didn't actually sing in it, he can.

He made his debut as a child actor, playing Robin Hood at Ealing Town Hall, and when he was 13, sang at Sadlers' Wells, later winning a choral scholarship to St Paul's which he didn't take up. Much of his childhood and adolescence was devoted to acting children's roles for the BBC.

It is doubtless his incessant sporting activities — riding, squash, skiing and running — which keep him looking about half his age. Or maybe it's his fairly carefree life. He is tee-total, unmarried, and is not above taking off without warning to walk by himself in Scotland or the Lake District.

In contrast to his close friend, Tommy Steele, he is not particularly dedicated to his profession: 'I don't like to act. That's not why I'm alive. I live to be happy. Every day I want to do something that turns me on'. If nothing else, he's certainly frank.

BRIAN WALDEN

Born: July 8, 1932.
Educated: West Bromwich Grammar School; Queens College, Oxford.

Walden was a natural choice to succeed Peter Jay as the presenter of *Weekend World* when 'the cleverest young man in Europe' went to Washington as Britain's Ambassador.

He had previously sat in the Labour interest for the Birmingham constituency of All Saints (renamed Ladywood in 1974) for 13 years. His patron was Hugh Gaitskell, who helped Walden to get the Labour nomination at the Coventry by-election in 1961. Walden lost and, by the time he got into Parliament, Gaitskell was dead. A founder member of The Campaign for Democratic Socialism, Walden was not very popular with many members of the Parliamentary Labour Party, who were to the left of him — that is to say, practically all of them. He was regarded as a flashy debater (he had been president of the Oxford Union), rather than as an earnest party man, as too individualistic a journalist and telly pundit, and too successful a businessman. It is doubtless no surprise to his former colleagues that he is now an admirer of Margaret Thatcher.

Walden was brought up in the industrial West Midlands. His father was a glass-worker, his mother a bookbinder. She was also a Catholic, and he describes himself as 'an intermittent and occasional Catholic'. Her death when he was in his teens was, he says, one of the great tragedies of

EDDIE WARING

Born: 1912, Dewsbury.
Educated: Dewsbury.

The doyen of rregbih leegah commentators — all right, the only rugby league commentator — is to the English language what Cliff Richard is to hod-carrying. This is what distinguishes him. The last thing of which Waring can be accused is the standard commentatorial voice. The fact that, for a sizeable chunk of Britain, he *is* rugby league (and as much a part of the North as fog, cloth caps, cow heel, slag heaps and belching chimneys) is a cause of some resentment. A few years ago, a petition signed by 10,000 people was delivered to the BBC, demanding that Waring be relieved of his duties because his commentaries were thought to be 'an insult to the English language, which turn the game into a music hall joke'. Just as he provokes this sort of antipathy, so he has many millions of devoted fans. There are numerous Eddie Waring appreciation societies in pubs, clubs and colleges all over Britain, and a northern comedian has made a record about him.

He first wrote about rugby league in his school magazine. His first job was on a local paper. He played both codes of rugby and was also good enough at soccer to get a trial with Nottingham Forest. He managed Dewsbury RLFC just before and during the

DENNIS WATERMAN

Born: February 24, 1948, Clapham.

Like John Thaw, who went from *The Sweeney* into Tom Stoppard's *Night and Day,* Waterman returned to the stage as well, playing the leading role in the Royal Shakespeare Company's production of *Saratoga.* It was not his first engagement with the company. When he was 12, he played in *A Winter's Tale* at Stratford. His career as a child actor was notably successful. One of the nine children of a ticket-collector, he made his first film, *Night Train to Inverness,* when he was 11. Two years later, he played one of the lead parts in *Music Man* in the West End. He had the title role in the first TV *Just William* series and, at 14, was a Hollywood star in a series called *Fair Exchange.* However, when he returned to England, he already looked too old for child parts, and the transition to theatrical and screen adulthood was not easily made. He eventually landed on his feet playing a tough in Edward Bond's *Saved,* and that led to *Up The Junction.* During his two years of more or less constant non-theatrical employment, he worked as a coat salesman and as a time and motion study man, watching over dustmen at their toilet.

Waterman, who is now married to the actress, Patricia Maynard (his second marriage), has two daughters, Hannah and Julia. His success in *The Sweeney* has enabled him to pursue a second career as a singer. He has released four records and, last year, made a show for Yorkshire Television. His latest TV show is *Minder,* which comes from Euston Films, who were responsible for *The Sweeney.* He says that his most enjoyable hobby is 'buying a lot of people a lot of drinks.'

his life. He joined the Labour Party at about that time, putting leaflets through doors, attending meetings, debating at schools. His Oxford career was spectacular enough to bring him to the attention of the national press on more than one occasion.

His life now is far from the 'vile slum' where he was raised. He earns a reputed £40,000 per annum, lives with his third wife in Little Venice, though makes no particular display of wealth. 'Money to Brian is symbolic', says a friend.

war. After it, he joined first the Sunday Pictorial and then the Sunday Mirror, and paid his own passage (£11 on an aircraft carrier) to Australia to report on the British rugby tour in 1946.

He did his first TV commentary in 1951 (he had previously done occasional radio stints) and has been at it ever since. In 1966 he presented the first English series of It's A Knockout and has been at that ever since.

Waring is a very private man, will reveal little about himself and is often to be found in his 'office', the Queen's Hotel in Leeds.

KENT WALTON

Born: 1925 (?), London or Canada.

Walton is probably half-Canadian, hence, perhaps, his mid-Atlantic accent. He may have been brought up in Surrey and was certainly an actor and a disc jockey before he introduced Cool For Cats, the first TV pop shop in the mid-'fifties. He enjoys the anonymity of a man the back of whose neck is as well-known as his voice.

Wrestling is not really his favourite sport. Soccer is what he likes and when Match of the Day or The Big Match is on, he refuses even to answer the door of his Haslemere home. He is a qualified FA coach and used to put his son's school team through its paces. Before he became the mouth of wrestling (his mouth, incidentally, is slightly dented as a result of having spoken into a lip mike for so many years), he commentated on both soccer and tennis in the days before Jimmy Hill entered the scene.

He is very keen on maintaining his privacy. 'I have one wife, one son, one dog—and', he said to the interviewer,

Gordon Burn, 'that girl who gave you my home number should know better. She's not working there any more. She's gone'. He is a director of Pyramid Films which has produced Can You Keep It Up For a Week, Keep It Up Downstairs, Virgin Witch, and other 'adult' works. His co-director is Hazel Adair who in earlier, more innocent days, was the originator of Crossroads.

GWEN WATFORD

Born: September 10, 1927. Educated: Orchard School, Hastings.

Miss Watford is the daughter of an RSM turned publican. She grew up wanting to be a pianist, and was hugely upset when she was told at the age of 16 that she would never make the grade. To comfort her, her headmistress, Miss Dorothy Catt, said that she ought to be an actress and gave her a leading role in a play she was putting on for the Red Cross. Her performance was impressive enough for John Gielgud, who was

casting Cradle Song, to travel to St Leonards to see it. She didn't get a part in that show, but was taken on by Sir Anthony Hawtrey's Embassy Theatre Company and was sent into rep at Buxton. It was there that she met her husband, Richard Bebb, by whom she has two sons. Her first TV appearance was as the Virgin Mary in 1955. Four years later, she won the first of her two awards as TV actress of the year. Her most recent TV appearances have been as George Cole's put-upon wife in Don't Forget To Write. She still plays the piano, and lives with her family in Hampstead Garden Suburb.

QUEENIE WATTS

Born: July 21st, 1926, London.

The Cockney character actress, who has played opposite Arfur Mullard in *Yus My Dear* and had the lead in *Waterloo Sunset,* made her acting debut in the film, *Sparrows Can't Sing,* in 1964. Before that, she had been a jazz and blues singer, beginning at the age of 14 and encouraged by her mother, who was a pianist. She married a publican called Slim, and hired an eight-piece band to back her and pull more punters into their pub. These appearances led to engagements on TV shows like *Stars and Garters* and *Time, Gentlemen, Please.* She and her husband have now moved pubs, and run the Rose and Crown, in Limehouse.

ALAN WEEKS

Born: September 8, 1923. Educated: Brighton, Hove and Sussex Grammar School.

The BBC's iceman is director of the Sports Aid Foundation, a post to which he was appointed by weatherman Dennis Howell after some of its earliest members had resigned following a disagreement with the then Minister. This is an administrative job of a sort to which Weeks is no stranger. After leaving the Navy as a lieutenant at the end of the war, Weeks became pro of Brighton Sports

Stadium and secretary to Brighton Tigers Ice Hockey team. He combined these posts with his BBC work, which began when Peter Dymock heard him making PA announcements and offered him an audition.

TIMOTHY WEST

Born: October 20, 1934, Bradford.
Educated: John Lyon School, Harrow; Regent Street Polytechnic.

The son of the actor Lockwood West, who tried to discourage him from going on the stage, West managed to contain his ambition for three years, during which he was a furniture salesman and recording engineer. He then got a part in a play in the Wimbledon Theatre, went into rep, to the RSC ('certain actors they pushed. Others they didn't. I was one of the latter') and on to his long-standing (14 years) association with the Prospect Theatre, of which he is now a director.

On TV, he has in recent years delighted his many admirers, and won new ones, with his Bounderby in *Hard Times* and in the role of *Edward VII.* He will soon be seen as Churchill in *Churchill and the Generals.* He is also much in demand on radio, and gives numerous recitals with his wife, Prunella Scales, who describes him as a chronic workaholic'.

ALAN WHICKER

Born: August 2, 1925, Cairo.
Educated: Haberdasher's Aske's School.

The alliterative traveller is a very rich man indeed. He lives as a 'taxile' in Jersey, where no one who is anyone carries a wallet thinner than the cream on a bottle of milk. Where the very rich rub shoulders with the very rich. He has never married, though some of his romances with the very rich have been widely publicised. He lived with the Dutch multi-millionairess, Olga Deterding, for four years, and it is rumoured – it always is – that he may marry his current companion, Valerie Kleeman.

Whicker has become very rich by holding a microscope to the even richer. Nevertheless, he is shyer than many of his subjects when quizzed about his fortune. He says that he lives in Jersey not in order to avoid taxes, but because he likes it there – 'not that I expect anyone to believe me'. No one disputes that he is a millionaire.

CHARLES WHEELER

Born: March 26, 1923.
Educated: Cranbrook School.

'If', said Wheeler when appointed presenter of *Panorama,* 'I were still the producer, I'd be the last man I'd choose'. His stint as producer of the programme during the mid-'fifties was an atypical interlude in his distinguished career as a foreign correspondent.

He joined *The Daily Sketch* as a tape boy straight from school and, after serving in the marines during the war – he attained the rank of captain – was recruited to the BBC Latin American service. His first overseas posting was to Berlin and, from 1958 until 1976 (when he officially retired from the Corporation),

was 12 and still has it) and articles to magazines like *Lilliput* and *Men Only* (in its former, less carnal, incarnation). Indeed, he can recall the astonishment of a Royal Navy officer, whom he met while on a story in the Far East, that a man known for his contributions to slightly *risqué* magazines should also be covering a hard news item. But then Whicker is nothing if not versatile. In Korea, he was forced to parachute from a plane that was about to crash and was reported dead. He said: 'The report disturbed almost nobody'.

Whicker went into TV in 1957 as *Tonight's* perambulating man. He quickly established himself as the pair of eyes through which millions of people got to see the world. He has now circumnavigated the globe three and a half times, and spends far more time on planes, in hotels (and in shanty shacks) than he does in Jersey or did in his London home in Regent's Park. He was once given the title 'The Room Service Man'.

Among his interests is a £500,000 stake in Yorkshire Television.

The only child of a father who died when Whicker was very young, he came back to England from Egypt, where he had lived, and was brought up by his mother in Richmond. He joined *The Manchester Guardian* as a tea boy, and worked on papers in Hampshire and Dorset before he was called up and commissioned into the Devon Regiment. He transferred to the Army film unit and covered the Eighth Army campaigns in North Africa, Sicily and Italy. After the war, he joined the Exchange Telegraph Agency as a 'fireman' – newspaper slang for a reporter sent off at a moment's notice to cover any sort of emergency.

During this period, he was also contributing stories (he had written his first when he

---

JUNE WHITFIELD

Born: 1927, Streatham.
Educated: R.A.D.A.

June Whitfield it was, who spoke Muir and Norden's immortal words: 'Ooooh, Ron'. As Eth Glum, she for years attempted to get the reluctant Dick Bentley to the altar in *Take It From Here*. Actually, she had never really wanted to be a comedienne but, even at drama school, found out that, somehow, she just wasn't cut out for serious parts. She toured with Wilfred Pickles, played in numerous pantos and comedies, and came to the West End in 1950.

At the same time as she was the hapless Eth, she was also making a name for herself in

he was successively in India, Berlin again, Washington for seven years and, finally, in Brussels as chief European correspondent.

Wheeler and his Indian wife have two daughters and live in a village in Sussex.

TV in Bob Monkhouse's *Fast and Loose*. Since then, she has been in countless TV series. She first worked with Terry Scott, her telly husband, in *Happy Ever After*, when he had his own show, *Scott On*. Her real husband is a surveyor, Tim Aitchison. They live in Wimbledon with their 19-year-old daughter, Susie, who wants to follow in her mother's footsteps.

RICHARD WHITMORE

Born: 1934, Hitchin.
Educated: Hitchin Grammar
School.

Whitmore, his wife, Wendy, and their four daughters still live near his place of birth in Hertfordshire, and he is an enthusiastic local historian. He has written two books about Hertfordshire during the nineteenth century, illustrated with contemporary photographs. He is also a stalwart of many amateur dramatic productions there and has played, among other roles, that of Al Capone in a musical—a Chicago typewriter and fedora become him admirably. His job as a newscaster evidently restricts his

Thespian urges, but he has demonstrated them on *Saturday Night At the Mill.*

A few years ago, he was dropped from reading the news for a few months, and it is some measure of his popularity that this decision of

the TV news editor was met with widespread disapproval. He is a former reporter, and it was thought that he might return to that trade, but his fear of flying put the kybosh on the possibility of foreign assignments.

He started as a journalist on the *Hertfordshire Express,* and it was while working for that paper that he met his wife. He returned to journalism after National Service, joining the BBC in 1964. For four years, until 1968, he was a roving reporter. While boarding a plane for the Winter Olympics in Grenoble, he was gripped with the conviction that it would crash. He has not flown since and is a great advocate of trains and ships.

DORIAN WILLIAMS

Born: July 1, 1914.
Educated: Harrow; Guildhall
School of Music and Drama.

The horse wallah is also an educationalist. He was left a prep school by an aunt and ran it as headmaster. Later on, he turned his family's huge Victorian house, Pendley, near Tring, into one of the country's first adult education centres. He still runs it. He may have been born with a silver spoon in his mouth, but he has evidently used it for the public good. He presented the town of Tring with a large plot of land for use as a sports field, etc. He has the reputation of being as respectful to horses as he is to a princess. As a child, he was used to having his parents entertain the Dukes of Windsor and Gloucester.

Before he was a school-master, he was an actor, and he recounts in his autobiography that a producer once attempted to entice him onto a casting couch. He began his successful broadcasting career from the Richmond Horse Show in 1951.

Named not after Wilde's interesting hero, but after a general, Williams and his wife live in a Jacobean pile near Buckingham. They have one son and one daughter. Williams is a former chairman

of the National Equestrian Council and MFH of the Whaddon Chase. He has in his time been invited by both the major parties and the Liberals to stand for them in Parliamentary elections.

SIMON WILLIAMS

Born: 1946.
Educated: Harrow.

The son of the actor-playwright, Hugh Williams, and his playwright wife, Margaret Williams has a brother called Hugo, a poet, and is married to the actress Belinda Carroll. She is the daughter of one actress, Hazel Bainbridge, and sister of another, Kate O'Mara. Williams, who is also a director, has been responsible for the production of one of his parents' plays at the Yvonne Arnaud Theatre, Guildford, and has also appeared there opposite his mother-in-law. He and Miss Carroll live quite close to the theatre with their two children. He is one of the numerous actors who became well-known in *Upstairs Downstairs.* He played James Bellamy, who eventually shot himself. He claimed that he modelled this not too congenial character on two prefects who bullied him while he was at Harrow, a school he disliked and which he left at the age of 16 to join Worthing rep. When he got the part in *Upstairs, Downstairs,* he was actually considering quitting the theatre. Since that series ended, he has had no further thought of turning to another career and, as well as doing film and theatre work, has been on the box in *Agony* and *Company and Co.*

FRANK WINDSOR

Born: 1926, Walsall.
Educated: Queen Mary's Grammar School, Walsall.

Unlike many actors who are associated with one role — he played John Watt in *Z Cars* and *Softly Softly* for more than 15 years — Windsor has been constantly in work since the latter series came to an end almost three years ago. He played the title part in the BBC series, *Head Master,* only a couple of months afterwards, and went on to co-star in *Middle Men* with Francis Matthews. He has also recently appeared in Stoppard's *Every Good Boy Deserves A Favour* (he had earlier played in the same author's *Travesties*) and sells cigars in TV commercials.

During his years in *Z Cars,* he had made certain of working between series. He has, he says, a massive fear of unemployment, a fear which he attributes to his secure background — his father was a local government official. He lives with his wife, a former dancer, and two children in Holland Park.

HENRY WINKLER

Born: October 30, 1946,
New York.
Educated: Lausanne; Emerson
College; Yale; Yale School of
Drama.

Arthur Fonzarelli is very wrong-side-of-the-tracks. Winkler is not. His father, who fled Germany in the 'thirties, is president of an international lumber corporation, and he was educated at expensive private schools and graduated in psychology before joining Yale's Drama Department: 'I did more school than God'. For five years, he acted in off-Broadway theatres (he got to Broadway once, but the play was a flop and closed after one performance), and did bit parts and commercials. He was the last actor to audition for the *Happy Days* producers, and was hardly what they were looking for. The script specified a blond

6ft 2ins youth. Winkler is far from blond and he is only 5ft 6ins. He claims that he actually modelled the Fonz on Sylvester Stallone's character in *The Lords of Flatbush*, in which Winkler himself appeared as a Brooklyn yob. He was, he says, 'a short Jewish kid who lived an insular life. If I had met the Fonz, I would have pretended to be blind, so that he would leave me alone'. The Fonz has been turned into a successful merchandising industry – underwear, posters, socks, hats, plates, magazines, perfume, etc. Winkler receives a 'substantial' royalty from all sales – not bad for an actor who was not even in the pilot show of *Happy Days* and had only a featured role in the first series. Winkler is teetotal and has worked in the rehabilitation of teenage alcoholics. He has been married for a year and a half to Stacy Weitzman and has an 8-year-old stepson.

ERNIE WISE

Born: November, 1925,
Ardsley, Yorkshire.

Wise's dilemma for some time has been what to do if Eric Morecambe is forced to retire. He could, he says, be a fat Des O'Connor, but his real ambition is to star in a Hollywood film. Meanwhile, he is working on two books. One of them is a series of recollections of the guests who have appeared with M and W, the other is a history of music hall double acts.

His own double act began in 1939, when he met Eric Morecambe on a bill in Swansea, and they became the best of friends. They appeared together for four years, before Wise was called up into the merchant navy – at the time they were appearing at the Prince of Wales Theatre in *Strike a New Note*. A few months later, Morecambe

became a Bevin boy, and they saw each other only rarely throughout the rest of the war. On those few occasions, their attempts to put together new stuff for their act were unsuccessful. Wise decided to go it alone when he left the merchant service, and didn't even bother to get in touch with Morecambe when he was discharged. One day, he was trekking from agent to agent in search of work, when he re-encountered Morecambe,

who was doing the same in Russell Square. They have been together ever since.

Wiseman's father was a railway signalman with a wife and five children to keep, and he used to do a song and dance act around working clubs to augment his £2 a week wage. Wise's father taught him to clog dance and, at the age of six, he joined the act. At the age of 12, he auditioned for a discovery show called *New Voices,* and Bryan Michie, who ran it, recommended him to Jack Hylton, who put him in *Band Wagon.* Hylton took him under his wing and used to invite him down to his home at Angmering, where Arthur Askey also lived.

He attributes to his odd, hard working and rather 'adult' childhood the fact that he and his wife Doreen, with whom he lives at Maidenhead, have never had any children.

TERRY WOGAN

Born: 1938, Limerick.
Educated: Belvedere College,
Dublin.

Flab, knickers, mild cracks about his employers—these are the things associated with the mild Irishman who is the housewife's choice for disc jockey, quiz master, host, etc. All these activities have made him a rich man, but he is not, he says, preoccupied with money.

He is used to counting it. He began life as a bank clerk. His first job in broadcasting was as an announcer of cattle prices on local radio in Dublin. He graduated to news—reading, interviewing and presenting quiz shows and, after a couple of years of hectic commuting, came to live in England permanently in 1969. His home is at Bray, near the Thames, in Berkshire. His wife, Helen, is a former model whom he met in Dublin, and they have three children, a brown Rolls and a swimming pool.

HARRY WORTH

Born: January 13, 1920,
Barnsley.

Worth was only five months old when his father, a miner, died from injuries received in an industrial accident. The youngest of eleven children, he himself became a miner at the age of 14. He was down the pits for eight years until he joined the RAF. During his teens, he had taught himself ventriloquism and, with his two dummies, Fortheringay and Clarence, set out round the halls after the war. However, his heart wasn't really in it: 'The ventriloquist goes through life talking to himself'. For a while, he toured with Stan Laurel and Oliver Hardy, then towards the

end of their career. Ollie told him that he ought to concentrate on being a comedian, and he eventually got his chance at the Newcastle Empire, where nerves got the better of him and he discovered his distinctive bumbling act by chance.

He became a popular figure on radio and TV, but turned down the opportunity of a film career when he declined to play a part written for him in *Those Magnificent Men In Their Flying Machines*. When he returned to TV this year with *How's Your Father?* after a four-year break, it wasn't for want of offers in the meantime. He simply hadn't been happy with the scripts he had been expected to do. His experience in an adaptation of Evelyn Waugh's *Scoop*, where he was bizarrely cast as Boot, no doubt contributed to his circumspection.

Worth admits to being a thrifty man, and is well able to afford the Rolls that he runs and the large house at Berkhamsted where he lives with his wife, Kay, who was a singer when they met, their daughter, Jobina, and their two grandchildren.

TESSA WYATT

Born: April 23, 1948, Woking.
Educated: Elmhurst School,
Camberley.

Though she has now learnt to cook, Miss Wyatt's only experience of working in a restaurant was ill-starred. She was employed when she was 18 in a restaurant in King's Road. She lasted two days before she got the sack. In that time, she let all the coffee in the place boil dry and tipped ice cream over one of the customers. However, she has some experience of the business, and runs a boutique in Old Windsor, together with her friend, Julie Samuel.

Tessa Wyatt's stockbroker father captained England at hockey. She and her four sisters and brothers were brought up in London and Surrey. She acted intermittently throughout her time at ballet school, playing parts in Cheltenham, Leatherhead and Bromley, and in *Mr Pastry* on TV. When she left school at 17, she lived in France for a few months and then failed to get into the Guildhall School of Drama More or less immediately, though, she landed the first of many TV parts.

After she married Tony Blackburn in 1972, she gave up work for three years. The break-up of their marriage came soon after she had started working again. She now lives alone with their son, Simon, and spends much time denying that she is romantically involved with Richard O'Sullivan.

MIKE YARWOOD

Born June 14, 1941,
Bredbury, Cheshire.
Educated: Bredbury Secondary
Modern School.

The country's leading mimic showed no particular aptitude for conventional entertaining as a youth, and was, more-over, extremely shy. Even when he was 20, his father, an engineering fitter, used to go to shops to buy things for him. However, he did entertain his parents with impressions of their friends and of his Irish maternal uncles, each of whom had a different accent. Neither he nor his parents had any inkling that he might even attempt to make his living in such a way.

He left school when he was 15 with no qualifications, the nickname 'Spiv' (he wore a handkerchief in his breast pocket), and a reputation for taking off the teachers. He worked in garment warehouses, starting as a messenger and ending up as a salesman. What he actually wanted to do was be a footballer (he got a trial with Oldham, but was too skinny) or a football reporter, but the local paper refused to take him on—which is, perhaps, as well. A former Tiller girl who used to model the garments he was selling was so impressed by his impressions of his workmates, that she suggested that he ought to try to get some professional experience. By this time, he was working in a raincoat shop, and he used to dash from it at night in order to enter talent contests. Surprisingly, he never won one. His first engagement was at The Salvage, a pub in the Manchester suburb of Colly-hurst, and he was amazed to find himself being paid 30 shillings to do two 15-minute spots. He went on working for Jacobs' Gown Shops and, on

a firm's Christmas outing to the Whisky a Go-Go in Manchester in 1962, met Wilf Fielding, who was to become his manager. From the Albion in Dukinfield, he progressed to The Ponderosa in Chorlton, with an act that was partly devised by Ray Mayoh (who went on to become a director of *This is Your Life*). Mayoh it was who got Yarwood to build up his repertoire of impressions, so that he could switch from one character to another without any scene set-ting. This is now common practice among mimics, of course, but it was then an innovation.

As his reputation in the North-West grew, so did his place of bills rise, and he eventually became a regular at the Whisky a Go-Go (which offered him a seven-year contract which would have precluded him from appearing elsewhere. He had to have his pen forcibly removed from him in order to prevent him from signing). He was booked by Billy 'Uke' Scott, a former radio star turned agent, as a warm-up man for the TV show,

Comedy Band Box. He scored such a success with the audience, that he was eventually given a slot in the show itself.

This was in 1963, the year Harold Wilson was elected leader of the Labour party and a year before he became Prime Minister. Yarwood has reason to be thankful for Wilson's comparatively long period in office, as well as for Ted Heath's equally protracted eminence. He calls Wilson 'my hit record', and made his reputation as Wilson's most accurate mimic. Wilson, of course, is a great fan and awarded him an OBE—one of the few uncontroversial awards in his Resignation Honours List three-and-a-half years ago. The actor, Clive Merrison, recalls that, on one occasion when he was recording a TV play at the BBC, he was having trouble with his role in a stage play that he was simultaneously rehearsing—he was required to impersonate Enoch Powell. Someone suggested that he should seek the advice of Yarwood, who was in a dressing room along the corridor. So he knocked, introduced himself to Yar-wood, who was just as nervous as he was, told him his problem and was treated to a 45-minute lesson in mimicry from the horse's mouth. Eventually, when Yar-wood had got Merrison doing Enoch pretty well, there came a knock at the door. It was none other than Harold Wilson. 'Ello Mike', said he. 'Ello Ereld', Yarwood replied, immediately going into his Wilson act, 'this is Clive, who's doing Enoch'. Merrison did Enoch. Wilson looked on impressed: 'But there's no one who can do Enoch like Enoch'.

Yarwood attributes his popularity with his subjects to the fact that his act lacks malice. This is a quality which some of his admirers would obviously like to see him introduce, but it would be entirely against his nature to do so. Nonetheless, it appears that, although imitation is in this case a form of flattery (as well as of entertainment), some people do not think so. Witness the number of the great and famous who decline invitations to his shows.

Two who are unlikely to have to decline are—an improbable couple—Margaret Thatcher and Les Dawson. Yarwood admits that he is stumped by both of them. He knows the lugubrious comedian well, but can't bring him off and was rather disappointed when Mrs T became Tory leader—he would have preferred William Whitelaw. He has on occasions done Mrs T, but he now leaves her to Janet Brown. He might, of course, have a go at Dennis Thatcher.

Yarwood takes his work home to Prestbury with him. A lot of his impersonations do not come easily and require protracted periods of rehearsal and change. Since he deals in individuals rather than cartoons (which is why he dislikes doing women—the physical barrier overcomes even him) he has to get the details right. He is not an impressionist, he is a living simulacrum. His two daughters, Charlotte and Claire, do not find him all that funny on the box apparently, but like having him do such favourites of theirs as Michael Crawford and Bruce Forsyth. (Yarwood's own preference is for Stanley Baxter.) His wife, Sandra, former dancer, sometimes gets a bit tired of having a husband who is about a hundred people. He even proposed in someone else's voice, and she knows when he's angry, because he puts on his Brian Clough voice—and she retaliates with her impersonation of him. He is not amused.

SUSANNA YORK

Born: 1941, London.
Educated: R.A.D.A.

Miss York's role as Maria Fitzherbert in *The Prince Regent* was her first on television for five years. During that time, she was in such movies as *The Shout* and such plays as *The Singular Life of Alfred Lobbs,* in which she played a young woman who sought to fend off the advances of men by dressing as a man and leading a bizarrely celibate life.

She was very successful very young. She made her first film, *Tunes of Glory,* when she was 18 and, the same year, married the actor and writer, Michael Wells. Her first leading film role came a year or so later, in *The Greengage Summer,* for which she received the sort of notice that all actors must dream about. Then came *Tom Jones, Kaleidoscope* and numerous others, certain of which made few demands on her talent and required that she do no more than wear a nice smile and a short skirt. This was London in the mid-'sixties,

when Miss York was living in Chelsea. She re-established herself in *The Killing of Sister George* ('disgusting'—*The Daily Sketch*).

Since her marriage to Michael Wells broke up, Miss York has lived with the Australian director, Tim Burstall, and the Cambridge zoologist, Nick Humphries. She has two children by Mr Wells, and her first book, *In Search of Unicorns,* was written for her daughter, Sacha. She has since written another called *Larks Rise.*

Susanna York's father is a man called Simon Fletcher, who has been described as Britain's most persistant litigant. When called up in the war, he was managing director of a Wolverhampton group of companies worth £600,000. When he was discharged from the Army, the companies were in the process of being sold to meet debts incurred under wartime management. Mr Fletcher has spent a fortune in a quixotic attempt to get successive governments to compensate him for the loss of his business.

INDEX

Picture Credits

The publishers wish to thank the following photographers and organisations who have supplied photographs for this book. Photographs have been credited by page number.

ABC Television: 7
Associated Newspapers: 30, 36, 45, 67, 79, 98
BBC: 8, 12, 16, 18, 21, 32, 33, 40, 45, 46, 47, 57, 60, 63, 66, 69, 76, 81, 82, 84, 85, 86, 92, 92, 93, 97, 98, 100, 100, 102, 105, 107, 108, 115, 116, 120, 121, 125
Camera Press: 6, 10, 11, 12, 13, 74, 84, 94, 119
Central Press Photos: 53, 55, 107, 119
Dominic Photography: 46
Doug McKenzie: 122
Epoque: 101, 110, 110, 124
George Wilkes: 9, 15, 20, 22, 26, 27, 52, 41, 48, 68, 78, 90, 95, 104, 106, 109, 112, 112, 113, 115, 117, 119, 123, 123
Granada Television: 32
Group 4 Syndication: 55, 62, 72
ITN: 22, 49, 96
Keystone: 6, 87, 88
London Weekend Television: 18, 24, 31, 40/41, 50, 61, 88, 93
Mirrorpic: 24
PIC Photos: 29, 38, 48, 53, 76, 79, 94
Press Association: 10, 74, 75
Rex Features: 28, 31, 33, 34, 35, 36, 37, 42, 51, 51, 53, 56, 58, 60, 64, 65, 66, 70, 71, 72, 80, 82, 86, 90, 91, 97, 103, 108, 110, 113, 114, 114, 122
Roy Jones: 39
The Sunday Telegraph: 77
Sport & General: 117
Syndication International: 7, 14, 14, 16, 17, 26, 43, 58, 66, 73, 83, 89, 108, 117
Thames Television; 10, 19, 25, 42, 47, 54, 63, 113
TV Times: 41
Universal Pictorial Press: 69, 114, 118, 120